The Role of EU Agencies in Fighting Transnational Environmental Crime

The Role of EU Agencies in Fighting Transnational Environmental Crime

New Challenges for Eurojust and Europol

By

Valsamis Mitsilegas and Fabio Giuffrida

BRILL

LEIDEN | BOSTON

Library of Congress Control Number: 2016960881

Typeface for the Latin, Greek, and Cyrillic scripts: "Brill". See and download: brill.com/brill-typeface.

ISBN 978-90-04-34154-8 (paperback)
ISBN 978-90-04-34155-5 (e-book)

Originally published as Volume 1(1) 2017, in *Transnational Crime*, DOI 10.1163/24680931-12340001.

This book is printed on acid-free paper and produced in a sustainable manner.

Contents

Acknowledgments

The authors are very grateful to the interviewees for their time and for sharing their invaluable experiences. Part of the research has been conducted in the frame of the scholarship awarded by the "Giovanni e Francesca Falcone" Foundation (Palermo, Italy) and it has benefitted from the support of David Ellero, Werner Gowitzke, Giovanni Grasso, and Francesco Lo Voi. Fabio Giuffrida must thank each of them and the Foundation for the inspiring opportunity to study such a challenging topic.

Abbreviations

ADBHU	Association de défense des brûleurs d'huiles usagées (referred to Case 240/83 of the Court of Justice)
AFSJ	Area of Freedom, Security and Justice
ASEAN-WEN	Association of Southeast Asian Nations Wildlife Enforcement Network
AWF	Analysis Working File
CAU	Case Analysis Unit
CFR	Charter of Fundamental Rights
CITES	Convention on the International Trade in Endangered Species
COSI	Standing Committee on Internal Security
DG	Directorate General
EAP	Environmental Action Programme
EAW	European Arrest Warrant
EC	European Community
EDP	European Delegated Prosecutor
EEC	European Economic Community
EFFACE	European Union Action to Fight Environmental Crime
EIO	European Investigation Order
EIS	Europol Information System
EJN	European Judicial Network
ELO	Europol Liaison Officer
ENPE	European Network of Prosecutors for the Environment
ENU	Europol National Unit
EnviCrimeNet	Environmental Crime Network
EPE	Europol Platform for Experts
EPPO	European Public Prosecutor's Office
EU	European Union
EU-TWIX	European Union Trade in Wildlife Information Exchange
FATF	Financial Action Task Force
FECT	Financial and Economic Crime Team
GENVAL	Council Working Party on General Matters including Evaluation
GNST	General nature and strategic type
HENU	Heads of the Europol National Units
IEEP	Institute for European Environmental Policy
IMPEL	European Union Network for the Implementation and Enforcement of Environmental Law

INECE	International Network for Environmental Compliance and Enforcement
IOCTA	Internet Organised Crime Threat Assessment
IPEC	Intelligence Project on Environmental Crime
ITOC	Europol's Focal Point on Italian Organised Crime
JHA	Justice and Home Affairs
JIT	Joint Investigation Team
LAFT	Lusaka Agreement Task Force
MARPOL	Convention on the Prevention of Pollution from Ships
MLA	Mutual Legal Assistance
MS	Member States
OAP	Operational Action Plan
OCG	Organised crime group
OCTA	Organised Crime Threat Assessment
ODS	Ozone-depleting substances
OHIM	Office for Harmonization in the Internal Market
OJ	Official Journal of the European Union
OLAF	European Commission Anti-Fraud Office
OUP	Oxford University Press
SCAN	Scanning, analysis, and notification
SEA	Single European Act
SIENA	Secure Information Exchange Network Application
SOC	Serious and Organised Crime
SOCTA	Serious and Organised Crime Threat Assessment
SWD	Staff Working Document
TE-SAT	European Union Terrorism Situation and Trend Report
TEC	Transnational environmental crime
TECUM	Tackling Environmental Crime through Standardized Methodologies
TEU	Treaty on European Union
TFEU	Treaty on the Functioning of the European Union
TOC	Transnational organised crime
UNCAC	United Nations Convention against Corruption
UNEP	United Nations Environmental Programme
UNICRI	United Nations Interregional Crime and Justice Research Institute
UNODC	United Nations Office on Drugs and Crim

The Role of EU Agencies in Fighting Transnational Environmental Crime: New Challenges for Eurojust and Europol

Valsamis Mitsilegas and Fabio Giuffrida
Queen Mary University of London
v.mitsilegas@qmul.ac.uk; f.giuffrida@qmul.ac.uk

Abstract

The last decades have witnessed a growing emphasis on the relationship between environmental law and criminal law. Legislation aimed at tackling environmental crime has been adopted at national, EU, and international level and has been gradually evolving over time. These developments notwithstanding, the current legal framework faces a number of challenges in tackling the largely inter-related phenomena of transnational, organised and economic environmental crime. This study of Valsamis Mitsilegas and Fabio Giuffrida addresses these challenges by focusing on the role of the European Union- and more specifically its criminal justice agencies (Europol and Eurojust)- in tackling transnational environmental crime. The study analyses the role of Eurojust and Europol in supporting and coordinating the competent national authorities dealing with investigations and/or prosecutions on transnational environmental crime, and it shows that, for the time being, the full potential of these agencies is not adequately fulfilled with regard to fighting this phenomenon effectively.

Keywords

Transnational environmental crime – Europol – Eurojust – judicial cooperation – police cooperation – European Public Prosecutor's Office (EPPO) – wildlife trafficking – waste trafficking – organised crime – European Union (EU)

* This is a co-authored publication. Valsamis Mitsilegas has taken the lead in drafting sections 2–4 and Fabio Giuffrida has taken the lead in drafting sections 5–7.

 | DOI 10.1163/9789004341555_02

1 Introduction

The last decades have witnessed a growing emphasis on the relationship between environmental law and criminal law. Legislation aimed at tackling environmental crime has been adopted at national, EU, and international level and has been gradually evolving over time. These developments notwithstanding, the current legal framework on environmental crime faces a number of challenges in tackling the largely inter-related phenomena of transnational, organised and economic environmental crime.

This study will address these challenges by focusing on the role of the European Union—and more specifically its criminal justice agencies—in tackling transnational environmental crime. The study will focus primarily on the two key operative EU agencies, Europol and Eurojust,[1] and in particular on their role in supporting and coordinating the competent national authorities dealing with investigations and/or prosecutions on transnational environmental crime.

Before embarking upon the analysis of the potential added value of Europol and Eurojust in the fight against cross-border environmental crime (sections 4, 5 and 6), some reflections are spent on the transnational nature of such a phenomenon (section 2) and on the relevant EU legislation in the field (section 3). After a forward-looking analysis of what could be expected in terms of legislative and operational developments in the short and medium term (section 7), we draw some conclusions (section 8), where we submit that, for the time being, the full potential of Eurojust and Europol is not adequately fulfilled with regard to fighting transnational environmental crime effectively.[2]

1 The term 'agencies' is used in the text to refer to Eurojust and Europol. As Busuioc points out, there are different definitions and classifications of the European agencies (M Busuioc, *European Agencies. Law and Practices of Accountability* (OUP 2013) 21ff). In the former three-pillar structure of the EU, agencies were usually divided in 'Commission agencies' and 'Council agencies'; Europol and Eurojust fell within the second category (ibid 21–22). However, whereas the recently adopted Regulation 2016/794/EU on Europol explicitly defines Europol as an agency, the 2009 Council Decision on Eurojust only refers to it as a 'unit' or a 'body' (see more *infra*, section 4.1). Nevertheless, Eurojust features many typical aspects of the former 'Commission agencies', including the funding by the EU budget and the application of the Staff Regulations of Officials of the European Union to its employees.

2 This work has been finalised in September 2016.

2 Transnational Environmental Crime and the EU Perspective: Preliminary Remarks

If one wonders what 'environmental crime' is, the only feasible reply seems to be that the boundaries of this notion are unclear; it is a broad and ambiguous concept, as it is that of environment itself.[3] For instance, according to the European Commission 'environmental crime covers acts that *breach* environmental legislation and cause significant *harm* or *risk* to the environment and human health'.[4]

The conducts that could potentially fall within the ambiguous category at stake are therefore multifarious: trafficking in waste, in protected species, or in ozone-depleting substances (ODS), pollution, fly-tipping, illegal fishing, and so on. However, since the EU agencies on which this work is focused are competent for cases of cross-border environmental crime, it seems more appropriate to discuss the transnational dimension of this phenomenon rather than lingering on the notion of environmental crime *per se*.

2.1 *Environmental Crime as a Transnational (Organised) Crime*

By and large, 'transnational crimes' are defined as 'crimes whose inception, prevention or effect involve more than one country'.[5] They are distinguished by their 'multinational nature and cross border impact'[6] and they are sometimes defined by way of exclusion. In fact, transnational crimes are not

---

3 For different views on this topic see, among the many, P Cleary Yeager and SS Simpson, 'Environmental Crime' in M Tonry (ed), *The Oxford Handbook of Crime and Public Policy* (OUP 2009) 325; S Chin, W Veening and C Gerstetter, 'EFFACE Policy Brief 1: Limitations and challenges of the criminal justice system in addressing environmental crime' (2014) 4–5; A Farmer, AR Germani and R Sollund, 'Conclusions of the EFFACE Case studies' (2015) 7–10; C Nellemann, R Henriksen, A Kreilhuber and others (eds), 'The Rise of Environmental Crime—A Growing Threat To Natural Resources Peace, Development And Security. A UNEP-INTERPOL Rapid Response Assessment' (United Nations Environment Programme and RHIPTO Rapid Response–Norwegian Center for Global Analyses, 2016) <http://unep.org/documents/itw/environmental_crimes.pdf> accessed 18 September 2016, 17–24. See also EnviCrimeNet, 'Report on Environmental Crime' (2016) <http://www.envicrimenet.eu/EN/reports> accessed 18 September 2016, 4. Some considerations of this section are based on the latter document, to whose drafting one of the authors has contributed. The Report also provides further bibliography on environmental crime.

4 <http://ec.europa.eu/environment/legal/crime/> accessed 18 September 2016. Emphasis added.

5 M Marmo and N Chazal, *Transnational Crime & Criminal Justice* (SAGE 2016) 15.

6 J Albanese, 'Deciphering the Linkages between Organized Crime and Transnational Crime' (2012) 66 *Journal of International Affairs* 1.

international core crimes (such as crimes against peace) and they are not judged before international tribunals, but they are not even purely 'national offences', ie those offences 'committed in and having effects solely within one jurisdiction, or not having an extraterritorial link due to the foreign nationality of the victim or the offender or the vessel and only of prosecutorial interest to one state'.[7] Therefore, when a crime affects more than one jurisdiction it can be regarded as 'transnational'.

The Latin term '*trans*' means 'across', 'beyond', 'over', so that transnational crime is usually understood as concerning more than one country. This is the nitty-gritty of the concept on which there is a broad consensus in the literature and which is also reflected in the 2000 United Nations Convention on Transnational Organised Crime ('Palermo Convention'), where it is stated that an offence is of transnational nature if:

> (a) It is committed in more than one State; (b) It is committed in one State but a substantial part of its preparation, planning, direction or control takes place in another State; (c) It is committed in one State but involves an organized criminal group that engages in criminal activities in more than one State; or (d) It is committed in one State but has substantial effects in another State.[8]

However, the involvement of more than one country is not always necessary according to some authors, provided that a given crime has at least 'transboundary moral impacts'.[9] For instance, recalling a previous work of Nadelmann, Boister argues that the notion of transnational crime refers to a behaviour that '(i) actually crosses borders or (ii) has substantial effects in other states' but it can also include '(iii) [...] *local crime* that has only the most tenuous potential extraterritorial impact but which is of *transboundary moral concern* sufficient to include this behaviour within the scope of treaty obligations obliging its criminalisation'.[10]

7 S Gless and JAE Vervaele, 'Law Should Govern: Aspiring General Principles for Transnational Criminal Justice' (2013) 9 *Utrecht Law Review* 1, 2. See also N Boister, *An Introduction to Transnational Criminal Law* (OUP 2012) 13ff; G Bruinsma, 'Criminology and Transnational Crime' in G Bruinsma (ed), *Histories of Transnational Crime* (Springer 2015) 1–2.

8 Article 2 Palermo Convention. For further reflections on the history and definition of transnational crime see MP Roth, 'Historical Overview of Transnational Crime' in P Reichel and J Albanese (eds), *Handbook of Transnational Crime and Justice* (2nd edn, SAGE 2014) 5–22.

9 N Boister, 'Further reflections on the concept of transnational criminal law' (2015) 6 *Transnational Legal Theory* 9, 13.

10 Ibid 12. Emphasis added.

Such a breadth of the concept endorsed by some authors seems to be balanced by the caveat of others, who argue that the focus on the transnational nature of some crimes should not lead to neglect the—still relevant—national dimension of these phenomena. For instance, with regard to cases of illicit trafficking, Fijnaut argues that 'often only the transport of the goods or people concerned is actually transnational, while the production and distribution of the goods or the supply of the services take place in specific locations in the world'.[11] He adds that in some cases of illegal control of economic sectors the illegal activities are not at all transnational.[12]

However, it does not seem necessary to linger further on the debated notion of 'transnational crime': since the EU agencies on which this work is focused are explicitly made competent for crimes affecting *two or more Member States*,[13] in the following analysis 'transnational crime' is used to refer to crimes affecting two or more Member States, in line with the core meaning of this concept. It is instead relevant to evaluate whether environmental crimes are transnational and, therefore, whether they can fall within the competence of Europol and Eurojust.

As the notions of 'environmental crime' and of 'transnational crime', also the one born from their union is not defined in a universally accepted way.[14] It also seems that transnational environmental crime (TEC) has been long ignored by the researchers: in 2007 Sheptycki argued that crimes against the environment were neglected by the criminological literature on transnational crime,[15]

---

11 C Fijnaut, 'Transnational Crime and the Role of the United Nations in Its Containment through International Cooperation: A Challenge for the 21st Century' (2000) 8 *European Journal of Crime, Criminal Law and Criminal Justice* 119, 120. For similar considerations on the need not to neglect the 'national dimension' of transnational crimes see also M Felson, 'Routine Activities and Transnational Crime' in M Natarajan (ed), *International Crime and Justice* (Cambridge University Press 2010) 11–18.

12 'The grip that the Calabrian Mafia, the "Ndrangheta", has on the economy is a purely local phenomenon. And the same can be said of the monopoly that the Mafia families in New York managed to acquire in the course of this century in a number of vital economic sectors' (C Fijnaut, 'Transnational Crime and the Role of the United Nations (n 11) 120). For some comments on this position of Fijnaut see N Boister, '"Transnational Criminal Law"?' (2003) 14 *European Journal of International Law* 953, 954ff.

13 See *infra*, section 4.1.

14 L Elliott and WH Schaedla, 'Transnational environmental crime: excavating the complexities—an introduction' in L Elliott and WH Schaedla (eds), *Handbook of Transnational Environmental Crime* (Edward Elgar 2016) 1.

15 JWE Sheptycki, 'Transnational Crime and Transnational Policing' (2007) 1 *Sociology Compass* 485, 488.

and the same did Bisschop in 2011.[16] Studies on TEC have become increasingly numerous in the most recent years and two volumes on the matter have been released in 2016.[17]

There are no doubts that many forms of environmental crime are transnational. Spapens and Huisman highlight some typical examples of environmental crimes crossing national borders:[18] i) pollution of air and water can be hardly limited to the place where the act of polluting is committed; in fact, 'environmental toxins move freely from one country to another. They travel on the wind, in surface and ground water, and through the movements of humans and animals';[19] ii) in cases involving *trafficking activities* (such as those in waste or protected species), the different rings of the chain can be located in different countries; iii) environmental crimes can be transnational when they take place in the cyberspace, such as in the cases of frauds in emission trading schemes or of online trade in endangered species; iv) the perpetrators may operate in more than one country, as in those cases where a ship dumps waste throughout its journey across the seas of different States; v) finally, criminals can take advantage of differences in the national legislations: for instance, 'a certain amount of soil may count as polluted according to the standards set in one country whereas it is not in another country. Thus, a company hired to clean the soil only needs to export it illegally, thereby avoiding a costly cleaning operation'.[20]

Likewise, Elliott submits that TEC involves

> the movement across borders of species, resources, and pollutants in contravention of domestic law or in violation of prohibition or regulation regimes established by multilateral environmental agreements. It includes the trafficking of illegally-logged timber; smuggling of endangered, threatened, and protected species; the black market in ODS and other prohibited or regulated chemicals; and the transboundary dumping of toxic and hazardous waste including electronic waste (e-waste).

16 L Bisschop, 'Transnational environmental crime: exploring (un)charted territory' in M Cools, B De Ruyver, M Easton and others (eds), *EU Criminal Justice, Financial & Economic Crime: new perspectives* (Maklu 2011) 156ff.

17 L Elliott and WH Schaedla (eds), *Handbook of Transnational Environmental Crime* (Edward Elgar 2016); T Spapens, R White and W Huisman (eds), *Environmental Crime in Transnational Context* (Routledge 2016).

18 T Spapens and W Huisman, 'Tackling Cross-Border Environmental Crime. A "Wicked Problem"' in T Spapens, R White and W Huisman (eds), *Environmental Crime in Transnational Context* (Routledge 2016) 27ff.

19 R Michalowski and R Kramer, 'Transnational Environmental Crime' in P Reichel and J Albanese (eds), *Handbook of Transnational Crime and Justice* (2nd edn, SAGE 2014) 189.

20 T Spapens and W Huisman, 'Tackling Cross-Border Environmental Crime' (n 18) 27.

> INTERPOL now formally recognizes the illegal exploitation of marine living resources, often referred to simply as "fisheries crime," as part of this broader suite of criminal enterprise.[21]

Therefore, as submitted by Boister, environmental crime is 'usually large in scale and transnational in nature'.[22] It seems that that not all the types of environmental crime can be regarded as transnational though. For instance, minor cases of fly-tipping usually do not involve more than one country.[23] In other words, it seems more correct to submit that the 'effects of *some* environmental crimes are global in nature'.[24]

In some circumstances, the transnational dimension of an environmental crime can emerge in a second stage. For instance, this is the case of 'wildlife crime', which usually refers to all those criminal activities concerning protected species, and especially their illegal trade. Wellsmith argues that wildlife crime can be considered 'as occurring at the *micro-level* (such as subsistence poaching and individual acts of cruelty), *meso-level* (such as domestic trade in resident vulnerable species and organised illegal hunts) and *macro-level* (notably import and export of endangered species for international trade)':[25] it seems clear that wildlife crime becomes transnational when it turns from the first two levels to the third one.

Some authors have also attempted to classify the forms of TEC. Whereas White lists four different types of transnational environmental crime (resource depletion, disposal problems, corporate colonisation of nature, and species decline),[26] Wright embraces the division of TEC in two categories suggested by the United Nations Office on Drugs and Crime (UNODC), namely *trafficking*

---

21 L Elliott, 'Fighting Transnational Environmental Crime' (2012) 66 *Journal of International Affairs* 87, 89.

22 N Boister, *An Introduction to Transnational Criminal Law* (n 7) 118.

23 E Watkins, 'A case study on illegal localized pollution incidents in the EU'. A study compiled as part of the EFFACE project (IEEP 2015).

24 G Wright, 'Conceptualising and combating transnational environmental crime' (2011) 14 *Trends in organized crime* 332, 333. Emphasis added.

25 M Wellsmith, 'Wildlife Crime: The Problems of Enforcement' (2011) 17 *European journal on criminal policy and research* 125, 128. Emphasis added. For similar considerations see SF Pires and WD Moreto, 'Preventing Wildlife Crimes: Solutions That Can Overcome the "Tragedy of the Commons"' (2011) 17 *European Journal on Criminal Policy and Research* 101, 104.

26 R White, 'Transnational Environmental Crime' in M Natarajan (ed), *International Crime and Justice* (Cambridge University Press 2010) 195–196.

in natural resources and *trafficking in hazardous substances*.[27] In his words, 'the former includes the trade in endangered species, illegal logging and illegal exploitation and trafficking of mineral resources while the latter includes the illegal trade in ozone depleting substances and the dumping and trafficking of waste'.[28]

It is true that usually these forms of trafficking represent the most serious cases of TEC and that they often raise the concerns of policy-makers, law enforcement agencies, populations, and academics. It is not a case, for instance, that the reports issued by Eurojust and Europol on environmental crime mainly deal with illegal trafficking in waste and in endangered species,[29] or that all the three forms of TEC included in a study on transnational crime launched under the auspices of the non-profit research organisation Global Financial Integrity in 2011 concern illegal trade (wildlife, fish, and timber).[30] However, Wright's two-fold distinction does not seem to capture the whole picture: a typical transnational environmental crime such as pollution, for instance, does not sit very well in any of the two above-mentioned categories (trafficking in natural resources and trafficking in hazardous substances). In the 2010 Transnational Organized Crime Threat Assessment issued by the UNODC, it is stated that the various forms of transnational organised environmental crime can fall within two subheadings, but 'trafficking in hazardous substances' is not a subheading *per se*, since this kind of trafficking is rather one of the main examples of the broader phenomenon referred to as 'pollution'.

Likewise, the other argument of Wright that transnational environmental crime is 'a form of *organised crime*'[31] is valid mainly when applied to trafficking

27 G Wright (n 24) 333. See Conference of the Parties to the United Nations Convention against Transnational Organized Crime, 'Expert consultation on the use of the Convention for combating emerging forms of crime'. Item 5 of the provisional agenda for the Fifth session, held in Vienna, 18–22 October 2010 (2010) CTOC/COP/2010/3, 9.

28 G Wright (n 24) 333.

29 Eurojust, 'Strategic Project on Environmental Crime. Report' (November 2014) <http://www.eurojust.europa.eu/press/pressreleases/pages/2014/2014-11-21.aspx> accessed 18 September 2016 (see more *infra*, section 6.2); Europol, 'Threat Assessment 2013. Environmental Crime in the EU' (2013) <https://www.europol.europa.eu/content/threat-assessment-2013-environmental-crime-eu> accessed 18 September 2016 (see more *infra*, section 5.1).

30 J Haken, 'Transnational Crime In The Developing World' (Global Financial Integrity 2011). On the illicit trafficking in waste see also: European Environment Agency, 'Movements of waste across the EU's internal and external borders' (2012) <http://www.eea.europa.eu/publications/movements-of-waste-EU-2012> accessed 18 September 2016.

31 G Wright (n 24) 332. Emphasis added.

activities.[32] For instance, the just mentioned 2010 Transnational Organized Crime Threat Assessment devotes a whole chapter to two relevant forms of organised transnational environmental crimes, namely the trafficking of endangered species from Africa and South-East Asia to Asia and the trafficking of timber from South-East Asia to Europe and Asia.[33] On the contrary, the involvement of organised crime is limited, or even absent, in other phenomena still falling within the broad notion of TEC, such as the surface water pollution.[34]

In other words, there are often—but not always—strong links between TEC and organised crime.[35] Likewise, in the literature concerning transnational crime in general it is argued that 'transnational crime is *heavily associated with organized crime*' although 'organization is *not a necessary condition* of transnational crime [...]'.[36]

---

32 See, for instance, Eurojust, 'Strategic Project on Environmental Crime. Report' (n 29) 14–15 and 19–20.

33 UNODC, 'The Globalization of Crime. A Transnational Organized Crime Threat Assessment' (Vienna 2010) 149–169. Among the many studies dealing with the involvement of organised crime groups (OCGs) in wildlife crime see, for instance, R Sollund and J Maher, 'The Illegal wildlife trade. A case study report on the illegal wildlife trade in the United Kingdom, Norway, Colombia and Brazil'. A study compiled as part of the EFFACE project (University of Oslo and University of South Wales 2015) 5–7.

34 Eurojust, 'Strategic Project on Environmental Crime. Report' (n 29) 36. Likewise, in the frame of a study on crimes occurring in the fishing sector, it is stated that 'not all forms of marine living resource crimes should be considered transnational organized crime' (E de Coning, 'Transnational Organized Crime in the Fishing Industry. Focus on: Trafficking in Persons, Smuggling of Migrants, Illicit Drugs Trafficking' (UNODC 2011) 98). The expression 'marine living resource crimes' refers to the criminal conducts that 'may impact negatively on the marine living environment' (ibid 96). Further in the same study it is underlined that the involvement of OCGs in the sector at stake is nevertheless relevant and alarming (ibid 109).

35 See L Elliott, 'Fighting Transnational Environmental Crime' (n 21) 92–95. For some remarks on the involvement of OCGs in the area of illegal, unreported and unregulated fishing see D Liddick, 'The dimension of a transnational crime problem: the case of iuu fishing' (2014) 17 *Trends in Organized Crime* 290, 295–297. For the analysis of some scenarios of the possible future involvement of OCGs in the energy supply sector see 'Report and Conclusions' of the Europol-OHIM Awareness Conference on Fake and Illicit Pesticides, held in Alicante, 26–28 November 2012 (2012) <https://euipo.europa.eu/tunnel-web/secure/webdav/guest/document_library/observatory/documents/Knowledge-building-events/1392909557_pesticides_report_en.pdf> accessed 18 September 2016.

36 N Boister, *An Introduction to Transnational Criminal Law* (n 7) 6. Emphasis added. See also J Albanese, 'Deciphering the Linkages between Organized Crime and Transnational Crime' (n 6) 3ff.

Also the concept of 'organised crime' is quite debated, under a criminological and a legal perspective. As submitted by Finckenauer, '[i]t seems that everyone has a view of what organized crime is'.[37] Defining and criminalising organised crime is admittedly a legally complex task, as it is difficult to translate into a legal norm providing a sufficient degree of legal certainty and precision the multifarious activities of organised criminals. Thorny issues in this respect involve the legal definition of organised criminal groups, in particular with regard to the degree of organisation, the structure (or not) of such groups and the number of people involved.[38]

However, there is strong evidence that organised crime groups (OCGs) are increasingly involved in some forms of environmental crime, especially illegal trafficking in waste and in protected species, where different countries feature as origin, transit and/or destination places.[39]

37 J Finckenauer, 'Organized Crime' in M Tonry (ed), *The Oxford Handbook of Crime and Public Policy* (OUP 2009) 304.

38 V Mitsilegas, 'The Council Framework Decision on the Fight against Organised Crime: What can be done to strengthen EU legislation in the field?'. Note for the European Parliament (2011) <http://www.europarl.europa.eu/document/activities/cont/201206/20120627ATT47779/20120627ATT47779EN.pdf> accessed 18 September 2016, 8–9. On the notion of organised crime at the EU level see *infra*, section 3.5.

39 See, for instance, M Luna and W Veening, 'EFFACE Policy Brief 2: Organised Environmental Crime' (2014); Report of the 'European action against the involvement of Organized Crime and Mafia-related crime in Waste Trafficking, in cooperation with Europol, owing to the emergence of the trans-national phenomenon', Council doc 16605/14, 8 December 2014, 31ff; G Giardi, 'Fighiting the European Ecomafia. Organised Trafficking in Waste and the Need for a Criminal Law Response from the EU' (2015) 6 *New Journal of European Criminal Law* 229, *passim*; I Rodopoulos, 'Les activités criminelles organisées en matière environnementale: quelque réflexion en vue d'une réponse pénale internationale' in L Neyret (ed), *Des écocrimes à l'écocide. Le droit pénal au secours de l'environnement* (Bruylant 2015) 165–182; GM Vagliasindi, 'Organised environmental crime' in A Farmer, V Mitsilegas, M Faure and others, 'Evaluation of the strengths, weaknesses, threats and opportunities associated with EU efforts to combat environmental crime'. Study in the framework of the EFFACE research project (2015) 87–104; E van Asch, 'Countering transnational organized wildlife crime: regional and sub-regional initiatives, global responses and the need for more effective coordination' in M Faure, P De Smedt and A Stas (eds), *Environmental Enforcement Networks. Concepts, Implementation and Effectiveness* (Edward Elgar 2015) 187–189 and 197–202; L Elliott and WH Schaedla, 'Transnational environmental crime: excavating the complexities—an introduction' (n 14) 4ff; C Gerstetter, C Stefes, A Farmer and others, 'Environmental crime and the EU Synthesis of the Research Project "European Action to Fight Environmental Crime" (EFFACE)' (2016) 40–41.

However, apart from OCGs, also individuals can be held responsible for the crimes at issue, such as in cases of transnational pollution following a shipwreck. The involvement of legal persons is not rare, too. Legitimate companies can often decide to 'behave' in an illegal way to avoid relevant costs inevitably linked with their activities, such as those concerning the waste disposal. In the literature, these phenomena are defined as 'organisation crime'[50] or 'organizational crime', which refers 'to violations of criminal statutes committed in the context or in pursuit of the goals of legitimate organizations, organizational subunits, or work groups'.[51] In theory, the difference between organisational crime and organised crime is crystal-clear: only in the latter case it would be necessary to punish all the members of the criminal syndicate, whereas in the case of a crime committed by a corporation it would be illogical to sanction all the employees.[52] Nevertheless, the boundaries between organised and organisational crime can become quite blurred in practice, 'as when legitimate businesses are converted gradually into criminal ones, or when they serve as nothing more than a respectable-appearing shell for activities that are largely, if not exclusively, criminal [...]'.[53]

This multiplicity of possible perpetrators is one of the reasons why TEC is different from the traditional forms of transnational organised crime (TOC), as argued by Wright.[54] Unlike traditional TOC, moreover, transnational environmental crime is a collective noun which refers to a raft of different phenomena, as noted above. In Wright's words, 'this is reflected by their multiple foundations in international law, with separate treaties for each issue, instead

50 T Fajardo del Castillo, 'Organised Crime and Environmental Crime: Analysis of EU Legal Instruments'. Study in the framework of the EFFACE Research Project (University of Granada 2015) 20–21.

51 N Shover and J Scroggins, 'Organizational crime' in M Tonry (ed), *The Oxford Handbook of Crime and Public Policy* (OUP 2009) 273. For further considerations on 'corporate environmental crime' see M Faure, 'Environmental Crimes' in G De Geest (ed), *Encyclopedia of Law and Economics*, vol 3 (2nd edn, Edward Elgar 2009) 330–333.

52 I Rodopoulos (n 39) 169–171.

53 N Shover and J Scroggins (n 51) 276. See also, for instance, G D'Alisa, PM Falcone, AR Germani and others, 'Victims in the "Land of Fires": case study on the consequences of buried and burnt waste in Campania, Italy'. Case study compiled as part of the EFFACE project (University of Rome "La Sapienza" 2015). The authors highlight the involvement of legal business in waste-related crimes, in addition to that of the OCGs. The importance to regulate the corporate liability in the field of environmental crime is also pointed out by M Faure and G Heine, *Criminal Enforcement of Environmental Law in the European Union* (Kluwer Law International 2005) 87–88.

54 On this 'multiplicity of perpetrators' see G Wright (n 24) 338.

of one in the case of the traditional forms of TOC, such as drugs and people smuggling'.[55] As it is argued below, however, the existing international treaties on environmental matters do not expressly impose on the States the duty to punish the illicit conducts thereof with *criminal* sanctions. This step forward has been taken by the EU legislation. At the time of writing, an international convention on transnational environmental crime (or one of its forms) is still missing, even though often advocated by scholars and practitioners.[56]

Moreover, in some areas falling within the notion of TEC, licit forms of trade do exist, so that it is not always easy for the national authorities to ascertain whether a given crime has been committed. The selling of any drugs is prohibited by international conventions, whereas wildlife trafficking legislation often criminalises the purchase and the selling only of *certain* protected species. Law enforcement authorities usually face the difficulty to correctly assess whether a given item falls within such a category: 'the presence of a licit market makes it particularly difficult for those on the ground to know whether what they are confronted with is legal or not'.[57]

Finally, TEC is regarded as a 'victimless' crime; subsequently, if no one complains because no one is directly affected, there is a misrepresented perception of its seriousness and of the impact of the phenomenon, with the further consequence that it is not considered as a priority by national authorities. The definition of 'victimless crime' is misleading, since, firstly, many species (flora and fauna) are the direct 'victims' of these crimes: they are on the verge of extinction and the continued illegal trade with them (or commodities derived from them) needs to be stopped to avoid unforeseeable consequences on different ecosystems.[58]

Second, the damages that TEC can produce can be not so easy to grasp on the short term, but they can turn out to be dramatic in the long run, and above all they can be *irreversible*: 'once an animal is poached, it is gone forever. […] once pristine rainforest is illegally logged it is irreplaceable and when ozone-depleting substances are released they cannot be stopped from damaging the

---

55 Ibid 337.

56 'Report of the Expert Groups', UNICRI-UNEP International Conference on 'Environmental Crime—Current and Emerging Threats', held in Rome, 29–30 October 2012 (2012) <http://www.unicri.it/topics/environmental/conference/Report_of_the_Conference.pdf> accessed 18 September 2016, 2.

57 G Wright (n 24) 337. For similar considerations see, among the many, Interpol, 'Assessment on Illegal Bear Trade' (2014) <http://www.interpol.int/contentinterpol/search?SearchText=assessment+on+illegal+bear+trade&x=0&y=0> accessed 18 September 2016, 4; C Gibbs, EF McGarrell and B Sullivan (n 40), 243; E van Asch (n 39) 209.

58 EnviCrimeNet, 'Report on Environmental Crime' (n 3) 5.

atmosphere'.[59] Environmental crimes affect the ecosystems and can cause environmental disasters, irreversible climate change, contamination of the food chain and diseases, reduced life expectancy and ultimately the death of human beings.[60]

Apart from organised crime, it is to be noted that transnational environmental crime has been found to go hand in hand with other forms of crime; among them, corruption appears to be the most common. Environmental crime has been defined as a 'catalyst for corruption', because 'in the same way that criminals perceive environmental crime as an easy option, so individuals in corporate or official positions of authority and power view environmental crime as a chance to cash in'.[61] Likewise, Elliott argues that

> [l]ocal officials, customs officers, police and the judiciary are bribed to overlook illegal shipments, to assist with false paper trails and forged documentation, to help evidence disappear during prosecutions, to delay or drop prosecutions, and even to return no convictions in the cases of those who are brought to trial.[62]

Acknowledging that environmental crime is a 'haven for corruption' could lead to a greater use of the instruments provided for in the United Nations Convention against Corruption (UNCAC).[63] It is not a case, therefore, that the Fourth Conference of States Parties to the UNCAC has been focused on the topic of 'Impact of corruption on the environment and the United Nations Convention against Corruption as a tool to address it'.[64]

---

59 G Wright (n 24) 339. See also L Elliott, 'Fighting Transnational Environmental Crime' (n 21) 89–90.

60 EnviCrimeNet, 'Report on Environmental Crime' (n 3) 5.

61 D Banks, C Davies, J Gosling and others, 'Environmental Crime. A threat to our future' (Environmental Investigation Agency 2008) 3. The extensive use of corruption in the illicit waste trafficking has been pointed out also in Europol, 'Threat Assessment 2013. Environmental Crime in the EU' (n 29) 17. For some reflections on corruption and organised crime in the area of wildlife crime see Environmental Investigation Agency, 'In Cold Blood. Combating organised wildlife crime' (2014) <https://eia-international.org/wp-content/uploads/EIA-In-Cold-Blood-FINAL.pdf> accessed 18 September 2016.

62 L Elliott, 'Fighting Transnational Environmental Crime' (n 21) 94. See also the 'Report of the Expert Groups' (n 56), 2–3.

63 D Banks, C Davies, J Gosling and others (n 61) 24.

64 For further considerations see TT Van Dinh, 'Addressing Corruption in the Environmental Sector: How the United Nations Convention against Corruption Provides a Basis

Moreover, the illegal forms of trafficking falling within the category of TEC sometimes follow the same routes of the trafficking of other illegal commodities.[65] Counterfeiting and fraud are also often committed along with environmental crimes, especially in those cases where some activities need specific documentation or certificates to comply with the existing regulations. As far as money laundering is concerned, environmental crime is considered as a predicate offence in the Financial Action Task Force (FATF) Recommendations and the importance to 'follow the money' coming from environmental crime is underlined in many studies.[66] Finally, there are reasons to believe that in some parts of the world the proceeds from environmental crime (especially wildlife crime) are used also to finance terrorist groups.[67]

In sum, TEC is a phenomenon (or rather a sum of different phenomena) which can have devastating environmental, economic, social, and political consequences. Most of the transnational environmental crimes are highly attractive for organised crime groups and are often committed together with other criminal activities. More details on TEC are given further in this work, whose aim is to analyse the role that Eurojust and Europol can play in the fight against this form of transnational crime. The following section explains the reasons of this choice.

2.2 *Between Transnational Criminal Law and EU Criminal Law: Why Focus on EU Agencies and Environmental Crime?*

The possible added value of Eurojust and Europol in the field at stake has not been discussed in depth in the current literature.[68] The increasing concerns

---

for Action' (2012) <http://www.unodc.org/documents/corruption/Publications/2012/Corruption_Environment_and_the_UNCAC.pdf> accessed 18 September 2016, 34–50.

65 L Elliott, 'Fighting Transnational Environmental Crime' (n 21) 93–94.

66 EnviCrimeNet, 'Report on Environmental Crime' (n 3) 8. For example, on the need to follow the money coming from forest crime see MP Goncalves, M Panjer, TS Greenberg and WB Magrath, *Justice for Forests. Improving Criminal Justice Efforts to Combat Illegal Logging* (World Bank Study 2012) <http://elibrary.worldbank.org/doi/abs/10.1596/978-0-8213-8978-2> accessed 18 September 2016, 20ff.

67 See L Elliott, 'Fighting Transnational Environmental Crime' (n 21) 95; M Luna and W Veening, 'EFFACE Policy Brief 2' (n 39) 2; 'Commission Staff Working Document accompanying the Communication on the EU Action Plan against Wildlife Trafficking' (n 45) 31–33; C Nellemann, R Henriksen, A Kreilhuber and others (eds) (n 3) *passim*.

68 At the time of writing, the topic has been briefly discussed in some works published in the frame of the recently concluded EU-funded Project EFFACE (European Union Action to Fight Environmental Crime). The studies compiled in the frame of this Project are

raised by TEC, which needs a strong and *coordinated* reaction from law enforcement agencies, call for further analysis on the role of the two agencies, also in light of their growing importance in the Area of Freedom, Security and Justice (AFSJ). It can actually be argued that the existence of supranational agencies supporting national investigations and prosecutions against cross-border crimes represents one of the key features of EU criminal law. This is especially true when the latter is compared with transnational criminal law, ie the legal counterpart of the criminological concept of 'transnational crime'.

The expression 'transnational criminal law' has been increasingly used in the last decade, mainly thanks to the studies of Boister, who has defined it as the '*indirect* suppression by *international* law through *domestic* penal law of criminal activities that have actual or potential *trans-boundary effects*'.[69] This definition is based on the assumption that transnational criminal law has a horizontal and a vertical component.

The *horizontal* one is represented by the so-called 'suppression conventions', namely those international treaties which usually feature both the *duty* for the State Parties *to criminalise* some illicit transnational conducts and the rules to streamline the *cooperation* among national authorities to curb such phenomena. An example is the already mentioned Palermo Convention.

The *vertical* component of transnational criminal law is instead represented by the *national implementation* of the suppression conventions. In a way, 'it is an example of subsidiarity: the state is left the task of criminalisation and enforcement because it is the most effective unit to take these steps [...]'.[70] Therefore, unlike international criminal law *stricto sensu*, transnational criminal law heavily relies on national criminal justice systems to punish transnational crimes: in other words, sovereignty is still important in this area of law.[71]

In a recent work, Boister has suggested that transnational criminal law can include norms and rules emerging from what he calls 'unfamiliar sources of

---

available at <http://efface.eu/> accessed 18 September 2016. Likewise, the issue at stake has been touched upon in some documents issued at the EU level by different institutions and bodies, including the two agencies themselves. All these sources are mentioned and taken into account in the analysis provided further in the text.

69 N Boister, '"Transnational Criminal Law"?' (n 12) 955. Emphasis added.

70 N Boister, 'Further reflections on the concept of transnational criminal law' (n 9) 19.

71 N Boister, '"Transnational Criminal Law"?' (n 12) 956. For similar considerations on the fact that the 'nation state [...] is still the cornerstone of international police and judicial cooperation' see C Fijnaut, 'The globalisation of police and judicial cooperation: drivers, substance and organisational arrangements, political complications' in S Hufnagel, C Harfield and S Bronitt, *Cross-Border Law Enforcement. Regional Law Enforcement Cooperation—European, Australian and Asia-Pacific Perspectives* (Routledge 2013) 6.

authority',[72] such as the FATF Recommendations, which reveal 'multiple examples of "soft" (formally non-binding) transnational criminal law'.[73] The FATF Recommendations have been already recalled, since they suggest the inclusion of environmental crime among the predicate offences for money laundering.

Apart from this 'unfamiliar source of authority', however, the growing concerns raised by transnational environmental crime do not seem to be adequately reflected in transnational criminal law: no 'suppression conventions' have been adopted and the existing instruments, such as the Palermo Convention, are insufficient to fill the gaps.[74] Bluntly put, this is a case of transnational crime without an adequate response of transnational criminal law.[75]

In this work we adopt the perspective of EU criminal law. Although the interplay between this area of EU law and transnational criminal law would deserve a more detailed analysis, a couple of points can be made on the topic.[76]

The EU system is completely different from the international scenario in which transnational criminal law is flourished. The latter is still the realm of sovereign States. On the contrary, by establishing the Communities (and then the EU) the Member States have decided to pool their sovereignty and to share it with the supranational organisation. Throughout the years, this contentious but unavoidable transfer of sovereignty has concerned also the extremely sensitive field of (substantive and procedural) criminal law: the economic integration could not go ahead without a corresponding integration in criminal matters. The story of the so-called 'spillover' effect is known and it does not deserve to be told again.[77] The bottom line is that nowadays the impact of EU legislation on national criminal justice systems is impressive. The European Arrest Warrant (EAW) and the other instruments of mutual recognition are

---

72 N Boister, 'Further reflections on the concept of transnational criminal law' (n 9) 22.

73 Ibid 23. However, Boister argues that this does not affect the nature of transnational criminal law as an area of law primarily composed by the transversal combination of the mentioned horizontal and vertical elements. See more ibid 21ff.

74 See more *infra*, section 3.5.

75 However, it is to be noted that Interpol is quite active in supporting national authorities in fighting environmental crime. See more at <http://www.interpol.int/Crime-areas/Environmental-crime/Environmental-crime> accessed 18 September 2016.

76 The issue is touched upon by Wade in a recent article, where she reflects on some potential general principles of 'transnationalised criminal justice' (a broad expression which refers both to transnational criminal law and EU criminal law): see M Wade, 'General Principles of Transnationalised Criminal Justice? Exploratory Reflections' (2013) 9 *Utrecht Law Review* 165.

77 See, for instance, V Mitsilegas, J Monar and W Rees, *The European Union and Internal Security* (Palgrave Macmillan 2003) 27ff.

tools of the every-day practice of criminal law,[78] *ne bis in idem* as enshrined in the Convention Implementing the Schengen Agreement (and now the Charter of Fundamental Rights of the European Union) bars further prosecutions on the same facts in other Member States, domestic legislators are in the process of implementing the EU Directives recently issued on some procedural rights, and so on.

Nothing similar exists in the frame of 'transnational criminal law'. It is true that one of the aims of the suppression conventions is to enhance the cooperation among domestic authorities dealing with transnational crime, but the level of integration is not comparable with the one reached at the EU level. Unless otherwise agreed, extraditions still follow the traditional, quite cumbersome political paths, there is no transnational *ne bis in idem* prohibiting two States to prosecute the same facts, the rights of the individuals potentially concerned by transnational criminal law are not adequately addressed, etc.[79]

Likewise, it is also true that, to a certain extent, the EU approach to cross-border crime follows the same pattern of transnational criminal law: EU legislation imposes on the Member States duties to criminalise some illicit conducts and provides for many rules to strengthen the cooperation among domestic authorities (*horizontal element*). Moreover, the *vertical element* is still of fundamental importance, because the effectiveness of EU criminal policy depends (also) on the implementation of Member States.

The following sections deal with these issues more in depth, but for the moment it needs to be highlighted that a fundamental difference between EU criminal law and transnational criminal law exists. Whereas the core components of transnational criminal law are the horizontal and the vertical ones, in the EU perspective a third dimension is also important, namely that of the *agencies*. In a way, agencies such as Europol and Eurojust are the clearest representation of the integration reached within the EU in the field of criminal law: the fight against cross-border crimes is ultimately a task of national authorities, who apply national substantive and procedural rules of their own Member State, even though in a growing number of cases such rules derive from supranational legislation. However, these authorities have a

78 See more *infra*, section 3.4.

79 On the fact that transnational criminal law traditionally neglects the rights of the individuals see N Boister, '"Transnational Criminal Law"?' (n 12) 959; M Wade, 'General Principles of Transnationalised Criminal Justice?' (n 76) 169ff.

further instrument in their toolbox to curb transnational phenomena in a more coordinated—European—way, ie Europol and Eurojust.[80]

Also in the frame of transnational criminal law, national authorities—still the kingpins of this area of law—can rely on some international law enforcement organisations, such as Interpol. In the words of Boister, Interpol 'is not an operational organization with powers of arrest in different states; it is a *network of national police organizations* that can be used to track suspected criminals'.[81] Its 'primary function is to serve as a conduit for requests for information from national law enforcement'[82] and it also 'serves as a resource centre for the collection and distribution of data and maintains databases on names, fingerprints, DNA profiles, etc which serve as useful sources of information'.[83] As shown below, these activities are by and large similar to those of Europol, which seems to be more focused on intelligence-related tasks. In addition, Europol plays a relevant role in shaping EU criminal policy. However, even though Interpol and Europol have similar tasks, the absence of something comparable to Eurojust at the international level cannot be ignored: 'it is [...] a salient point that members of the judiciary—in particular public prosecution services—now often cooperate with their counterparts abroad, but that their efforts have not yet led to serious initiatives to set up an 'Interjust' so as to hasten and improve such worldwide cooperation'.[84]

Therefore, as argued by Wade, 'there can be little doubt that the density and frequency of the involvement of European bodies and agencies marks this area of law and criminal justice out as a *specific phenomenon*'.[85]

---

80 Other bodies and agencies act in the frame of the AFSJ, such as the European Commission Anti-Fraud Office (OLAF) and Frontex. This work does not focus on them since Frontex mainly deals with migration issues, whereas OLAF is competent for the *administrative* investigations on the frauds affecting the financial interests of the EU. However, the latter body in some cases has played a relevant role in the field of trafficking of pesticides, which is a conduct that could fall within the broad notion of 'environmental crime'. OLAF's mandate, indeed, 'includes investigations related to counterfeit goods that enter the EU through its external borders. The trade of such products generates vast illicit profits and huge losses of tax revenues' (<https://ec.europa.eu/anti-fraud/media-corner/press-releases/substantial-quantities-smuggled-counterfeit-pesticides-seized-poland_mt> accessed 18 September 2016).

81 N Boister, *An Introduction to Transnational Criminal Law* (n 7) 173. Emphasis added.

82 Ibid.

83 Ibid.

84 C Fijnaut, 'The globalisation of police and judicial cooperation' (n 71) 9.

85 M Wade, 'General Principles of Transnationalised Criminal Justice?' (n 76) 168. Emphasis added. See more ibid 172.

In other words, the establishment of agencies has been a key feature of the development of EU criminal law in the past twenty years, so that an adequate evaluation of the EU's response to transnational crimes needs to adequately take into account their role and their (real or potential) added value. This is precisely what the following analysis attempts to do, focusing on the more limited field of transnational environmental crime.

3 Environmental Crime in the EU

EU environmental law and EU criminal law share a similar history. Whereas the founding Treaties did not provide any competence of the Communities on environmental and criminal matters, now the EU is empowered to adopt legislation in both sectors. In the following section, we summarily go through the history of the protection of the environment within the EU, which is necessary to introduce the contentious issue of the possibility to guarantee such a protection by means of criminal law (section 3.2). Section 3.3 gives a short overview of the two most relevant EU instruments in the field, namely Directive 2008/99/EC and Directive 2009/123/EC, whereas in section 3.4 the applicability of EU instruments on mutual recognition to environmental crime cases is examined. Then, EU legislation on organised (environmental) crime is discussed in section 3.5. The last two sections focus on the perspectives and challenges introduced by the Treaty of Lisbon in the field of environmental crime (section 3.6) and on the so-called 'multi-disciplinary approach' to this phenomenon (section 3.7). Against this backdrop, full of light and shade, it will be then possible to discuss the role of Eurojust and Europol in curbing TEC.

3.1 *The Protection of the Environment within the EU: A Short History*

The environment first appeared in the Treaties with the Single European Act (SEA), signed in 1986 and entered into force in 1987. Article 25 SEA introduced Title VII in the Treaty Establishing the European Economic Community ('EEC Treaty'): that title was composed of three articles explicitly devoted to the environment (Articles 130r, 130s, and 130t EEC Treaty). Nowadays, after the entry into force of the Treaty of Lisbon (2009), the Treaty on the Functioning of the European Union (TFEU) still features a title entirely dedicated to the environment and made up of three articles, which are very similar to the original ones.

Article 191 TFEU sets out the *objectives* of the Union policy on the environment, namely those to preserve, protect and improve the quality of the environment, to protect human health, to guarantee a prudent and rational utilisation of natural resources, and to promote measures at international level to deal with environmental problems.[86] The first three objectives were already mentioned in the SEA, whereas the fourth has been added by the Treaty of Maastricht, signed in 1992 and entered into force in 1993.

Article 191 TFEU also lists the *principles* on which the Union policy on the environment shall be based, as well as the *elements* to be taken into account when preparing such a policy. As far as the former are concerned, they are the precautionary principle and the principles that preventive action should be taken, that environmental damage should as a priority be rectified at source, and that the polluter should pay.[87] These principles already featured in the SEA, with the only exception of the precautionary principle which was introduced by the Treaty of Maastricht. The elements to be taken into account in the Union policy on the matter are instead entirely identical to those listed in the SEA: 'available scientific and technical data, environmental conditions in the various regions of the Union, the potential benefits and costs of action or lack of action, the economic and social development of the Union as a whole and the balanced development of its regions'.[88]

Finally, as Article 130r EEC Treaty, Article 191(4) TFEU allows the Union and the Member States to cooperate with third countries and competent international organisations. Since the beginning, therefore, the *external dimension* of the EU action in the field of environmental protection has been extremely important. As it is shown below, the Communities first, the Union then, have taken part to different international agreements and conventions concerning the protection of the environment.[89]

---

86 Article 191(1) TFEU.

87 Article 191(2) TFEU. For further considerations on the listed principles, as well as on the historical development of EU environmental law, see E Orlando, 'The evolution of EU Policy and Law in the Environmental Field: Achievements and Current Challenges' (2013) Transworld Working Paper 21 <http://www.iai.it/sites/default/files/TW_WP_21.pdf> accessed 18 September 2016; N de Sadeleer, *EU Environmental Law and the Internal Market* (OUP 2014) 7ff; M Lee, *EU Environmental Law, Governance and Decision-Making* (2nd edn, Hart 2014) 1–27; R Pereira, *Environmental Criminal Liability and Enforcement in European and International Law* (Brill 2015) 173ff. On the precautionary principle see also the 'Communication from the Commission on the precautionary principle' COM(2000) 1 final, 2 February 2000.

88 Article 191(3) TFEU.

89 See *infra*, section 3.3. See also T Fajardo del Castillo, 'Revisiting the External Dimension of the Environmental Policy. Some Challenges Ahead' (2010) 7 *Journal of European Environmental Law* 365; E Morgera (ed), *The External Environmental Policy of the European Union. EU and International Law Perspectives* (Cambridge University Press 2012).

Whereas Article 193 TFEU, as Article 130t EEC Treaty, acknowledges the possibility for the Member States to maintain or introduce more stringent protective measures, insofar as they are compatible with the Treaties, Article 192 TFEU regulates the decision-making procedure to follow when actions need to be taken in order to achieve the above-mentioned EU objectives.

In that regard, it is to be noted that the Treaty of Lisbon has finally classified the competences of the Union, dividing them in exclusive competences, shared competences, and competences to support, coordinate or supplement the actions of the Member States.[90] The environment falls within those areas in which the EU shares its competences with the Member States,[91] with the consequence that the latter could regulate the matter inasmuch as the EU has not exercised its competences. The EU is therefore allowed to adopt legally binding acts in the field, but only and in so far as the objective of the proposed action cannot be sufficiently achieved by the Member States; in other words, EU actions need to comply with the principle of *subsidiarity*.[92]

Against this backdrop, and in line with the changes brought by the Treaty of Amsterdam (entered into force in 1999), Article 192 TFEU now provides that, when the EU exercises its competence in environmental matters, the *ordinary legislative procedure* applies, namely that procedure where the Council and the European Parliament have the role of *co-legislators*. In Article 130s EEC Treaty as introduced by the SEA, the rule was instead that the Council had to act unanimously. In some sensitive fields, the Council can still act unanimously, simply after having consulted the European Parliament, the Economic and Social Committee, and the Committee of the Regions: such a special legislative procedure applies, for instance, when provisions primarily of a fiscal nature—still concerning the environment though—have to be adopted.[93]

Apart from the three mentioned Articles, however, the importance of the protection of the environment at the EU level emerges also from *other provisions* of the Treaties. For instance, Article 2 EEC Treaty was modified by the Treaty of Maastricht so as to include a reference to the *respect of the environment* among the principles to be observed in the establishment of the common market. The Treaty of Amsterdam included in the same Article also a reference

---

90 Respectively, Articles 3, 4, and 6 TFEU.

91 Article 4(2)(e) TFEU.

92 Article 5(3) Treaty on European Union. On subsidiarity in EU environmental law see N de Sadeleer, 'Principle of subsidiarity and the EU Environmental Policy' (2012) 9 *Journal of European Environment and Planning Law* 63; M Lee (n 87) 20ff.

93 Article 192(2)(a) TFEU. Article 192(2) TFEU lists the cases in which the special legislative procedure applies.

to the *improvement of the quality of the environment*; this Article has been in substance replaced by Article 3 of the Treaty on European Union (TEU), whose para 3 now reads as follows:

> [t]he Union shall establish an internal market. It shall work for the sustainable development of Europe based on balanced economic growth and price stability, a highly competitive social market economy, aiming at full employment and social progress, and a *high level of protection and improvement of the quality of the environment*.[94]

The Treaty of Amsterdam had also inserted a new Article 3c in the Treaty establishing the European Community, which had repealed the EEC Treaty since the entry into force of the Treaty of Maastricht. The content of that provision can now be found in Article 11 TFEU, which states that 'environmental protection requirements must be integrated into the definition and implementation of the Union's policies and activities, in particular with a view to promoting sustainable development'.[95] This is the so-called *environmental integration principle*.[96]

Therefore, it is clear that the protection of the environment has become a horizontal interest of the EU, to be respected in the frame of all its actions. In this scenario, the Treaty of Lisbon has not brought any relevant change concerning the issue as such. However, with its entry into force, the Charter of Fundamental Rights of the European Union (CFR or 'Charter') has been recognised the same legal value as the Treaties.[97] The analysis of the consequences of this innovation would fall far beyond the scope of this work; just a few points need to be made.

The mentioned 'upgrade' of the Charter could have by and large relevant effects, since it can be assumed that individuals can now directly rely on the rights listed in the CFR before domestic courts. This seems to be possible, however, only when the Member States are implementing EU law[98] and only when a *right*—and *not a principle*—comes into play. The Charter distinguishes the two categories: the principles have to be 'observed' and have to be implemented either by EU institutions and bodies or by acts of Member States, whereas the

94 Article 3(3) TEU. Emphasis added.
95 Article 11 TFEU.
96 See, for instance, M Lee (n 87) 24.
97 Article 6(1) TEU.
98 Article 51(1) CFR.

rights have to be 'respected'.[99] For instance, in a decision concerning the right to *ne bis in idem* (enshrined in Article 50 CFR), the Court held that in cases of a conflict between provisions of domestic law and rights guaranteed by the Charter, 'a national court which is called upon, within the exercise of its jurisdiction, to apply provisions of European Union law is under a duty to give *full effect* to those provisions, if necessary *refusing of its own motion to apply any conflicting provision* of national legislation [...]'.[100]

Nevertheless, as argued by Lee, the expected impact of the Charter on the environmental field is very limited for a number of reasons. It is true that Article 37 CFR regulates the principle of environmental protection, stating that '[a] high level of environmental protection and the improvement of the quality of the environment must be integrated into the policies of the Union and ensured in accordance with the principle of sustainable development'. It is also true, however, that Article 37 CFR is clearly phrased as a *principle*, and not a right, so that it does not seem directly enforceable before domestic courts. As it is stated also in the explanations to the Charter, the content of Article 37 CFR is based on the above-mentioned Article 3(3) TEU and Article 191 TFEU,[101] as well as on Article 11 TFEU. In other words, 'given its similarity to existing language, and its status as a principle, it seems *unlikely* that Article 37 CFR will have a *dramatic effect* on environmental law'.[102]

The importance of the protection of the environment at the EU level has been so far discussed by means of reference to Treaties and Charter provisions, especially looking at the period that followed the Single European Union Act. However, in the history of EU environmental law some measures have been adopted also *beyond* the frame of above-mentioned Articles, and even *before* the entry into force of the SEA.

For instance, the first Environmental Action Programme (EAP) was launched in 1973.[103] Even though it 'provided only a broad framework of principles and

---

99 See Article 51 CFR, as well as the explanation to this Article in the 'Explanations relating to the Charter of Fundamental Rights' [2007] OJ C303/17, 35.

100 Case C-617/10 *Åklagaren v Hans Åkerberg Fransson*, para 45. Emphasis added.

101 'Explanations relating to the Charter of Fundamental Rights' (n 99) 27.

102 M Lee (n 87) 24. Emphasis added. For further reflections on Article 37 CFR see N de Sadeleer, *EU Environmental Law and the Internal Market* (n 87) 108ff.

103 'Declaration of the Council of the European Communities and of the representatives of the Governments of the Member States meeting in the Council of 22 November 1973 on the programme of action of the European Communities on the environment' [1973] OJ C112/1.

objectives', 'it inaugurated what has become an *established practice*':[104] since that Programme, other six EAPs have been adopted in the EU. At the time of writing, the 7th EAP is still in force; it covers the period until 2020 and it has been adopted by the Council and the Parliament on the basis of the ordinary legislative procedure.[105]

As far as legally binding instruments are concerned, because of the lack of specific provisions until the entry into force of the SEA, the Council had resorted to the Articles of the Treaties on the *common market* and on the *flexibility clause* to regulate environmental issues. In particular, since the national environmental regulations could represent a burden on the undertakings and therefore hamper their fair competition and enjoyment of the fundamental freedoms, the Community institutions began to *approximate* national legislations on the matter thanks to the competence they had—and still have, according to Articles 114 and 115 TFEU—in the field of the common (now internal) market.[106] This choice was also supported by the Court of Justice.

In *Commission v Italy* (1980), adjudicating on the failure of Italy to implement a Council Directive on the approximation of the laws relating to the sulphur content of certain liquid fuel, the Court held that that measure was well founded on Article 100 EEC Treaty (now Article 115 TFEU), since 'provisions which are made necessary by considerations relating to the *environment* and health may be a *burden* upon the undertakings to which they apply and if there is no harmonization of national provisions on the matter, *competition* may be appreciably distorted'.[107]

104 E Orlando (n 87) 4. Emphasis added.

105 Decision No 1386/2013/EU of the European Parliament and of the Council of 20 November 2013 on a General Union Environment Action Programme to 2020 'Living well, within the limits of our planet' [2013] OJ L354/171. For some considerations on the Programme, including its silence on environmental crime, see T Fajardo del Castillo, 'EU Environmental Law and Environmental Crime: An Introduction'. Study in the framework of the EFFACE research project (University of Granada 2015) 11–13. The competence of the European Parliament and of the Council to adopt the Programme, acting in accordance with the ordinary legislative procedure, is enshrined in Article 192(3) TFEU.

106 See N de Sadeleer, *EU Environmental Law and the Internal Market* (n 87). See also I von Homeyer, 'The Evolution of EU Environmental Governance' in J Scott (ed), *Environmental Protection: European Law and Governance* (OUP 2009) 12ff; N Giovannini, L Melica, M Giannotta and M Zingoni, 'Compendium of International and EU Law Instruments' (Droit au Droit 2013) <http://www.dadinternational.org/images/PDF/DRD-Compendium.pdf> accessed 18 September 2016, 19ff.

107 Case 92/79 *Commission v Italy* [1980] ECR 1115, para 8. Emphasis added. The Directive at stake was the Council Directive 75/716/EEC of 24 November 1975 on the approximation of

Whereas in this judgment the Court mainly looked at the environment through economic lens, five years later it took a step further in *ADBHU* (1985), where it upheld the validity of a Directive which imposed that the undertakings that wanted to dispose of waste oils had to obtain a permit. The limits to the free trade deriving from the Directive were necessary to guarantee an adequate protection of the environment, which was defined as '*one of the Community's essential objectives*'.[108] The Court recalled this judgment in some subsequent decisions, such as the so-called *Danish Bottle* case (1988), where it underlined that the view on the protection of the environment as an essential objective of the Community 'is [...] confirmed by the Single European Act'.[109]

As mentioned, indeed, the SEA introduced in the EEC Treaty an *ad hoc* Title on the environment. However, this did not imply that measures concerning environmental issues could have not been adopted anymore pursuant to other legal bases. In the so-called *Titanium Dioxide* case (1991), for instance, the Court annulled a Directive adopted on the basis of the above-mentioned Article 130s EEC Treaty (now Article 192 TFEU), ie that provision—introduced by the SEA—which was devoted to regulate the decision-making procedure to be followed in the environmental field. In that case, the Court found that the Directive at stake should have been adopted on the basis of the Article on the harmonisation of national regulations for the better functioning of the internal market.[110] The difference in the legal basis was not irrelevant since, according to Article 130s EEC Treaty, the Council acted at the unanimity, whereas on the basis of Article 100a EEC Treaty (now Article 114 TFEU), the so-called 'cooperation procedure' applied; under this procedure, explained the Court,

> the Council acts by a qualified majority where it intends accepting the amendments to its common position proposed by the Parliament and included by the Commission in its re-examined proposal, whereas it must secure unanimity if it intends taking a decision after its common

the laws of the Member States relating to the sulphur content of certain liquid fuels [1975] OJ L327/22.

108 Case 240/83 *Procureur de la République v Association de défense des brûleurs d'huiles usagées* [1985] ECR 00531, para 13. Emphasis added. The Directive whose validity was questioned was the Council Directive 75/439/EEC of 16 June 1975 on the disposal of waste oils [1975] OJ L194/23.

109 Case 302/86 *Commission v Denmark* [1988] ECR 4607, para 8.

110 Case C-300/89 *Commission v Council* [1991] ECR I-02867.

position has been rejected by the Parliament or if it intends modifying the Commission's re-examined proposal.[111]

In this judgment the Court argued that the Directive on procedures for harmonising the programmes for the reduction and eventual elimination of pollution caused by waste from the titanium dioxide industry should have been adopted as a measure related to the internal market. The reasons of such a conclusion are the following: i) pursuant to Article 130r(2) EEC Treaty (now Article 191 TFEU), the environmental protection shall be a component also of *other policies* of the Community; ii) the harmonisation of national measures on environment can be necessary to avoid unnecessary burdens on the undertakings and the distortion of fair competition (as already pointed out in *Commission v Italy*); iii) the provision on the harmonisation of national actions for the functioning of the internal market (then Article 100a(3) EEC Treaty, now Article 114(3) TFEU) expressly requires that the Commission, in its proposal for the measures intended to pursue such an harmonisation, should take as a base a *high level of protection*, when these measures concern environmental protection.[112]

Therefore, also this decision seems to confirm the nature of the environmental protection as a horizontal interest of the EU, to be protected in the frame of any EU policy. Moreover, this was not the only case where the environmental matters featured as a field of battle among the EU institutions. In fact, the dispute on the correct legal basis for the adoption of EU legislation aimed at the protection of the environment by means of criminal law lies at the heart of two landmark decisions of the Court of Justice, discussed in the following section.

3.2 *The Environmental Crime and the Ship-Source Pollution Cases*

The founding Treaties did not regulate the powers of the Communities in the field of criminal law. After the entry into force of the Treaty of Lisbon, the Communities have been incorporated in the European Union and no more dualism exists. However, at the times of the Treaty of Amsterdam, the European Community represented the first pillar of the three-pillar structure of the EU and within its frame it was not possible for the European legislator (European Parliament and the Council) to define criminal offences and impose criminal

111 Ibid, para 19.

112 Ibid, paras 22–24. For further considerations on the case-law mentioned in this section see E Orlando (n 87) 5ff.

sanctions;[113] provisions obliging Member States to criminalise some conducts could be adopted only in the context of the former *intergovernmental* third pillar, by means of legal instruments such as the Framework Decisions.

In this frame, a question arose: in light of the growing importance of the protection of the environment at the European level, was it possible for the Community to adopt first-pillar legal instruments to oblige the Member States to sanction environmental violations with *criminal* penalties? The story that followed is well-known.

In 2003, the Council had adopted a Framework Decision on the protection of the environment through criminal law, with the intent to harmonise the legislation of the Member States in the field.[114] The content of this Framework Decision had been mainly inspired by the 1998 Council of Europe Convention on the Protection of the Environment through Criminal Law, which never entered into force.[115] Arguing that the protection of the environment was a first pillar objective, the Commission challenged the legality of the legal basis of the 2003 Framework Decision before the Court of Justice. The judges of Luxembourg shared the view of the Commission and annulled the Framework Decision in the landmark ruling known as *Environmental Crime* case.[116]

Recalling both the *ADBHU* (1985) and the *Danish Bottle* (1988) cases, the Court focused on the protection of the environment as an *essential objective* of the Community. It also reminded that, according to settled case law, the choice of legal basis must rest on objective factors that are amenable to judicial review, including in particular the *aim* and the *content* of the measure. In those circumstances, the aim was the protection of the environment and the content particularly serious environmental offences.[117]

---

113 See more in V Mitsilegas, *EU Criminal Law* (Hart 2009) 65ff.

114 Council Framework Decision 2003/80/JHA of 27 January 2003 on the protection of the environment through criminal law [2003] OJ L29/55. On this Framework Decision see, among the others, HE Zeitler, 'Environmental Criminal Law' (2006) 77 *Revue Internationale de Droit Pénal* 255.

115 Convention on the Protection of the Environment through Criminal Law, ETS No 172, Strasbourg, 4 November 1998. The Convention was signed by 13 out of 47 Parties to the Council of Europe and ratified only by Estonia. On the Convention and its relations with the 2008 Directive on environmental crime see R Pereira (n 87) *passim*; GM Vagliasindi, 'Directive 2008/99/EC on Environmental Crime and Directive 2009/123/EC on Ship-source Pollution'. Study in the framework of the EFFACE research project (University of Catania 2015) 6–8 and 16–17.

116 Case C-176/03 *Commission v Council* [2005] ECR I–7879.

117 Ibid, paras 41 and 45–47.

Therefore, the essential character of environmental protection as a Community objective was crucial in this decision for determining whether criminal law could be used to achieve such an objective in the Community pillar. According to the Court, the fact that the Community did not enjoy any direct power in the field of criminal law did not prevent the Community itself,

> when the application of effective, proportionate and dissuasive criminal penalties by the competent national authorities is an *essential* measure for combating serious environmental offences, from taking measures which relate to the criminal law of the Member States which it considers *necessary* in order to ensure that the rules which it lays down on environmental protection are fully effective.[118]

The European Community was therefore deemed to be competent—in the circumstances pointed out by the Court—to adopt *directives* which contained provisions of *criminal* law, namely provisions imposing on the Member States the duty to criminalise some conducts affecting the environment.[119] The legal basis was represented by Article 175 of the Treaty on the European Community, ie what was in its first version Article 130s EEC Treaty and what is now Article 192 TFEU.

After this seminal ruling, a number of questions remained open. Among the others, the Court did not specify whether the Community competence in criminal law was limited to the definition of *criminal offences* or extended also to the definition of *criminal sanctions*.[120] This issue was dealt with by the Court in another relevant judgment, known as the *Ship-Source Pollution* case.

In 2005, the European Parliament and the Council adopted the Directive 2005/35/EC,[121] which aimed to incorporate international standards for ship-source pollution into Community law (Article 1), namely those provided for

118 Ibid, para 48. Emphasis added. For further considerations on the judgment and the reactions thereof see, among the many, V Mitsilegas, *EU Criminal Law* (n 113) 70ff; R Pereira (n 87) 186 ff.

119 V Mitsilegas, M Fitzmaurice and E Fasoli, 'The relationship between EU criminal law and environmental law' in V Mitsilegas, M Bergström and T Konstadinides (eds), *Research Handbook on EU Criminal Law* (Edward Elgar 2016) 275.

120 V Mitsilegas, *EU Criminal Law* (n 113) 74.

121 Directive 2005/35/EC of the European Parliament and of the Council of 7 September 2005 on ship-source pollution and on the introduction of penalties for infringements [2005] OJ L255/11.

in the 1973 Convention on the Prevention of Pollution from Ships (MARPOL).[122] Adopted on the basis of Article 80(2) of the Treaty on the European Community on the *transport* policy of the Communities, the 2005 Directive (first-pillar instrument) had been originally accompanied by the Framework Decision 2005/667/JHA (third-pillar instrument),[123] which imposed on the Member States the duty to *criminalise* some conducts defined in the Directive. The adoption of these two instruments was prompted by the dramatic shipwreck of the tanker 'Prestige' in 2002.[124]

Once again, the Commission challenged the legality of the adoption of a third-pillar instrument on ship-source pollution, arguing that parts of that Framework Decision should have been adopted under the first pillar. However, the Commission did not bring to the fore the articles on the environmental policy of the Communities, rather it focused its arguments on Article 80 of the Treaty on the European Community concerning the transport policy. Also in this case, the Court of Justice shared the view of the Commission and annulled the Framework Decision 2005/667/JHA.

In its decision, the Court restated what it had ruled in the *Environmental Crime* case, but it clarified that the competence of the Community in the field of criminal law could *not* include the determination of the *type and level of sanctions*.[125] In evaluating whether the Framework Decision affected the Community's competence on transport under Article 80(2) of the Treaty on the European Community, the Court followed a twofold approach: it examined the nature of Community competence on transport in the general Treaty framework; and it linked the Community transport policy with the objective of *environmental protection*.[126] On the latter issue, the Court reminded that environmental protection, one of the essential objectives of the Community, had to be integrated in the definition and implementation of the Community policies, according to the above-mentioned Article 6 of the Treaty on the European

122 MARPOL 1973, the original Treaty, was modified by a 1978 Protocol and the combined instrument (sometimes referred to as 'MARPOL 73/78') entered into force in 1983.

123 Council Framework Decision 2005/667/JHA of 12 July 2005 to strengthen the criminal-law framework for the enforcement of the law against ship-source pollution [2005] OJ L255/164.

124 See recitals Nos 2–4 of the Council Framework Decision 2005/667/JHA. For broader considerations on the effects of this dramatic shipwreck on EU and international environmental law see V Frank, 'Consequences of the *Prestige* Sinking for European and International Law' (2005) 20 *The International Journal of Marine and Coastal Law* 1. See also *infra*, section 6.1.

125 Case C-440/05 *Commission v Council* [2007] ECR I-09097.

126 V Mitsilegas, *EU Criminal Law* (n 113) 82.

Community (now Article 11 TFEU). Of course, such a provision concerned also the common transport policy: '[t]he Community legislature may therefore, on the basis of Article 80(2) EC and in the exercise of the powers conferred on it by that provision, *decide to promote environmental protection* [...]'.[127]

This link between the environmental protection and Community policies is pinned down even better when the Court specified that, since some Articles of the Framework Decision were 'designed to ensure the efficacy of the rules adopted in the field of maritime safety, noncompliance with which may have serious *environmental consequences*, by requiring Member States to apply criminal penalties to certain forms of conduct', those Articles must have been regarded as 'being essentially aimed at improving maritime safety, as well as *environmental protection*, and could have been validly adopted on the basis of Article 80(2) EC'.[128]

Against this backdrop, it is possible to conclude that the protection of the environment has been of utter importance in the history of the European Communities, and then of the European Union: not only the supranational organisation has paid an increasing attention to such a matter despite the silence of the founding Treaties, but its criminal competences have been acknowledged for the first time in the field of the environmental protection. However, such a protection by means of criminal law has turned out to be largely unsatisfactory, as it is shown in the next sections.

3.3 *Substantive EU Criminal Law on Environmental Crime: An Overview*

After the annulment of the above-mentioned 2003 Framework Decision on the protection of the environment through criminal law, the Council and the Parliament decided to transpose some of its provisions in the Directive 2008/99/EC on the protection of the environment through criminal law ('2008 Directive on environmental crime').[129] Likewise, the 2005 Framework Decision on ship-source pollution was repealed by the Directive 2009/123/EC ('2009 Directive on ship-source pollution').[130] In this section, the content of these

127 Case C-440/05 (n 125) para 60. Emphasis added.

128 Ibid, para 69. Emphasis added.

129 Directive 2008/99/EC of the European Parliament and of the Council of 19 November 2008 on the protection of the environment through criminal law [2008] OJ L328/28.

130 Directive 2009/123/EC of the European Parliament and of the Council of 21 October 2009 amending Directive 2005/35/EC on ship-source pollution and on the introduction of penalties for infringements [2009] OJ L280/52. On these Directives see, among the many, A Gouritin and P De Hert, 'Directive 2008/99/EC: A new start for criminal law in the

Directives is briefly discussed, in order to have a better understanding of the meaning of 'environmental crime' in the EU perspective.

Article 3 of the 2008 Directive on environmental crime obliges Member States to ensure that the nine conducts listed therein constitute *criminal* offences, which have to be punishable by 'effective, proportionate and dissuasive *criminal* penalties',[131] if they are 'committed intentionally or with at least serious negligence'.[132]

Four of these conducts have to be punished when they cause, or are likely to cause: i) death or serious injury to any person; or ii) substantial damage to the quality of air, soil, water, or to animals or plants. When transposed into national substantive criminal law, this cause-effect relationship between a conduct and its (potential) impact on persons or environment usually represents a real challenge for national authorities, since in most of the cases it is very difficult to prove this link in a satisfactory way.[133]

As Mégret underlines,

> environmental crime often lacks the single-event character typical of ordinary localized crime, and consequently may be *much more about process than a one-time occurrence.* [...] While crimes against the environment may be committed gradually, the criminal law traditionally looks to an identifiable event (an actus reus) and, more often than not, clearly and relatively immediately ascertainable damage (e.g., bodily harm, death, or damage to property). The problem that this presents for the criminalization of environmental harm is magnified when the damage is not only

European Community?' [2009] *Environmental Law Network International Review* 22; R Meeus, 'Fill in the Gaps: EU Sanctioning Requirements to Improve Member State Enforcement of EU Environmental Law' (2010) 7 *Journal for European Environmental & Planning Law* 135; PJ Cardwell, D French and M Hall, 'Tackling environmental crime in the European Union: the case of the missing victim?' (2011) 23 *Environmental Law and Management* 113; GM Vagliasindi, 'The European Harmonisation in the Sector of Protection of the Environment through Criminal Law: the Results achieved and Further Needs for Intervention' (2012) 3 *New Journal of European Criminal Law* 320; Ead, 'Directive 2008/99/EC on Environmental Crime and Directive 2009/123/EC on Ship-source Pollution' (n 115). National reports on the implementation of the Directives in the Member States can be found on the Commission website (<http://ec.europa.eu/justice/criminal/criminal-law-policy/environmental-protection/index_en.htm> accessed 18 September 2016).

131 Article 5 Directive 2008/99/EC. Emphasis added.

132 Article 3 Directive 2008/99/EC.

133 See, for instance, Eurojust, 'Strategic Project on Environmental Crime. Report' (n 29) 55–56.

> *geographically* but also *temporally diffuse*. In some cases, for example, the existence of harm may only be ascertainable with a substantial passage of time, and might only affect future generations.[134]

The conducts for which the Directive requires the above-mentioned causal relationship are: the discharge, emission or introduction of materials or ionising radiation into air, soil or water; various activities concerning *waste* and *nuclear* or *radioactive substances* (such as collection, transport, and disposal of them); the operation of plants in which dangerous activities are carried out or dangerous substances are used.[135]

Another conduct to be criminalised is the *illegal shipment of waste*, as regulated by Article 2(35) Regulation 1013/2006, when the illegal shipment is undertaken in a non-negligible quantity.[136] Regulation 1013/2006 is also known as the 'Basel Regulation' since it implements, in the EU, a Multilateral Environmental Agreement concluded at the international level, namely the 1989 Convention on the Control of Transboundary Movements of Hazardous Wastes and their Disposal (the 'Basel Convention').[137] Whereas the Basel Regulation is quite vague on the penalties to apply in cases of illegal shipment of waste,[138] the Directive 2008/99/EC makes it clear that they have to be of *criminal* nature.

Two of the other conducts mentioned in Article 3 Directive 2008/99/EC concern *protected species*; more precisely, Article 3(f) refers to the killing, destruction, possession, and taking of specimens of protected wild fauna or

134 F Mégret, 'The Problem of an International Criminal Law of the Environment' (2011) 36 *Columbia Journal of Environmental Law* 195, 222. Emphasis added. Similarly, E Pirjatanniemi, 'Desperately Seeking Reason—New Directions for European Environmental Criminal Law' (2009) 54 *Scandinavian Studies in Law* 409, 418.

135 Respectively, Article 3(a), (b), (e) and (d) Directive 2008/99/EC.

136 Article 3(c) Directive 2008/99.

137 Regulation (EC) No 1013/2006 of the European Parliament and of the Council of 14 June 2006 on shipments of waste [2006] OJ L190/1. It has been amended by the Regulation (EU) No 660/2014 of the European Parliament and of the Council of 15 May 2014 amending Regulation (EC) No 1013/2006 on shipments of waste [2014] OJ L189/135. The European Union is party to the Basel Convention since 1994 (<http://www.basel.int/Countries/StatusofRatifications/PartiesSignatories/tabid/4499/Default.aspx#enote1> accessed 18 September 2016). For some considerations on the trafficking of waste in Europe and the legislation thereof see European Environment Agency, 'Movements of waste across the EU's internal and external borders' (n 30).

138 Article 50(1) Basel Regulation states: '1. Member States shall lay down the rules on penalties applicable for infringement of the provisions of this Regulation and shall take all measures necessary to ensure that they are implemented. The penalties provided for must be effective, proportionate and dissuasive. [...]'.

flora species, whereas Article 3(g) concerns the *trading* in such specimens. In both cases, however, the conduct may not be punished by means of criminal law if it 'concerns a negligible quantity of such specimens and has a negligible impact on the conservation status of the species'.[139]

As the illegal shipments of waste, also the illegal *trade* in protected species had been regulated at the international level already before the adoption of the 2008 Directive on environmental crime. The landmark multilateral agreement in the field is represented by the 1973 Convention on the International Trade in Endangered Species (CITES), which aims to 'ensure that international trade in specimens of wild animals and plants does not threaten their survival'.[140] Even though the EU has formally become a party to the CITES Convention only in 2015,[141] already in 1982 the Convention had been implemented in the Community with Regulation 3626/82, subsequently repealed by Regulation 338/97.[142] Whereas all these instruments provided vague rules on the measures to take against the phenomenon at issue,[143] the 2008 Directive on environmental crime has clarified that such measures should be of *penal* nature.

Moreover, Member States are requested to sanction any conduct which causes the 'significant deterioration of a *habitat* within a protected site'.[144] Finally, also the 'production, importation, exportation, placing on the market or use of *ozone-depleting substances*' have to be sanctioned by means of criminal law.[145]

---

139 Article 3(f) and (g) Directive 2008/99/EC. On the ambiguous notions of 'negligible impact' and 'negligible quantity' see M Faure, 'Vague notions in environmental criminal law (part 1)' (2010) 18 *Environmental Liability, Law Practice and Policy* 119, 122ff.

140 <https://www.cites.org/eng/disc/what.php> accessed 18 September 2016.

141 See <https://www.cites.org/eng/disc/parties/chronolo.php> accessed 18 September 2016.

142 Council Regulation (EEC) No 3626/82 of 3 December 1982 on the implementation in the Community of the Convention on international trade in endangered species of wild fauna and flora [1982] OJ L384/1. It was repealed by the Council Regulation (EC) No 338/97 of 9 December 1996 on the protection of species of wild fauna and flora by regulating trade therein [1997] OJ L61/1.

143 Article 16(1) Regulation 338/97 provides that Member States shall take 'appropriate measures' to ensure the imposition of sanctions for at least some of the infringements of the Regulation listed therein, whereas Article 16(2) specifies that such measures 'shall be appropriate to the nature and gravity of the infringement and shall include provisions relating to the seizure and, where appropriate, confiscation of specimens'. See also L Elliott, 'Fighting Transnational Environmental Crime' (n 21) 96.

144 Article 3(h) Directive 2008/99/EC. Emphasis added.

145 Article 3(i) Directive 2008/99/EC. Emphasis added.

This overview confirms that 'environmental crime' is a broad concept encompassing very different conducts, and not all of them are included in Article 3. For instance, crimes concerning food safety or animal welfare are not addressed in the Directive.[146] It is to be noted that those nine conducts have to be criminalised when they are 'unlawful'.[147] It means that they have to be punished when they infringe either the legislation adopted pursuant to the European Treaties to be found in Annexes A or B to the Directive, or a national piece of legislation, a national regulation or a decision taken by a national authority giving effect to the legislation adopted pursuant to the Treaties.[148] In Annex A, for instance, the above-mentioned Regulation 338/97 implementing the CITES Convention can be found.

Choosing to impose a duty of criminalisation when the conducts are *unlawful*, the EU has followed the path of many national legislators. In most jurisdictions, environmental criminal law is strictly intertwined with other branches of law (usually administrative law), so that it looks as an 'accessory' to them, rather than a self-standing matter. In other words, in many legal systems

> the major part of environmental criminal law simply consists of provisions incorporated in environmental statutes of an administrative nature (for example, a Clean Water Act) and have as their main function the enforcement of compliance with administrative obligations. A great deal of environmental criminal law is therefore not formulated in an independent manner but is rather formulated as *accessory* to regulation. In legal practice, an important part of environmental criminal law will therefore consist of violations of a regulatory nature. For example, the polluter will be prosecuted for discharging certain substances into the environment without a permit or for violating permit conditions.[149]

The duty imposed on the Member States to criminalise some conducts only when they are 'unlawful' confirms such an accessory nature of environmental criminal law, which does not sit very well with the principle of legal

146 EnviCrimeNet and Europol, 'Intelligence Project on Environmental Crime. Report on Environmental Crime in Europe' (2015) <http://www.envicrimenet.eu/EN/reports> accessed 18 September 2016, 11. On this Project see more *infra*, section 5.1.

147 Article 3 Directive 2008/99/EC.

148 Article 2(a) Directive 2008/99/EC.

149 M Faure, 'Environmental Crimes' (n 51) 320. Emphasis added.

certainty.[150] In many instances, it is not immediately clear when a given conduct is criminal or not. This also makes very hard to prove the intentional subjective element of the illegal conduct.

More in general, the technical complexity of the legislation makes it difficult to ascertain that an environmental crime has occurred.[151] As already mentioned, for instance, for a prosecutor or a police officer to realise that a crime of illegal trading in protected species has been committed, it is first necessary to evaluate if a specimen falls within those endangered species whose trade is forbidden. Whereas this can be clear-cut in some instances, in others it could be not so easy and this evaluation could take some time. As a consequence, the investigations could begin with a quite substantial delay from the commission of the facts, when it has become even harder to gather sufficient evidence and when the crime can be on the verge to become time barred.[152]

That environmental criminal law is not a stand-alone subject emerges even better from the other Directive adopted in the field by the EU. Directive 2009/123/EC does not contain a list of conducts to be criminalised, but it rather modifies an existing piece of EU legislation concerning ship-source pollution (the above-mentioned Directive 2005/35/EC), introducing in it some articles which provide that (some) infringements of the Directive itself have to be punished by the Member States with *criminal* penalties.

It deserves to be further noted that, in line with the previously discussed case law of the Court of Justice, neither Directive 2008/99/EC nor Directive 2009/123/EC regulates the possible sanctions to be issued. They only require that the mentioned offences have to be punished by means of 'effective, proportionate and dissuasive *criminal* penalties', when committed by *individuals*.[153] As shown above, this constitutes a step forward in comparison with the existing international agreements.

Similarly, as far as *legal persons* are concerned, the Directives do provide some rules for their liability, whereas similar provisions are absent at the

150 See also P Beauvais, 'Les limites de l'internationalisation du droit pénal de l'environnement' in L Neyret (ed), *Des écocrimes à l'écocide. Le droit pénal au secours de l'environnement* (Bruylant 2015) 13–14.

151 See, for instance, L Lotti, 'Complessità degli illeciti ambientali ed evoluzione di metodi e strategie di accertamento' in B Romano (ed), *I reati ambientali alla luce del Diritto dell'Unione Europea* (CEDAM 2013) 89.

152 On the technical complexity of environmental criminal law in the EU Member States and on the negative consequences for an effective fight against this phenomenon, see Eurojust, 'Strategic Project on Environmental Crime. Report' (n 29) *passim*.

153 Article 5 Directive 2008/99/EC and Article 8a Directive 2005/35/EC (as inserted by Article 1(6) Directive 2009/123/EC). Emphasis added.

conventional level; however, the nature of the penalties is not specified: they have to be 'effective, proportionate and dissuasive'.[154] This choice was welcomed by some commentators, since it allowed the introduction of forms of corporate liability in those countries where a criminal responsibility of legal persons would be problematic.[155]

The wording of the provisions of the Directives on *penalties*—for natural and legal persons—leaves a considerable *margin of discretion* to the Member States. Therefore, it comes as no surprise that the impact of the mentioned EU legislation on national systems has been *very limited* and that they still bear *significant differences*.[156] According to some stunning data, it seems that at the Member States' level criminal law sanctions range from six months to life imprisonment for natural persons and from 200.000 to 60.000.000 Euros for legal persons.[157]

Even though in some countries the penalties for environmental crime can be high, on average they are deemed to be quite mild in most of the EU Member States.[158] In that regard, a further remark is necessary. The high sanctions that could be provided for environmental crimes would not *per se* guarantee that the fight against them is more efficient, since 'the legally defined maximum sentence says relatively little on the sanctions that are *effectively* imposed by the judiciary'.[159] However, the choice of keeping the penalties for environmental crimes (too) low can hamper an effective response to these crimes under different perspectives.

On a practical level, low penalties are usually understood as a clue of low importance of a crime, so that resources and people are thought to be better employed in the fight against more serious offences. On a legal ground, in many countries the possibility to undertake some investigative measures

---

154 Article 7 Directive 2008/99/EC and Article 8c Directive 2005/35/EC (as inserted by Article 1(6) Directive 2009/123/EC).

155 GM Vagliasindi, 'Directive 2008/99/EC on Environmental Crime and Directive 2009/123/EC on Ship-source Pollution' (n 115) 16–17.

156 Eurojust, 'Strategic Project on Environmental Crime. Report' (n 29) 36; S Chin, W Veening and C Gerstetter, 'EFFACE Policy Brief 1' (n 3) 2; G Giardi (n 39) 248ff; C Gerstetter, C Stefes, A Farmer and others, 'Environmental crime and the EU' (n 39) 31–34.

157 V Mitsilegas, M Fitzmaurice and E Fasoli, 'The relationship between EU criminal law and environmental law' (n 119) 286. This data has been presented by H Wagner of the Directorate-General for Justice of the European Commission during the EFFACE project meeting held in Berlin on 24 January 2014.

158 See, among the many, EnviCrimeNet, 'Report on Environmental Crime' (n 3) 11–13.

159 C Gerstetter, C Stefes, A Farmer and others, 'Environmental crime and the EU' (n 39) 34. Emphasis added.

depends on the amount of the *maximum* penalty provided for a crime: only if a given threshold is exceeded those measures can be adopted. For instance, this is usually the case of wiretappings. Similarly, also the limitation period of the crime can depend upon the *maximum* penalty applicable, with the consequence that the lower is the sanction the shorter is the period needed for the crime to become time barred.

In other words, in different studies and surveys it is emerged that environmental crime is generally *under-investigated* at the national level. Effective investigations on such crimes would require time, expertise, and resources which often judicial and police authorities do not have.[160]

As the next section shows, such scenario is even more discouraging than it seems at first sight, since the low penalties for environmental crimes can also hamper the procedures of judicial cooperation at the supranational level.

3.4 *National Investigations and Mutual Recognition: The Limits of the Environmental Criminal Legislation*

As far as judicial cooperation is concerned, the procedures of mutual recognition at the EU level can be triggered only if a given crime is punished with a *maximum* penalty which exceeds certain thresholds. The most known example in the field is represented by the European Arrest Warrant, which has replaced the political and cumbersome procedures of extradition among EU Member States.[161] The EAW is a judicial decision issued by a Member State ('issuing Member State') with a view to the arrest and the surrender by another Member State ('executing Member State') of an individual for purposes of conducting a criminal prosecution or executing a custodial sentence or detention order.[162] The EAW Framework Decision regulates the procedure of issuing and executing the EAW, which is marked by automatisation and speed. A judicial authority of an EU Member State must give effect to a decision by a similar authority in another Member State with a minimum of formality: suspects or convicted

160 See, for instance, EnviCrimeNet and Europol, 'Intelligence Project on Environmental Crime. Report on Environmental Crime in Europe' (n 146) 12; E van Asch (n 39) 203–204; C Gerstetter, C Stefes, A Farmer and others, 'Environmental crime and the EU' (n 39) 34–37; K Klaas and S Sina, 'Contribution to conclusions and recommendations on environmental crime: Functioning of enforcement institutions and cooperation between them (MS/EU level)'. Study in the frame of the EFFACE Project (2016) 3.

161 Council Framework Decision of 13 June 2002 on the European arrest warrant and the surrender procedures between Member States (2002/584/JHA) [2002] OJ L190/1.

162 Article 1(1) Framework Decision 2002/584/JHA.

persons must be surrendered as soon as possible, on the basis of completed forms, and ideally without the executing authorities looking behind the form.[163]

However, some requirements concerning the amount of the penalties for the crimes under investigation (or prosecution) need to be met. More precisely, according to the EAW Framework Decision, such an amount is relevant for two reasons.

On the one hand, the EAW may be issued 'for acts *punishable* by the law of the issuing Member State by a custodial sentence or a detention order for a *maximum period of at least 12 months* or, where a sentence has been passed or a detention order has been made, for sentences of at least four months'.[164] Therefore, for crimes with a lower maximum penalty, the EAW cannot be used by national authorities.

On the other hand, for a list of 32 offences listed in Article 2 of the Framework Decision, the EAW can be executed *without verification of the dual criminality of the act*. This innovation represented one of the most ground-breaking novelties in the field of the extradition procedures. The list mentions 'environmental crime, including illicit trafficking in endangered animal species and in endangered plant species and varieties' and 'illicit trafficking in nuclear or radioactive materials'.[165] If this inclusion is certainly positive, since it allows the use of such an important instrument in the field at issue, it cannot be forgotten that those 32 offences can lead to the surrender of a person pursuant to an EAW without the verification of double criminality *only* when in the issuing Member State they are punishable 'by a custodial sentence or a detention order for a *maximum period of at least three years*'.[166] Therefore, if the national penalties for environmental crime fall below this threshold, or if they are only pecuniary, the surrender of the requested person should pass through a previous verification of the double criminality of the act, which can either delay the execution of the EAW or even lead to a refusal of the surrender, if in the executing Member State that specific act is not criminalised. This could happen in the matter at issue, in light of the differences among national legislations in the definition of environmental crime, which have not been overcome by the 2008 Directive on environmental crime and the 2009 Directive on ship-source pollution.

For all these reasons, coupled with the already mentioned limited priority given to this crime and the difficulties often detected in the fight against it, it

163 V Mitsilegas, *EU Criminal Law* (n 113) 121.

164 Article 2(1) Framework Decision 2002/584/JHA. Emphasis added.

165 Article 2(2) Framework Decision 2002/584/JHA.

166 Ibid. Emphasis added.

has been noted that the resort to EAWs with regard to environmental offences is quite limited.[167]

The same list of 32 conducts of Article 2 EAW Framework Decision, with the same exemption from the verification of the dual criminality if the crimes are punishable in the issuing State with a maximum penalty of at least *three* years of imprisonment, can be found in other EU instruments, such as the Framework Decisions on the *mutual recognition* of: i) orders freezing of property or evidence;[168] ii) confiscation orders;[169] iii) judgments in criminal matters imposing custodial sentences or measures involving deprivation of liberty;[170] iv) judgments and probation decisions;[171] v) decisions on supervision measures.[172] In the last three cases, however, Member States retain the option not to abolish dual criminality and some of them have decided to exercise it.[173]

---

167 L Salazar, 'European judicial cooperation in the fight against environmental crime' in 'Summary of the EFFACE Workshop "Environmental Crime and the Criminal Justice System"' (Catania, 23 June 2014) 6.

168 Article 3(2) Council Framework Decision 2003/577/JHA of 22 July 2003 on the execution in the European Union of orders freezing property or evidence [2003] OJ L196/45. The provisions of this Council Framework Decision as regards freezing of evidence are replaced by the Directive 2014/41/EU on the European Investigation Order, for those States which are bound by this Directive (see n 175).

169 Article 6(1) Council Framework Decision 2006/783/JHA of 6 October 2006 on the application of the principle of mutual recognition to confiscation orders [2006] OJ L328/59.

170 Article 7(1) Council Framework Decision 2008/909/JHA of 27 November 2008 on the application of the principle of mutual recognition to judgments in criminal matters imposing custodial sentences or measures involving deprivation of liberty for the purpose of their enforcement in the European Union [2008] OJ L327/27.

171 Article 10(1) Council Framework Decision 2008/947/JHA of 27 November 2008 on the application of the principle of mutual recognition to judgments and probation decisions with a view to the supervision of probation measures and alternative sanctions [2008] OJ L337/102.

172 Article 14(1) Council Framework Decision 2009/829/JHA of 23 October 2009 on the application, between Member States of the European Union, of the principle of mutual recognition to decisions on supervision measures as an alternative to provisional detention [2009] OJ L294/20.

173 See, respectively, Article 7(4) Council Framework Decision 2008/909/JHA, Article 10(4) Council Framework Decision 2008/947/JHA and Article 14(4) Council Framework Decision 2009/829/JHA. For further details on the States which have used this option see the 'Commission Staff Working Document. Tables "State of play" and "Declarations". Accompanying the document Report from the Commission to the European Parliament and the Council on the implementation by the Member States of the Framework Decisions 2008/909/JHA, 2008/947/JHA and 2009/829/JHA on the mutual recognition of judicial decisions on custodial sentences or measures involving deprivation of liberty, on

For those 32 areas of conduct, moreover, the Framework Decision on the mutual recognition of decisions imposing financial penalties exempts the executing State from previously verifying the double criminality, even though in these cases—quite obviously since the matter concerns *financial* penalties—there are no references to a minimum threshold of imprisonment to trigger the procedure of mutual recognition.[174]

Finally, also Annex D to the recent Directive on the European Investigation Order (EIO) displays the same list of 32 conducts.[175] The EIO is a judicial decision issued by national judicial authorities of a Member State to have one or more specific investigative measure(s) carried out in another Member State, with the aim to obtain evidence. As the EAW, in practical terms the EIO is a form to be completed by a national competent authority, who will send it to the executing State where the needed evidence can be found. Once the EIO is executed, the executing authority shall, without undue delay, transfer the evidence obtained or already in its possession to the issuing State.[176]

For instance, the EIO can be issued: i) 'for the temporary transfer of a person in custody in the executing State for the purpose of carrying out an investigative measure with a view to gathering evidence for which the presence of that person on the territory of the issuing State is required, provided that he shall be sent back within the period stipulated by the executing State';[177] ii) in order to hear a witness or an expert by videoconference or other audiovisual transmission, when this person is in the territory of the executing State;[178] and iii) 'in

---

probation decisions and alternative sanctions and on supervision measures as an alternative to provisional detention' COM(2014) 57 final, SWD(2014) 34 final, 5 February 2014.

174 Article 5(1) Council Framework Decision 2005/214/JHA of 24 February 2005 on the application of the principle of mutual recognition to financial penalties [2005] OJ L76/16.

175 Directive 2014/41/EU of the European Parliament and of the Council of 3 April 2014 regarding the European Investigation Order in criminal matters [2014] OJ L130/1. For those States that are bound by the EIO Directive, this instrument has replaced the previous Council Framework Decision 2008/978/JHA of 18 December 2008 on the European evidence warrant for the purpose of obtaining objects, documents and data for use in proceedings in criminal matters [2008] OJ L350/72. At the time of writing, the Council Framework Decision 2008/978/JHA has been implemented by less than a half of the EU Member States (<https://www.ejn-crimjust.europa.eu/ejn/EJN_Library_StatusOfImpByCat.aspx?CategoryId=40> accessed 18 September 2016). As far as the freezing of evidence is regarded, the EIO Directive has also replaced the Framework Decision 2003/577/JHA for those States that are bound by the Directive.

176 Article 13(1) Directive 2014/41/EU.

177 Article 22(1) Directive 2014/41/EU.

178 Article 24(1) Directive 2014/41/EU.

order to determine whether any natural or legal person subject to the criminal proceedings concerned holds or controls one or more accounts, of whatever nature, in any bank located in the territory of the executing State, and if so, to obtain all the details of the identified accounts'.[179]

The EIO Directive modernises the system of judicial cooperation at the EU level, as it emerges from the fact that the corresponding provisions of the three traditional conventions in the field will be replaced as of 22 May 2017, ie from the date by which the Member States bound by the Directive are required to implement it.[180] The conventions replaced are: a) the 1959 Convention on Mutual Assistance in Criminal Matters of the Council of Europe and its two additional protocols, as well as the bilateral agreements concluded pursuant to Article 26 thereof; (b) the Convention implementing the Schengen Agreement; and (c) the Convention on Mutual Assistance in Criminal Matters between the Member States of the European Union and its protocol.[181]

Moreover, in the panorama of mutual recognition, the EIO Directive is characterised by some interesting features. It expressly includes non-compliance with fundamental rights as a ground of non-recognition or non-execution of an EIO and it introduces a proportionality check in the issuing State, so that the issuing authority may only issue an EIO when this is necessary and proportionate and when the investigative measures indicated in the EIO could have been ordered under the same conditions in a similar domestic case.[182] The Directive thus links proportionality with the requirement to avoid abuse of law via the undertaking of 'fishing expeditions' by the authorities of the issuing State.[183]

---

179 Article 26(1) Directive 2014/41/EU.

180 Articles 34(1) and 36(1) Directive 2014/41/EU. As we can read in recitals Nos 43–45, UK is bound by the Directive, whereas Ireland and Denmark are not. At the time of writing, the effects of the referendum on the exit of the UK from the EU are not known and the UK has not yet notified its intention to withdraw from the Union pursuant to Article 50 TEU.

181 Respectively, European Convention on Mutual Assistance in Criminal Matters, ETS No 030, Strasbourg, 20 April 1959; Convention implementing the Schengen Agreement of 14 June 1985 between the Governments of the States of the Benelux Economic Union, the Federal Republic of Germany and the French Republic on the gradual abolition of checks at their common borders [2000] OJ L239/19; Council Act of 29 May 2000 establishing in accordance with Article 34 of the Treaty on European Union the Convention on Mutual Assistance in Criminal Matters between the Member States of the European Union [2000] OJ C197/1 ('MLA Convention').

182 See, respectively, Articles 11(1)(f) and 6(1) Directive 2014/41/EU.

183 V Mitsilegas, 'Mutual recognition, mutual trust and fundamental rights after Lisbon' in V Mitsilegas, M Bergström and T Konstadinides (eds), *Research Handbook on EU Criminal Law* (Edward Elgar 2016) 154.

Despite these innovations, the EIO Directive sticks to the traditional list of 32 offences. When the EIO concerns one of them, it can be executed even though the conduct does not constitute an offence under the law of the executing State, provided that is punishable in the issuing State by a custodial sentence or a detention order for a *maximum period of at least three years*.[184] Moreover, the execution of the EIO may be refused by the executing State if 'the use of the investigative measure indicated in the EIO is restricted under the law of the executing State to a list or category of offences or to offences punishable by a *certain threshold*, which does not include the offence covered by the EIO'.[185]

Against this normative backdrop, it is evident that the *level* of penalty provided for environmental crimes in national legislations can have noteworthy consequences in the procedures of judicial cooperation.[186] However, when environmental crime is committed in the frame of criminal organisations, there are some possibilities to circumvent similar problems.

3.5 *The EU Legislation on Organised (Environmental) Crime*

When environmental crimes are committed by an OCG, national prosecution and police authorities could deal with them as *forms of organised crime*. This different 'labelling' of the phenomena (organised environmental criminality rather environmental crime *per se*) can have relevant practical consequences, bearing in mind that penalties for organised crimes are usually higher than those for environmental ones. As a consequence, the possibilities to refuse the execution of mutual recognition instruments significantly decrease and national authorities can adopt more intrusive and effective *investigation measures*. In some countries, specialised units with more extensive powers conduct the investigations on organised crime.[187]

Nevertheless, the 2008 Directive on environmental crime and the 2009 Directive on ship-source pollution do not encompass any provision on

184 Article 11(1)(g) Directive 2014/41/EU.

185 Article 11(1)(h) Directive 2014/41/EU. Emphasis added.

186 See also 'Communication from the Commission to the Council and the European Parliament on the EU Approach against Wildlife Trafficking' COM(2014) 64 final, 7 February 2014, 8.

187 C Gerstetter, C Stefes, A Farmer and others, 'Environmental crime and the EU' (n 39) 41. More in general, for some considerations on special measures available to national authorities in the fight against organised crime see, among the many, M Fichera, 'Organised crime: development and challenges for an enlarged European Union' in C Eckes and T Konstadinides (eds), *Crime within the Area of Freedom, Security and Justice. A European Public Order* (Cambridge University Press 2011) 177ff.

organised crime,[188] so that it has been argued that 'environmental criminal law is only *integrated to a very small extent into organised crime legislation* at the *international, European* and national level (with the exception of Italy)'.[189]

More in detail, as far as the international scenario is concerned, the most known piece of legislation in the matter is represented by the already mentioned Palermo Convention. The aim of the Convention is to promote cooperation to prevent and combat transnational organised crime more effectively (Article 1). To this end, it provides rules concerning mutual legal assistance (Article 18), joint investigations (Article 19), and special investigative techniques (Article 20).

The Palermo Convention applies only in cases of 'serious crimes', if the offence is transnational in nature and an organised criminal group is concerned (Article 3(1)). If some forms of environmental crime can be definitely transnational in their very essence,[190] the problems in the application of the Convention concern the concept of 'serious crime', since it 'shall mean conduct constituting an offence punishable by a *maximum deprivation of liberty* of *at least four years* or a more serious penalty'.[191] For the purposes of the Convention, the notion of 'serious crime' is also recalled in the definition of '*organised criminal group*', since the latter 'shall mean a structured group of three or more persons, existing for a period of time and acting in concert with the aim of committing one or more *serious crimes* or offences established in accordance with this Convention, in order to obtain, directly or indirectly, a financial or other material benefit'.[192]

Therefore, and once again, if national legislations on environmental crimes do not provide for high penalties, it seems that the domestic judicial and police authorities cannot rely on the Palermo Convention to fight the phenomena at issue.[193] The Preamble of the Convention itself mentions the 'illicit trafficking in endangered species of wild flora and fauna' as one of those crimes against

188 T Fajardo del Castillo, 'Organised Crime and Environmental Crime' (n 50) 11–12.

189 C Gerstetter, C Stefes, A Farmer and others, 'Environmental crime and the EU' (n 39) 40. Emphasis added. See also L Krämer, *EU Environmental Law* (7th edn, Sweet & Maxwell 2012) 413; I Rodopoulos (n 39) 175ff.

190 See above, section 2.1.

191 Article 2(b) Palermo Convention. Emphasis added.

192 Article 2(a) Palermo Convention. Emphasis added.

193 Eurojust, 'Strategic Project on Environmental Crime. Report' (n 29) 93. On the limited applicability of the Palermo Convention to TEC see A Cabrejo le Roux, T Reitano and M Shaw, *Tightening the Net: Toward a Global Legal Framework on Transnational Organized Environmental Crime* (WWF-Global Initiative Against Transnational Organized Crime

which the tools provided by the Convention can be used; however, since often the penalties for wildlife crime are not high enough, this instrument has not been applied frequently.[194] For similar reasons, the idea of a Protocol to the Palermo Convention on environmental crime has been put forward, since it should allow the application of the Convention even if the high thresholds provided therein are not met.[195]

The EU has taken part to the negotiations for the drafting of the Convention and it is part to it.[196] On its basis, the 2008 Framework Decision on the fight against organised crime has been adopted.[197] It provides a sophisticated framework of criminalisation on participation in a criminal organisation,[198] but *no specific reference to environmental crime can be found*. The definition of 'criminal organisation' recalls that of the Palermo Convention, since it

> means a structured association, established over a period of time, of more than two persons acting in concert with a view to committing *offences* which are punishable by deprivation of liberty or a detention

---

2015) <http://d2ouvy59podg6k.cloudfront.net/downloads/tightening_the_net__1.pdf> accessed 18 September 2016, 30ff.

194 See 'Communication from the Commission. EU Action Plan Against Wildlife Trafficking' (n 45) 5–6. See also L Elliott, 'Fighting Transnational Environmental Crime' (n 21) 95.

195 A Cabrejo le Roux, T Reitano and M Shaw (n 193) 35.

196 On the peculiarities of the EU's participation to the procedures which led to the adoption of the Palermo Convention see V Mitsilegas, 'The European Union and the Global Governance of Crime' in V Mitsilegas, P Alldridge and L Cheliotis (eds), *Globalisation, Criminal Law and Criminal Justice. Theoretical, Comparative and Transnational Perspectives* (Hart 2015) 157ff.

197 Council Framework Decision 2008/841/JHA of 24 October 2008 on the fight against organised crime [2008] OJ L300/42. This Framework Decision repealed the previous Joint Action of 21 December 1998 adopted by the Council on the basis of Article K.3 of the Treaty on European Union, on making it a criminal offence to participate in a criminal organisation in the Member States of the European Union (98/733/JHA) [1998] OJ L351/1. On the Joint Action and on its relations with the Palermo Convention see V Mitsilegas, 'Defining organised crime in the European Union: the limits of European criminal law in an area of "freedom, security and justice"' (2001) 26 *European Law Review* 565. For a recent detailed overview of the EU legal scenario on organised crime see S Hufnagel, 'Organized crime' in V Mitsilegas, M Bergström and T Konstadinides (eds), *Research Handbook on EU Criminal Law* (Edward Elgar 2016) 355–375.

198 V Mitsilegas, 'The Council Framework Decision on the Fight against Organised Crime' (n 38) 5.

> order of a *maximum of at least four years* or a more serious penalty, to obtain, directly or indirectly, a financial or other material benefit.[199]

As the 2008 Directive on environmental crime and the 2009 Directive on ship-source pollution, the Framework Decision has left a wide margin of discretion to the Member States, since the elements of a criminal organisation are defined very broadly and with flexible, *ambiguous* criteria.[200] Some authors have argued that this choice is not necessarily blameworthy, since 'legal diversity can in fact promote the fight against cross-border organized crime, providing practitioners with a high level of flexibility in choosing strategies and jurisdictions to carry out certain measures (e.g. wiretapping, surveillance, arrest)'.[201]

However, the impact of this instrument on national legislations has been very limited, as acknowledged by the Commission in the Report on the implementation of the Framework Decision, issued in July 2016.[202] It emerges a quite patchy implementation in the Member States as far as the *predicate offences* of the criminal organisation are concerned: only four Member States have implemented the provision of the Framework Decision on the minimum level of maximum penalty of *four* years, whereas some of the others have chosen a lower threshold, some a higher one, some others have not indicated at all the level of the predicate offence, so that every criminal offence can be covered.[203] Given the mild penalties provided for environmental crimes on average, the latter choice to make the application of the legislation on organised crime independent from the limits of the penalties provided for the predicate offence seems to allow a better fight against organised environmental crime, at least on paper.

---

199 Article 1(1) Framework Decision 2008/841/JHA. Emphasis added.

200 V Mitsilegas, 'The Council Framework Decision on the Fight against Organised Crime' (n 38) 5–6. See also M Fichera (n 187) 173ff; F Calderoni, 'A definition that does not work: The impact of the EU Framework Decision on the fight against organized crime' (2012) 49 *Common Market Law Review* 1365.

201 S Hufnagel, 'Organized crime' (n 197) 367. It is a common view in the literature that the concept of 'organised crime' is quite ambiguous under both a criminological and a legal perspective (ibid 355; see also, among the many, J Finckenauer (n 37) 304–307; A Goldsmith, 'Organized crime' in M Marmo and N Chazal, *Transnational Crime & Criminal Justice* (SAGE 2016) 117–118).

202 'Report from the Commission to the European Parliament and the Council based on Article 10 of Council Framework Decision 2008/841/JHA of 24 October 2008 on the fight against organised crime' COM(2016) 448 final, 7 July 2016, 10.

203 Ibid 4–5.

The Report is based on information provided by the Member States and on a very detailed external study on the implementation of the Framework Decision, which confirms that when national authorities deal with organised crime they are better equipped to curb criminal phenomena.[204] In similar circumstances, national authorities are usually allowed to use special and effective investigative tools, to impose increased penalties or other penalties such as confiscation, etc. The study also shows that the provisions on the participation to a criminal organisation are deemed to be very useful in cases of OCGs involved in illegal *trafficking*, be it of drugs or human beings. In general, it emerged that 'the more "intellectual" the crime was, the more difficult it was to prove participation and therefore such offences became less useful' and that 'the usefulness was highest for offences whose commission in practice required some *sort of criminal organisation behind it*'.[205]

Even though neither the Report nor the study takes into account organised environmental crime, it can however be argued that the application of the provisions on organised crime can be useful to combat *environmental crimes in their organised dimension*, namely in cases of illegal *trafficking* (either of waste or of protected species). These activities are often transnational, as seen above, and they usually require a criminal organisation behind them.

Apart from the participation to a criminal syndicate as a criminal offence as such, EU law has provided that this conduct constitutes an *aggravating circumstance* for a series of other offences where there has been harmonisation at EU level. Participation in a criminal organisation has been used as an aggravating circumstance for offences such as attacks against information systems[206] and trafficking in human beings.[207] The use of participation in a criminal organisation as an aggravating circumstance reflects a view of the value of participation not as a 'self-standing' criminal offence, but rather as conduct which may be taken into account when other offences are prosecuted. This could be the

---

204 A Di Nicola, P Gounev, M Levi and others, 'Study on paving the way for future policy initiatives in the field of fight against organised crime: the effectiveness of specific criminal law measures targeting organised crime. Final report' (Rand 2015) <http://www.rand.org/randeurope/research/projects/organised-crime.html> accessed 18 September 2016, 207. See also ibid 223–337.

205 Ibid 207–208. Emphasis added.

206 Article 9(4)(a) Directive 2013/40/EU of the European Parliament and of the Council of 12 August 2013 on attacks against information systems and replacing Council Framework Decision 2005/222/JHA [2013] OJ L218/8.

207 Article 4(2)(b) Directive 2011/36/EU of the European Parliament and of the Council on preventing and combating trafficking in human beings and protecting its victims, and replacing Council Framework Decision 2002/629/JHA [2011] OJ L101/1.

case of environmental crime, so that it is disappointing that such an aggravating circumstance has not been provided in the 2008 Directive, since some of the conducts provided therein can be (and actually often are) undertaken in the frame of a criminal organisation.[208] On the contrary, the involvement of OCGs in cases of water pollution seems quite limited, so that the silence of the 2009 Directive on the matter is less surprising.

To complete the analysis of the EU regulation on environmental crime, especially in its organised form, the *economic nature* of the phenomenon needs to be stressed once more. As mentioned before, OCGs show a growing interest in the field of environmental crime because it has turned out to be a very lucrative activity. After all, it is common knowledge that the 'principal goal of criminal organizations is to make money'.[209] As a consequence, it seems necessary that the EU adopts effective legislation aimed to 'follow the money' coming from these crimes. Also in that regard, however, the EU current legal framework seems to be quite unsatisfactory, since an express link between environmental criminal law and anti-money laundering law is lacking.[210] This could hinder the effectiveness of environmental criminal law both within the EU and at the level of law enforcement co-operation with third states, as it is not always clear that proceeds from environmental offences are considered to be proceeds of crime for the purposes of anti-money laundering law.

The recently adopted fourth anti-money laundering Directive contains a broad definition of predicate offences including, on the one hand, *all* offences which are punishable by deprivation of liberty or a detention order for a maximum of more than one year or, as regards Member States that have a minimum threshold for offences in their legal system, all offences punishable by deprivation of liberty or a detention order for a minimum of more than six

---

208 On the need to introduce an aggravating circumstance in the Directive 2008/99/EC for cases in which environmental crime is committed in the frame of an OCG see GM Vagliasindi, 'Directive 2008/99/EC on Environmental Crime and Directive 2009/123/EC on Ship-source Pollution' (n 115).

209 J Finckenauer (n 37) 315.

210 V Mitsilegas, 'Contribution to conclusions and recommendations on environmental crime: Harmonisation of substantive environmental criminal law at EU level'. Study in the framework of the EFFACE research project (Queen Mary University of London 2016) 3. See also J Saunders and J Hein, 'EUTS, CITES and money laundering: A case study on the challenges to coordinated enforcement in tackling illegal logging'. A study for the EFFACE project (Chatham House 2015).

months.[211] The extensive scope of the predicate offences to include serious crime as defined above would include a number of environmental offences, provided that they meet the mentioned thresholds. On the other hand, the Directive includes among the predicate offences the activities of a criminal organisation as defined in Article 1 of the 2008 Framework Decision on organised crime. As a consequence, once more, dealing with environmental crime as a form of organised crime could allow the application of the Directive without further problems, but—as shown above—this is not always possible due to the mild choices of criminalisation adopted by the Member States.

Expressly including environmental crime in the list of money laundering predicate offences would have overcome differences in national legal approaches to the criminalisation of environmental crime and focused the mind of investigative and prosecutorial authorities on pursuing the proceeds of environmental crime.[212] Moreover, it would also have allowed the EU legislation to align with the most known international (soft) law instrument in the field, namely the already mentioned 40 FATF Recommendations, which provide that environmental crime has to be included among the predicate offences of money laundering.

In the context of the fight against the 'economic side' of environmental crimes, also the *confiscation* of proceeds deriving from these illegal activities needs to be guaranteed, in order to ensure that 'crime does not pay'.[213] However, the EU legal framework does not address this issue. Environmental crime is not mentioned in the recent Directive 2014/42/EU, which has the aim to establish minimum rules on the freezing of property with a view to possible subsequent confiscation and on the confiscation of property in criminal matters.[214]

211 Article 3(4)(f) Directive (EU) 2015/849 of the European Parliament and of the Council of 20 May 2015 on the prevention of the use of the financial system for the purposes of money laundering or terrorist financing, amending Regulation (EU) No 648/2012 of the European Parliament and of the Council, and repealing Directive 2005/60/EC of the European Parliament and of the Council and Commission Directive 2006/70/EC [2015] OJ L141/73. On this Directive see V Mitsilegas and N Vavoula, 'The Evolving EU Anti-Money Laundering Regime. Challenges for Fundamental Rights and the Rule of Law' (2016) 23 *Maastricht Journal of European and Comparative Law* 261.

212 V Mitsilegas, 'Contribution to conclusions and recommendations on environmental crime' (n 210) 7.

213 'Communication from the Commission to the European Parliament and the Council. Proceeds of organized crime. Ensuring that "crime does not pay"' COM(2008) 766 final, 20 November 2008.

214 Article 1 Directive 2014/42/EU of the European Parliament and of the Council of 3 April 2014 on the freezing and confiscation of instrumentalities and proceeds of crime in the European Union [2014] OJ L127/39.

Quite surprisingly, the list of offences already harmonised at the EU level to which the Directive applies does not contain any reference to the 2008 Directive on environmental crime.[215] As the fourth anti-money laundering Directive, the Directive on confiscation applies to the offences covered by the 2008 Framework Decision on organised crime; however, for the same above-mentioned reasons, it is deemed to be 'practically unable to indirectly cover organised environmental crime'.[216]

In conclusion, it seems that neither the current EU legislation on organised crime nor that on environmental crime is satisfactory.[217] However, especially after the entry into force of the Treaty of Lisbon, the EU is in a position to improve such a situation, even though it can be already anticipated that at the time of writing nothing is really changed.

3.6 *Environmental Crime and the Treaty of Lisbon: Hope Dies Last*

Among the most relevant innovations of the Treaty of Lisbon, those enshrined in Article 83 TFEU need to be mentioned. This provision allows the European Parliament and the Council to adopt *directives* providing for *minimum rules* concerning the definition of *criminal offences* and *sanctions* thereof. Since the choice of what to punish, and how to punish, is done at the EU level by means of a directive, which needs to be implemented at the national level, some commentators have referred to such a competence as an 'integrated' one.[218] Others prefer to underline the fact that the EU is still not competent to lay down penal legislation *directly* applicable in the Member States, so that they envisage an 'indirect criminal competence' of the EU in the aftermath of the Treaty of Lisbon.[219]

Article 83 TFEU features two different scenarios. Article 83(1) TFEU confers upon the Union competence to establish, by means of directives, 'minimum rules concerning the definition of criminal offences and sanctions in the areas of *particularly serious crime* with a *cross-border dimension* resulting from the nature or impact of such offences or from a special need to combat them on a

---

215 See also T Fajardo del Castillo, 'Organised Crime and Environmental Crime' (n 50) 17–18.

216 GM Vagliasindi, 'Contribution to conclusions and recommendations on environmental crime: Organised Environmental Crime'. Study in the framework of the EFFACE research project (University of Catania 2016) 5.

217 For similar considerations, as far as the trafficking in waste is concerned, see G Giardi (n 39) 248ff.

218 R Sicurella, '«Prove tecniche» per una metodologia dell'esercizio delle nuove competenze concorrenti dell'Unione europea in materia penale' in G Grasso, L Picotti and R Sicurella (eds), *L'evoluzione del diritto penale nei settori d'interesse europeo* (Giuffrè 2011) 6.

219 See, for instance, G Grasso, 'Il Trattato di Lisbona e le nuove competenze penali dell'Unione europea' in *Studi in onore di Mario Romano* (Jovene 2011) 2326.

common basis'.[220] Article 83(1) TFEU, therefore, reflects what could be called the 'securitised criminalisation approach'[221] in determining EU competence in substantive criminal law. In other words, EU competence to criminalise is justified as necessary to combat specified areas of criminality the majority of which have been elevated after the Cold War by the international community and the Union as global security threats.

Such areas are enumerated exhaustively in Article 83(1) TFEU, and among them *organised crime* is included. However, although in 2011 the European Parliament urged the Commission to submit a proposal for a directive on organised crime, acknowledging the failure of the 2008 Framework Decision in harmonising national legislations,[222] nothing is changed at the time of writing. Since the entry into force of the Treaty of Lisbon, in its annual work programmes and annexes thereof the European Commission has never mentioned its intention to issue a proposal on the matter. In the above-mentioned 2016 Report on the implementation of the Framework Decision on organised crime, the Commission has only stated—in a quite vague and ambiguous fashion—that 'this work will also contribute to the assessment of the necessity and the opportunity to review the Framework Decision'.[223]

Whereas it mentions organised crime, as well as money laundering,[224] Article 83(1) TFEU is on the contrary *silent on environmental crime*. However, unanimously and after the consent of the Parliament, the Council may adopt a decision identifying other areas of crime that meet the criteria mentioned in Article 83(1) TFEU, namely the cross-border dimension resulting from the nature or impact of the offences or from a special need to combat them on a common basis.

Similar criteria have led some commentators to argue that the justification for EU criminal law under Article 83(1) TFEU resides in its added-value function, drawing on a common capability to address the scale and nature of

220 Article 83(1) TFEU. Emphasis added.

221 V Mitsilegas, *EU Criminal Law after Lisbon. Rights, Trust and the Transformation of Justice in Europe* (Hart 2016) 58.

222 European Parliament resolution of 25 October 2011 on organised crime in the European Union (2010/2309(INI)), para 7.

223 'Report from the Commission to the European Parliament and the Council based on Article 10 of Council Framework Decision 2008/841/JHA' (n 202) 11.

224 However, the above-mentioned fourth anti-money laundering Directive has been adopted on the basis of Article 114 TFEU, concerning the approximation of laws in the field of the internal market, rather than Article 83 TFEU.

threats posed by *transnational* criminality.[225] In that regard, for instance, it can be easily argued that the trafficking of waste or of endangered species demonstrates a cross-border dimension which meets the legal basis requirements of Article 83(1) TFEU and complies with the principle of subsidiarity.

However, the applicability of Article 83(1) TFEU to areas of serious crime with a cross-border dimension resulting from the nature or impact of such offences or from a special need to combat them on a common basis must be read as conferring on the Union also the competence to define criminal offences and adopt criminal sanctions in areas of crime which have a cross-border dimension but which do not involve cross-border or transnational criminality as such. Examples of areas of crime with a cross-border dimension resulting from their nature or impact or need to combat on a common basis—but which may involve criminality conducted purely at national level—include terrorism and corruption. The same could be said with regard to some environmental offences, such as those cases of (national) pollution that can seriously affect the quality of (global) air, water or soil. Similarly, serious cases of *national* wildlife trafficking could fall within this broad reading of Article 83(1) TFEU, especially when the amount of specimens traded is considerable: in similar instances, wildlife trafficking can endanger ecosystems and biodiversity and can sometimes also facilitate the diffusion of diseases.[226] In this way, the scope of Article 83(1) TFEU is broader than it appears at first sight.[227]

Moreover, such a broad scope of Article 83(1) TFEU is confirmed by the fact that EU competence is defined on the basis of *areas of crime*, rather than on the basis of specific criminal offences. These areas of crime may actually correspond to a wide range of criminal offences or sanctions. A clear example of the potential to overstretch EU criminal law competence under Article 83(1) TFEU involves the use of the concept of organised crime, which can also be used as a legal basis for harmonisation of a wide range of specific criminal offences and sanctions linked to the activities of a criminal organisation: this could be the

---

225 C Harding and JB Banach-Gutierrez, 'The Emergent EU Criminal Policy: Identifying the Species' (2012) 37 *European Law Review* 758.

226 EnviCrimeNet, 'Report on Environmental Crime' (n 3) 23. In an article on the World Bank website concerning the risks of the recent Ebola virus disease, which is transmitted from animals to humans, it has been stated that '[a]s wildlife is traded between hunters, middle marketers, and consumers, there are, quite literally, billions of opportunities for disease transmission among wildlife, humans, and domestic animals each year' (T Bouley and S Thompson, 'Trafficking wildlife and transmitting disease: Bold threats in an era of Ebola' [2014] <http://blogs.worldbank.org/voices/trafficking-wildlife-and-transmitting-disease-bold-threats-era-ebola> accessed 18 September 2016).

227 V Mitsilegas, *EU Criminal Law After Lisbon* (n 221) 59.

case of (the most serious) environmental crimes, such as those forms of illicit trafficking which have proven to be very attractive for OCGs.[228]

However, more realistic possibilities for the EU to adopt harmonisation instruments concerning environmental crime are rooted in Article 83(2) TFEU,[229] which states that

> [i]f the approximation of criminal laws and regulations of the Member States proves *essential* to ensure the effective implementation of a Union policy in an area which has been *subject to harmonisation measures*, directives may establish minimum rules with regard to the definition of criminal offences and sanctions in the area concerned.[230]

Article 83(2) TFEU flows naturally from the Court interpretation of the Union's (than the Community's) criminalisation competence under the first pillar in the above-mentioned *Environmental Crime* and *Ship-Source Pollution* cases. Unlike the Court, the Treaty has also provided a competence on the sanctions.

Article 83(2) TFEU regulates what could be called a 'functional criminalisation'.[231] Rather than assuming the status of a self-standing Union policy, criminal law is thus perceived as a means to an end, the end being the effective implementation of other Union policies. In light of the peculiar history of this provision and of its strict relations with the environmental matters, it can be assumed that the existing doubts on the exact interpretation of Article 83(2) TFEU—such as those concerning the meaning of 'essential' and of 'effective' implementation of an area already harmonised—do not actually concern environmental crime. On the contrary, the adoption of a new harmonisation instrument pursuant to Article 83(2) TFEU in the field of environmental crime is highly desirable.

However, at the time of writing, neither the Commission nor the Member States have tabled any proposal to implement Article 83(1) or (2) TFEU as far as environmental crime is concerned.[232] Nothing is said in that regard in the

---

228 Ibid. See also G Giardi (n 39) 251ff; G Grasso, 'Article 83' in G Grasso, R Sicurella and V Scalia, 'Articles 82–86 of the Treaty on the Functioning of the European Union and Environmental Crime'. Study in the framework of the EFFACE research project (University of Catania 2015) 31–32.

229 See also R Pereira (n 87) 203; GM Vagliasindi, 'Directive 2008/99/EC on Environmental Crime and Directive 2009/123/EC on Ship-source Pollution' (n 115) 17–19.

230 Article 83(2) TFEU. Emphasis added.

231 V Mitsilegas, *EU Criminal Law After Lisbon* (n 221) 60.

232 The adoption of a directive pursuant to Article 83 TFEU could be proposed also by a quarter of the Member States, which enjoy the right of initiative in the AFSJ together with the Commission (Article 76(b) TFEU).

annual work programmes of the Commission and the annexes thereof adopted since the entry into force of the Treaty of Lisbon.

Therefore, even though the Treaty of Lisbon could lead to an improvement of the EU's response to transnational environmental crime, the scenario described above has not improved. Only the approach towards criminal phenomena at the EU level is changing, since there is now a shared belief that they are better curbed through the so-called 'multidisciplinary approach', which is briefly discussed in the next section.

3.7 *Perspectives on a Multidisciplinary and Multiagency Approach to Transnational Environmental Crime*

Nowadays, the expression '*multidisciplinary approach*' is quite trendy.[233] It suggests that crimes are better fought by means of a combined approach of criminal, administrative, and sometimes even civil measures. As a consequence, it implies a coordinated action of different bodies, such as law enforcement agencies, administrative entities, and private actors when possible. In this sense, 'multidisciplinary' can be used as a synonym for 'multiagency'.

For instance, an Informal Network of contact points on the *administrative approach to prevent and disrupt organised crime* has been set up at the European level. Even though the Network was established on the basis of the 2010 Council conclusions which concerned only the fight against crimes committed by mobile (itinerant) criminal groups, it concerns all forms of organised criminality.[234] The Commission, the Council Secretariat, and the 28 EU Member States are part of the Network, as well as Europol and Eurojust.[235] As we can read in a recent report on the activity of the Network, its purposes are those to 'promote, strengthen and develop the role of administrative authorities in the increasingly *multidisciplinary* fight against (organised) crime at EU level'.[236]

---

233 For a recent overview of this approach, especially in the field of organised crime, see T Fajardo del Castillo, 'Organised Crime and Environmental Crime' (n 50) 29–33.

234 See 'Draft Council Conclusions on the fight against crimes committed by mobile (itinerant) criminal groups', Council doc 15875/10, 5 November 2010. On this note, see also the outcome report of the meeting 'A Multidisciplinary Approach to Organised Crime: Administrative Measures, Judicial Follow-up, and the Role of Eurojust', Copenhagen, 11–13 March 2012, Council doc 11298/12, 14 June 2012.

235 'The Informal Network of contact points on the administrative approach to prevent and disrupt organised crime. A multi-annual Work Programme (2015–2017)', Council doc 16407/14, 9 December 2014 (document partially accessible to the public) 8. See also Eurojust, 'Annual Report 2012' (2013) <http://www.eurojust.europa.eu/doclibrary/corporate/Pages/annual-reports.aspx> accessed 18 September 2016, 31.

236 'Activity Report on the Administrative Approach to Prevent and Fight Organised Crime', Council doc 13498/13, 16 September 2013, 4. Emphasis added.

On a practical level, as explained in a very detailed study on the matter,[237] administrative approaches to crime cover three different kinds of measures and forms of cooperation. First, those aimed 'to *prevent* persons with a criminal background, or persons who can be linked to organized crime groups, from entering specific types of business or economic activity in general'.[238] Second, in some circumstances, the concept of 'administrative approach' implies the adoption of administrative measures, as well as the cooperation of law enforcement agencies and administrative bodies.[239] Finally, such a cooperation can be also institutionalised in some permanent or semi-permanent bodies, in which different agencies work together, such as the Dutch Regional Information and Expertise Centres, where 'the police, the public prosecution service, the tax authorities and the local administrative authorities have representatives'.[240] The study sums up its findings underlining the positive effects of a multidisciplinary approach in the fight against serious and organised crime and stressing the need of a stronger cooperation between law enforcement agencies and administrative bodies, and even private persons when possible and necessary.[241]

The increasing importance to adopt this approach has also led to issue a Handbook on complementary measures and actions to prevent and combat *organised crime*, drafted in 2011 by a group of specialists coming from some EU countries (Belgium, Finland, Hungary, Italy, the Netherlands, Poland, Sweden, the United Kingdom), the Commission, Europol, and the Secretariat of the Council.[242] A second version of this Handbook has been realised on behalf of the above-mentioned Informal Network.[243] Both documents are currently

237 ACM Spapens, M Peters and D Van Daele (eds), 'Administrative approaches to crime. Administrative measures based on regulatory legislation to prevent and tackle (serious and organized) crime. Legal possibilities and practical applications in 10 EU Member States' (2015) <http://ec.europa.eu/dgs/home-affairs/e-library/documents/policies/organized-crime-and-human-trafficking/crime-prevention/docs/final_report_eu_study_administrative_approaches_to_crime_en.pdf> accessed 18 September 2016, 469ff.

238 Ibid 469. Emphasis added.

239 'The latter may for example carry out sanitary inspections of businesses, impose fines and even revoke licences if local and business regulations have been infringed' (ibid).

240 Ibid.

241 Ibid 548.

242 'Complementary approaches and actions to prevent and combat organised crime. A collection of good practice examples from EU Member States', Council doc 10899/11, 30 March 2011 (document partially accessible to the public) 5.

243 'EU Handbook—Part II. Complementary Approaches and Actions to Prevent and Disrupt Organised Crime', Council doc 17600/13, 12 December 2013 (document partially accessible to the public).

partially accessible to the public. As far as the first version of the Handbook is concerned, its index is publicly available and it is possible to read that a section is devoted to *environmental crime*, with a specific sub-section on the 'illegal processing of waste'.[244]

The inclusion of this phenomenon in the Handbook allows to infer that there is a tendency to address also organised environmental criminality by means of a multidisciplinary approach. Actually, environmental crime seems a perfect candidate for such an approach, for two intertwined reasons.

On the one hand, as mentioned, environmental criminal law *per se* is often connected to environmental (administrative) law and it requires knowledge and expertise that is not easy to find among prosecutors and police officers. Therefore,

> easily accessible support from experts or specialised departments should be possible when faced with technically difficult investigations, e.g. customs officials with regard to the export of waste, the control of relevant certificates accompanying the transfer of protected species, specialised personnel from environmental agencies, etc.[245]

On the other hand, in light of the mentioned growing agreement on the fact that an effective fight against *organised crime* needs to pass through a strategy which puts together different agencies,[246] and since OCGs have shown an increasing interest in areas such as illegal trafficking of waste and of protected species, it seems reasonable to believe that also the efforts to curb organised environmental criminality could benefit from a multidisciplinary approach.[247]

4 Eurojust, Europol and Environmental Crime: Setting the Scene

The mission of Eurojust and Europol is to support and to coordinate, respectively, competent national prosecutors and national police forces dealing with

244 'Complementary approaches and actions to prevent and combat organised crime' (n 242) 4.

245 Ibid.

246 See also the recent 'Council conclusions on the administrative approach to prevent and fight serious and organised crime', Council doc 9935/16, 9 June 2016.

247 See Eurojust, 'Strategic Project on Environmental Crime. Report' (n 29) 35. As far as wildlife crime is concerned, the multidisciplinary approach is supported by E van Asch (n 39) 218.

investigations and/or prosecutions concerning cross-border crimes. It has already been shown that environmental crime falls within this category but the EU legislation does not address the issue in a satisfactory way. Against this backdrop, it is now possible to evaluate whether the two EU agencies can have an added value in the fight against TEC.

Section 4.1 deals with the legal basis and with the competences of Europol and Eurojust, providing a classification of their tasks. More in detail, the activities that the two agencies carry out to achieve their *core* tasks will be defined as 'operational', whereas the others will be referred to as 'non-operational' or 'strategic'. Then, the structure and the operational activities of Eurojust and Europol are discussed respectively in sections 4.2 and 4.3. The focus of section 4.4 is instead on the strategic tasks of the two agencies, whereas section 4.5 puts forward some final considerations on the suggested classification. It will be argued that, in practice, the boundaries between the 'operational' and 'non-operational' activities are quite blurred. Moreover, even though Eurojust and Europol do not enjoy direct coercive powers vis-à-vis the individuals, the importance that their contribution can have for the success of national investigations and prosecutions will be stressed. These considerations will be further confirmed in the sections addressing the role of the two agencies in the fight against TEC.

4.1 *Competence of the Agencies and Framing of Their Activities ('Operational' and 'Non-operational')*

Despite their similar mission, the ways Europol and Eurojust achieve their objectives are quite different, as well as their history, structure, and powers.

Europol was set up before what has been perceived by some authors as its 'judicial counterpart',[248] with a Convention dating back to 1995,[249] repealed in 2009 by a Council Decision ('Europol Council Decision')[250] which as will be

248 M Fletcher, R Lööf and B Gilmore, *EU Criminal Law and Justice* (Edward Elgar 2008) 69.

249 Council Act of 26 July 1995 drawing up the Convention based on Article K.3 of the Treaty on European Union, on the establishment of a European Police Office (Europol Convention) [1995] OJ C316/1. Different Protocols have amended this Convention over the years: for further references to them see V Mitsilegas, *EU Criminal Law* (n 113) 164ff. Europol began its activities in 1999, replacing the previous Europol Drugs Unit, established in 1995 by the Joint Action 95/73/JHA of 10 March 1995 adopted by the Council on the basis of Article K.3 of the Treaty on European Union concerning the Europol Drugs Unit [1995] OJ L62/1.

250 Council Decision 2009/371/JHA of 6 April 2009 establishing the European Police Office (Europol) [2009] OJ L121/37. For a comprehensive evaluation of the implementation of this Decision see E Disley, B Irving, W Hughes and B Patruni, 'Evaluation of the

seen below has been 'Lisbonised' since. The idea of a European Union's Judicial Cooperation Unit (Eurojust, hereinafter also the 'Unit') was instead conceived in Tampere during the 1999 European Council meeting,[251] but a Council Decision officially established the Unit only in 2002.[252] The latter instrument was amended in 2003 and in 2009,[253] and the consolidated text representing the current legal basis of Eurojust will be referred to as the 'Eurojust Council Decision'.

Following the entry into force of the Lisbon Treaty, in May 2016 the Council and the European Parliament have adopted the new Regulation on Europol.[254] Unless otherwise specified, the following analysis on Europol is based on this Regulation, which will be effective as of 1 May 2017.[255]

As far as their competence is concerned, the two agencies can carry out their activities with regard to the same areas of crime, since the Eurojust Council Decision states that 'the general competence of Eurojust shall cover: (a) the types of crime and the offences in respect of which Europol is at all times competent to act [...]'.[256] In turn, Europol is competent for 'serious crime affecting *two or more Member States*, terrorism and forms of crime which affect a

implementation of the Europol Council Decision and of Europol's activities'. Report for Europol Management Board (Rand Europe 2012) <https://www.europol.europa.eu/content/publication/evaluation-implementation-europol-council-decision-and-europol%E2%80%99s-activities-1677> accessed 18 September 2016.

251 See the 'Presidency Conclusions of the Tampere European Council', 15 and 16 October 1999 <http://www.europarl.europa.eu/summits/tam_en.htm> accessed 18 September 2016, Conclusion No 46.

252 Council Decision 2002/187/JHA of 28 February 2002 setting up Eurojust with a view to reinforcing the fight against serious crime [2002] OJ L63/1. An embryonic version of Eurojust ('pro-Eurojust') was established with the Council Decision of 14 December 2000 setting up a Provisional Judicial Cooperation Unit [2000] OJ L324/2. Located in Brussels, pro-Eurojust began its activities in March 2001 and ceased to exist with the entry into force of the 2002 Council Decision on Eurojust (6 March 2002).

253 Respectively, Council Decision 2003/659/JHA of 18 June 2003 amending Decision 2002/187/JHA setting up Eurojust with a view to reinforcing the fight against serious crime [2003] OJ L245/44; Council Decision 2009/426/JHA of 16 December 2008 on the strengthening of Eurojust and amending Council Decision 2002/187/JHA setting up Eurojust with a view to reinforcing the fight against serious crime [2009] OJ L138/14.

254 Regulation (EU) 2016/794 of the European Parliament and of the Council of 11 May 2016 on the European Union Agency for Law Enforcement Cooperation (Europol) and replacing and repealing Council Decisions 2009/371/JHA, 2009/934/JHA, 2009/935/JHA, 2009/936/JHA and 2009/968/JHA [2016] OJ L135/53.

255 Article 77(2) Europol Regulation.

256 Article 4(1)(a) Eurojust Council Decision.

common interest covered by a Union policy, as listed in Annex I'.[257] Annex I to the Europol Regulation expressly mentions 'environmental crime, including ship-source pollution'. In that regard, the only difference with the previous Europol Council Decision concerns the addition 'including ship-source pollution' after 'environmental crime'. However, there is no doubt that such a phenomenon already fell within the competence of Europol, and consequently of Eurojust.[258]

Even though the formulation of the Europol Regulation is not entirely clear on the fact that the forms of crime affecting a common interest covered by a EU policy and listed in Annex I—such as environmental crime—have to be of cross-border nature, this seems obvious, in light of the history and powers of the two agencies, created with the aim to support and coordinate the authorities of *different* countries dealing with *cross-border* cases. Moreover, also the sixth recital of the Europol Regulation states that '[a]s serious crime often occurs across internal borders, Europol should support and strengthen Member States' actions and their cooperation in preventing and combating serious crime affecting two or more Member States'.

Therefore, environmental crime falls within the competence of Eurojust and Europol when it concerns two or more Member States, ie when it is *transnational*. Moreover, Annex I to the Europol Regulation also mentions, as separate entries from 'environmental crime', 'illicit trafficking in endangered animal species' and 'illicit trafficking in endangered plant species and varieties'. Among the forms of environmental crime, as shown, wildlife trafficking represents one of the most serious threats in the EU, also because of the increasing involvement of OCGs.

Annex I to the Europol Regulation also lists 'organised crime', which in the past featured in the text of the Decision itself (Article 4(1) Europol Council Decision) rather than in the Annex. This change does not bear any practical effect and the consistency of the Regulation with the past emerges from the already mentioned sixth recital: '[a]mong the forms of crime with which Europol is competent to deal, organised crime will continue to fall within the scope of Europol's main objectives, as, given its scale, significance and consequences, it also calls for a common approach by the Member States'.

Against this backdrop, the response of Eurojust and Europol against transnational crime in general needs to be briefly sum up.

---

257 Article 3(1) Europol Regulation. Emphasis added.

258 In section 6.1 of this work, for instance, a well-known case of ship-source pollution dealt with by Eurojust already in 2003 is discussed.

According to the Europol Regulation, the objective of this agency is to '*support and strengthen* action by the competent authorities of the Member States and their mutual *cooperation* in preventing and combating'[259] serious cross-border crime. Likewise, the mission of Eurojust is to '*support and strengthen coordination and cooperation* between national investigating and prosecuting authorities'[260] with regard to transnational criminality.

The two agencies do not have the 'coercive' powers of national judicial authorities, such as the powers to arrest people, to search houses, to launch their own investigations or prosecutions.[261] The Treaty itself affirms the primary competence of domestic authorities in the field: pursuant to Article 85(2) TFEU (on Eurojust), 'formal acts of judicial procedure shall be carried out by the competent national officials', whereas Article 88(3) TFEU (on Europol) states that 'the application of coercive measures shall be the exclusive responsibility of the competent national authorities'. Therefore, the two agencies are only called to *help* domestic bodies in their investigations and prosecutions concerning transnational crimes.

Notwithstanding the similarity of their goals and of the inherent limits they have, the two agencies act in a different way. In this work, we will define 'operational' the activities that Eurojust and Europol carry out to achieve their *core* tasks.

Therefore, since Eurojust is mainly thought as an instrument to facilitate the *coordination* of national prosecutors, its 'operational activities' are those aimed to such an objective. Also the internal Rules of Eurojust label the provisions on the tasks of Eurojust aimed at facilitating the coordination among national authorities as 'operational rules'.[262]

With regard to Europol, its 'operational activities' seem two-fold. Until the adoption of the recent Regulation, Europol's core activity was represented by the *analysis* of (personal) data relevant for the ongoing investigations at the national level. The Regulation now defines '*operational* analysis' as encompassing 'all methods and techniques by which information is collected, stored, processed and assessed *with the aim of supporting criminal investigations*'.[263]

---

259 Article 3(1) Europol Regulation. Emphasis added.

260 Article 85(1) TFEU. Emphasis added. This provision basically rephrases—in a much more synthetic and clear way—the wording of Article 3(1) Eurojust Council Decision.

261 Eurojust features a limited exception in this regard, when its national members act in their capacity as *competent national authorities* according to Articles 9b, 9c, and 9d Eurojust Council Decision (see section 4.2).

262 See Title II ('operational rules') of the 'Rules of Procedure of Eurojust' [2002] OJ C286/1.

263 Article 2(c) Europol Regulation. Emphasis added. See more *infra*, section 4.3.

This will remain the kingpin of Europol's identity: in other words, 'Europol puts analysis at the centre of its activities'.[264]

Compared to the previous Council Decision, the Regulation pays more attention also to the *coordination* role which can be played by Europol. The Europol Council Decision only stated that Europol should have the power 'to ask the competent authorities of the Member States concerned to initiate, conduct or coordinate investigations and to suggest the setting up of joint investigation teams in specific cases'.[265] On the contrary, among the tasks of the agency, the Regulation now mentions those of coordinating, organising and implementing 'investigative and operational actions to support and strengthen actions by the competent authorities of the Member States, that are carried out: (i) jointly with the competent authorities of the Member States; or (ii) in the context of joint investigation teams [...]'.[266] Within these strict boundaries, which are consistent with the traditional unwillingness of Member States to surrender their sovereignty in the sensitive field of criminal justice, the Regulation has enhanced the role that could be played by Europol in the coordination of national authorities.

In sum, Eurojust's operational activities are those connected with its role of coordination of national investigations and prosecutions. Such a coordination role of national authorities falls also within the operational activities of Europol, even though its main task is the operational analysis of data provided by domestic law enforcement agencies.

---

264 See the EU informative document 'The EU justice and home affairs agencies' (2014) <http://ec.europa.eu/justice/about/files/jha_agencies_en.pdf> accessed 18 September 2016, 19. Similarly, on the website of Europol itself it is possible to read that 'analysis is the cornerstone of all modern intelligence-led law enforcement activities and critical to all Europol activities' (<https://www.europol.europa.eu/content/page/intelligence-analysis-1852> accessed 18 September 2016).

265 Article 5(1)(d) Europol Council Decision.

266 Article 4(1)(c) Europol Regulation. This wording had already been suggested by the Commission when it issued the Proposal for the Council Decision 2009/371/JHA on Europol, but it was not agreed by the Council (A De Moor and G Vermeulen, 'The Europol Council Decision: Transforming Europol into an Agency of the European Union' (2010) 47 *Common Market Law Review* 1089, 1109–1110). Therefore, commenting the Europol Council Decision when it came into force in 2010, these authors underlined that Europol's core activities remained those linked with the exchange and analysis of information, whereas the possibilities it had to support national investigations were defined 'semi-operational tasks' (ibid 1109).

Beyond this 'operational dimension', however, Eurojust and Europol carry out other activities, which mainly consist in gathering and spreading *knowledge* on areas of crimes within their competence, on the instruments to cope with them, on recurring legal issues in the frame of judicial and police cooperation, etc. This side of their activities could be defined as 'strategic' or 'non-operational'.

Throughout the last Eurojust Annual Report (2015), for instance, operational and strategic activities are often juxtaposed.[267] However, as shown below, especially Europol's strategic activities are relevant in the frame of EU criminal law[268] and some of them are clearly listed in the Regulation. For example, it is stated that Europol is empowered to 'prepare threat assessments, *strategic* and operational *analyses* and general situation reports'.[269] More in detail, '*strategic analysis*' means 'all methods and techniques by which *information* is collected, stored, processed and assessed with the aim of *supporting* and *developing* a *criminal policy* that contributes to the efficient and effective prevention of, and the fight against, crime'.[270] The difference with the above-mentioned 'operational analysis' seems crystal-clear: whereas the latter is thought to support (ongoing) criminal investigations, strategic analysis is a tool for criminal policy.

The multifaceted role of the two agencies and their activities to support national investigations are analysed in the following sections, before focusing on their efforts in the fight against transnational environmental crime.

However, it deserves to be already underlined that, especially with regard to Europol, it has been questioned whether it makes sense to continue to consider that this agency does not have any coercive power, since its contribution—in

---

267 'Eurojust's *operational* and *strategic* activities in the field of counter-terrorism [...]' (Eurojust, 'Annual Report 2015' (2016) <http://www.eurojust.europa.eu/doclibrary/corporate/Pages/annual-reports.aspx> accessed 18 September 2016, 23; emphasis added); 'Eurojust supported, both at *operational* and *strategic* levels [...]' (ibid 66, emphasis added). Similarly, Europol's current agreements with its partners are classified as 'strategic' if they do not allow the exchange of personal data, 'operational' if they do (see section 4.3). A distinction between 'operational' and 'policy' work of Eurojust can be found in M Coninsx, 'Eurojust' in V Mitsilegas, M Bergström and T Konstadinides (eds), *Research Handbook on EU Criminal Law* (Edward Elgar 2016) 446. See also M Groenleer, *The Autonomy of the European Union Agencies* (Eburon 2009) 317ff; F Lo Voi and F Giuffrida, 'The Dual Role of Eurojust in the Fight Against Transnational Crime: An Overview' (2014) 1 *The European Review of Organised Crime* 129.

268 See section 4.4.

269 Article 4(1)(f) Europol Regulation. Emphasis added.

270 Article 2(b) Europol Regulation. Emphasis added.

some circumstances—can be of extreme relevance for the measures adopted on the ground by national authorities.[271]

The present work submits that environmental crime is an area where the support of the two bodies can be of such an importance for the success of domestic investigations and prosecutions that the boundaries between the 'coercive' powers of national authorities and those of the EU agencies seem to be quite blurred in practice. Moreover, it is argued that also the dividing line between 'operational' and 'non-operational' tasks of Eurojust and Europol, theoretically quite useful to categorise their powers and tasks, is quite difficult to draw when looking more closely at their activities. It seems that given the limited operational activities carried out by the two agencies in the field of environmental crime, their strategic tasks somehow try to bridge the existing operational gaps.

4.2 *Eurojust: Structure and Operational Activities*

Within Eurojust, each of the EU countries has its own Representative, the so-called Desk, which is composed by the national member and, usually, by his(her) deputy and/or his(her) assistant(s).[272] According to paras (1) and

271 See V Mitsilegas, *EU Criminal Law* (n 113) 169; S Gless, 'Europol' in V Mitsilegas, M Bergström and T Konstadinides (eds), *Research Handbook on EU Criminal Law* (Edward Elgar 2016) 464.

272 In this work, only the main features of this body are discussed. For a broader analysis on the functioning of Eurojust see, among the others, D Flore, 'Eurojust ou Ministère public européen : un choix de politique criminelle' [2000] *Agon* 9; NLC Thwaites, 'Eurojust autre brique dans l'édifice de la coopération judiciaire en matière pénale ou solide mortier?' [2003] *Revue de science criminelle et de droit pénal comparé* 45; C Van den Wyngaert, 'Eurojust and the European Public Prosecutor's Office: Water and Fire?' in N Walker (ed), *Europe's Area of Freedom, Security and Justice* (OUP 2004) 201–240; H Xanthaki, 'Eurojust: Fulfilled or Empty Promises in EU Criminal Law?' [2006] *European Journal of Law Reform* 175; G De Amicis, 'Eurojust' in G Grasso and R Sicurella (eds), *Lezioni di diritto penale europeo* (Giuffrè 2007) 467–536; A Suominen, 'The Past, Present and the Future of Eurojust' (2008) 15 *Maastricht Journal of European and Comparative Law* 217; JAE Vervaele, 'The Shaping and Reshaping of Eurojust and OLAF' [2008] *Eucrim* 180; M Groenleer (n 267); V Mitsilegas, *EU Criminal Law* (n 113) 187–209; F Spiezia, 'Le linee evolutive della cooperazione giudiziaria penale in ambito europeo' in E Aprile and F Spiezia, *Cooperazione giudiziaria penale nell'Unione europea prima e dopo il Trattato di Lisbona* (IPSOA 2009) 167–260; T Marguery, 'Eurojust II: Un tiens vaut mieux que deux tu l'auras?' in L Besselink, F Pennings and S Prechal (eds), *The Eclipse of the Legality Principle in the European Union* (Kluwer Law International 2011) 249–272; S Peers, *EU Justice and Home Affairs Law* (3rd edn, OUP 2011) 855–858; P Jeney, 'The future of Eurojust'. Study for the LIBE Committee (2012) <http://www.europarl.europa.eu/RegData/etudes/etudes/join/

(5) of Article 2 Eurojust Council Decision, they all could be prosecutors, judges, or police officers of equivalent competence, seconded by Member States. Nevertheless, 'a majority of the current national members have a background in the prosecution service'.[273] All the national members form the leading body of Eurojust, ie the College, which elects among its members the President and the Vice-Presidents of the Unit.

When Eurojust is requested by national authorities to assist them in the coordination of investigations and prosecutions concerning cross-border crimes, it strives to help them in solving the typical problems arising in such cases: choice of jurisdiction, collection of evidence abroad, risks of *bis in idem*, competing EAWs, etc.

As an example, Eurojust can 'ask the competent authorities of the Member States concerned, giving its reasons, to: [...] ii) accept that one of them may be in a better position to undertake an investigation or to prosecute specific acts'.[274] The College can be asked to issue a non-binding written opinion in cases in which the national members cannot find an agreement on a conflict of jurisdiction.[275] Similar opinions are usually based on the guidelines attached to the Eurojust 2003 Annual Report,[276] which have been correctly defined as 'a list of emerging problems and their possible solutions' rather than 'a real tool

---

2012/462451/IPOL-LIBE_ET(2012)462451_EN.pdf> accessed 18 September 2016; A Klip, *European Criminal Law. An Integrative Approach* (2nd edn, Intersentia 2012) 448–452; A Weyembergh, 'Coordination and initiation of investigations prosecutions through Eurojust' (2013) 14 *ERA Forum* 177; M Coninsx, 'Eurojust' (n 267).

273 'Final report on the 6th round of mutual evaluations on "The practical implementation and operation of the Council Decision 2002/187/JHA of 28 February 2002 setting up Eurojust with a view to reinforcing the fight against serious crime and of the Council Decision 2008/976/JHA on the European Judicial Network in criminal matters"', Council doc 14536/2/14 REV 2, 2 December 2014, 23. This round of mutual evaluation was carried out under the aegis of the Council Working Party on General Matters including Evaluation (GENVAL) and the outcomes have been collected in single Reports for each country, plus the final Report just mentioned (all of them are available at <http://www.eurojust.europa.eu/Practitioners/objectives-tools/Pages/6thRME.aspx> accessed 18 September 2016). Hereinafter, the final Report will be referred to as 'GENVAL final report'.

274 Article 6(1)(a)(ii) (Eurojust acting through its national members) and Article 7(1)(a)(ii) (Eurojust acting as a College) Eurojust Council Decision. Eurojust can act through its national members or as a College (see, respectively, Articles 6 and 7 Eurojust Council Decision), but in both cases the powers bestowed on the Unit are almost the same.

275 Article 17(2) Eurojust Council Decision.

276 'Guidelines for deciding which jurisdiction should prosecute'. Annex to Eurojust, 'Annual Report 2003' (2004) <http://www.eurojust.europa.eu/doclibrary/corporate/Pages/annual-reports.aspx> accessed 18 September 2016.

to settle a conflict'.[277] In fact, EU binding rules to solve conflicts of jurisdiction do not exist for the time being.

For the purpose of this work, it is not necessary to list in detail all the measures that Eurojust (through the College or through the national members) could suggest to the domestic authorities, whereas it is important to remind that the Unit, at least in principle, has not *direct powers* in the frame of national ongoing investigations. The Eurojust Council Decision is clear in stating that Eurojust can only '*ask*' national authorities to do or accept something, but it cannot *compel* these authorities in any way.[278]

Nevertheless, in order to increase the effectiveness of the Unit, some specific powers have been bestowed upon national members with the 2009 Council Decision. National members shall be entitled: i) to exercise *ordinary* powers such as those to 'receive, transmit, facilitate, follow up and provide supplementary information in relation to the execution of requests for, and decisions on, judicial cooperation';[279] ii) to exercise even more intrusive powers, but *only with the agreement of national authorities* (such as *executing* in their Member State, or issuing and completing, 'requests for, and decisions on, judicial cooperation'[280]); and iii) in *urgent cases*, when national authorities cannot be identified or contacted swiftly, to act even without their consent, authorising and coordinating controlled deliveries in their Member State or *executing*, in relation to their Member State a request for, or a decision on, judicial cooperation.[281]

The listed powers are quite far-reaching, so that one could argue that the exercise of these powers by Eurojust national members may go beyond Eurojust's stated coordination role. It is true that, first, national members are allowed to carry out the above-mentioned activities only if their Member States have implemented accordingly the provisions at stake and that, second, in those cases they act 'in their capacity as *national authorities*'.[282] However, since they intervene *because of* their role at Eurojust, in those cases and within the limits set out by the above-mentioned provisions, the operational activities of

277 I Patrone, 'Conflicts of jurisdiction and judicial cooperation instruments: Eurojust's role' (2013) 14 *ERA Forum* 215, 223. For some data on the role of Eurojust with regard to the conflicts of jurisdiction see: Eurojust, 'Report of Eurojust's casework experience in the field of Prevention and Resolution of Conflicts of Jurisdiction' (2015) <http://www.eurojust.europa.eu/doclibrary/corporate/Pages/caseworkpublications.aspx> accessed 18 September 2016.

278 V Mitsilegas, *EU Criminal Law* (n 113) 196.

279 Article 9b Eurojust Council Decision.

280 Article 9c Eurojust Council Decision.

281 Article 9d Eurojust Council Decision.

282 Articles 9b, 9c(1), and 9d(1) Eurojust Council Decision. Emphasis added.

Eurojust—or rather, those of the national members, still members of Eurojust but acting as national authorities—overlap with the typical coercive powers of national prosecution bodies.

However, two further considerations are due on the enhanced powers of the national members. First, Member States have implemented the 2009 Council Decision in a very fragmented way, so that 'the powers of the national members vary considerably from one desk to another' and 'some national members are not even provided with the ordinary, basic powers set out in Article 9b)'.[283] Second, given the high sensitivity of the matter, it comes as no surprise that Article 9e Eurojust Council Decision leaves the Member States a certain freedom not to comply with the Decision, if granting those powers to the national members would infringe upon constitutional principles or some fundamental aspects of national criminal justice systems.

Apart from this 'law in books' perspective, the most straightforward way for Eurojust to cope with the requests of assistance coming from national authorities involved in the same case is to have all of them around a table, in order to find common solutions to the detected problems. Eurojust not only gives its logistical and financial support in the organisation of these so-called '*coordination meetings*', but during them its members offer their expertise in the field of judicial cooperation in criminal matters.

In addition, the competent national authorities could even decide to carry out, contemporarily and in a given day (the 'action day'), measures such as arrests, seizures, searches, and so on. In these cases, a '*coordination centre*' is usually set up at Eurojust: representatives of the involved Desks take part to it,[284] with the aim to monitor the activities, to facilitate the communications between authorities, and to solve possible legal problems raised by the ongoing actions. Once the day is over, a final document is drafted and on its basis the concerned authorities agree on the further steps.[285]

---

283 'GENVAL final report' (n 273) 28.

284 Sometimes also members of Europol and of the Eurojust's Case Analysis Unit (CAU) are present.

285 For a brief explanation of the functioning of the coordination centres see S Petit Leclair, 'Justice et sécurité en Europe: Eurojust ou la création d'un parquet européen' [2012] *Cahiers de la sécurité* 42. The description of some cases dealt with by Eurojust can be found in F Spiezia, 'La cooperazione investigativa e giudiziaria nell'Unione Europea per il contrasto alla contraffazione ed al contrabbando. Un caso riuscito: la vicenda Gomorrah' in L Camaldo (ed), *La circolazione e il contrabbando di prodotti contraffatti o pericolosi. La tutela degli interessi finanziari dell'Unione Europea e la protezione dei consumatori* (Giappichelli 2013) 71–78; F Lo Voi and F Giuffrida (n 267) 135ff.

Coordination meetings and coordination centres represent the clearest examples of the added value of Eurojust, but in some cases they are not even necessary to allow the agency to achieve its goals. It happens that the issues faced by domestic prosecutors are easily solved once Eurojust is contacted: this can be through a meeting of the representatives of the involved Desks[286] or even by a simple exchange of information between them (eg the national Desk at Eurojust can inform the requesting national authority on the person to contact in another country or could transmit the request for mutual assistance to another Desk). Actually, this *informal* way of cooperation is highly appreciated by the practitioners,[287] even though it makes the work of Eurojust not always transparent and raises serious questions in terms of legal certainty, especially when controversial issues such as the identification of the competent authority are concerned.[288]

On the contrary, a more structured way of cooperation is represented by the Joint Investigation Teams (JITs).[289] National members could ask the

---

286 Only the members of Eurojust take part to these meetings (called 'level two'), without the participation of national authorities. The coordination meetings are also known as 'level three'. 'Level one' instead refers to the formal opening of a case by the College. Levels one, two and three are regulated, respectively, in Articles 15, 16, and 17 of the 'Rules of Procedure of Eurojust' (n 262).

287 '[...] the vast majority of cases are resolved with the assistance of Eurojust and *without the registration of a formal request* to the concerned Member States' (Eurojust, 'Annual Report 2012' (n 235) 19–20; emphasis added). See also P Jeney (n 272) 94–95; 'GENVAL final report' (n 273) 43–44.

288 Article 6(1)(a)(iv) Eurojust Council Decision. See V Mitsilegas, 'The third wave of third pillar law: which direction for EU criminal justice?' (2009) 34 *European Law Review* 555. It is not surprising, therefore, that Eurojust has been 'invited to reflect on how to render more transparent the real workload of national members and national desks' ('GENVAL final report' (n 273) 44).

289 JITs are regulated by Article 13 2000 MLA Convention and by the Council Framework Decision 2002/465/JHA of 13 June 2002 on joint investigation teams [2002] OJ L162/1. On this topic, see M Plachta, 'Joint Investigation Teams. A New Form of International Cooperation in Criminal Matters' (2005) 13 *European Journal of Crime, Criminal Law, and Criminal Justice* 284; C Rijken and G Vermeulen, *Joint Investigations Teams in Europe: from theory to practice* (TMC Asser Press 2006); C Gualtieri, 'Joint Investigation Teams' (2007) 8 *ERA Forum* 233; T Spapens, 'Joint Investigation Teams in the European Union: Article 13 JITS and the Alternatives' (2011) 19 *European Journal of Crime, Criminal Law, and Criminal Justice* 239; L Block, 'EU Joint Investigation Teams; political ambitions and police practices' in S Hufnagel, C Harfield and S Bronitt, *Cross-Border Law Enforcement. Regional Law Enforcement Cooperation—European, Australian and Asia-Pacific Perspectives* (Routledge 2013) 87–108.

competent domestic authorities to set up a JIT,[290] and more in general Eurojust supports the establishment and the functioning of Joint Investigation Teams also under a *financial* point of view, something which is more than welcomed by national authorities, which are therefore not requested to bear extra-financial costs in similar cases.[291]

A JIT is usually composed of prosecutors and/or police officers coming from different countries, involved in the same investigations on cross-border crimes. The main advantages of JITs have been summarised as it follows:

> [...] requests for mutual legal assistance are *no longer necessary*. Instead, if investigative action is required in a state that is party to the JIT, a team member from that country can instigate such an action directly, exactly as they would have done in their home country. Furthermore, team members can *freely exchange* all the information acquired.[292]

For the time being, national authorities have resorted only occasionally to the establishment of JITs.[293] However, when it has been the case, JITs turned out to be a very useful instrument of cooperation, highly appreciated by the practitioners.[294] To promote the use of such a tool, in 2005 a JITs Network has been established.[295] It is composed of experts located in each Member State, whereas the Secretariat of the Network is hosted by Eurojust. Usually, also Europol can be called to play an important role with regard to JITs, offering its support before and during the activities of the team, analysing the information collected, facilitating the exchange of information among national authorities, etc.[296]

---

290 The same can be done by the College pursuant to Article 7(1)(a)(iv) Eurojust Council Decision.

291 For broader considerations on the role of Eurojust with regard to JITs see M Helmberg, 'Eurojust and Joint Investigation Teams: How Eurojust can support JITs' (2007) 8 *ERA Forum* 245. Further information on the financing of JITs by the Unit is available on the dedicated page of Eurojust's website: <http://www.eurojust.europa.eu/Practitioners/JITs/Eurojust-JITsFunding/Pages/Eurojust-JITs-funding.aspx> accessed 18 September 2016.

292 T Spapens (n 289) 249. Emphasis added.

293 See S Hufnagel, *Police Cooperation Across Borders: Comparative Perspectives on Law Enforcement within the EU and Australia* (Ashgate 2013) 214–230.

294 'GENVAL final report' (n 273) 16 and 50–52.

295 See 'Joint Investigation Teams—Proposal for designation of national experts', Council doc 11037/05, 8 July 2005.

296 See B De Buck, 'Joint Investigation Teams: The participation of Europol officials' (2007) 8 *ERA Forum* 253; see also T Schalken and M Fronk, 'On Joint Investigation Teams, Europol

Europol can also participate to the coordination meetings organised by Eurojust; in these circumstances, Europol has usually carried out a previous analysis on the case, thanks to which national authorities can be even more aware of the transnational dimension of the crimes at stake, of the criminal network(s) involved, of the existing links between criminals, and so on.[297] Europol is the most important partner of Eurojust and their mutual relations are now regulated by an Agreement signed in October 2009.

Moreover, the Unit benefits from the cooperation of other partners, first of all the European Judicial Network (EJN).[298] Pursuant to Articles 26 and 26a Eurojust Council Decision, the Unit has also signed agreements with other EU bodies, as well as with international organisations and with various third countries;[299] some of the latter, on the basis of Article 26a(2) Eurojust Council Decision, have posted liaison magistrates at Eurojust (e.g. Norway, Switzerland, and USA), with the aim to facilitate the cooperation between them and the Unit, for instance *streamlining the exchange of rogatory letters*. Nevertheless, before transferring information to third countries and international organisations, Eurojust shall obtain the consent of the Member State that provided that information.[300] In this frame of the *external* action of Eurojust, it can be

---

and Supervision of Their Joint Actions' (2002) 10 *European Journal of Crime, Criminal Law, and Criminal Justice* 70.

297 Similar analysis is sometimes carried out by the analysts working in the Eurojust's Case Analysis Unit. Moreover, when the cases pose complex legal issues that need a further study, Eurojust can rely on the expertise of the Legal Service. More details on the cooperation between Eurojust and Europol can be found in A Weyembergh, I Armada and C Brière, 'The inter-agency cooperation and future architecture of the EU criminal justice and law enforcement area'. Study for the LIBE Committee (2014) <http://www.europarl.europa.eu/thinktank/en/document.html?reference=IPOL_STU(2014)510000> accessed 18 September 2016, 11–26.

298 The EJN was established with Joint Action 98/428/JHA of 29 June 1998 adopted by the Council on the basis of Article K.3 of the Treaty on European Union, on the creation of a European Judicial Network [1998] OJ L191/4, which has been repealed by Council Decision 2008/976/JHA of 16 December 2008 on the European Judicial Network [2008] OJ L348/130.

299 For more details on Eurojust's agreements and memoranda (or letters) of understanding (more than fifteen for the time being) see <http://www.eurojust.europa.eu/doclibrary/Eurojust-framework/Pages/agreements-concluded-by-eurojust.aspx> accessed 18 September 2016.

300 Article 27 Eurojust Decision. On the relations between Eurojust and its partners see V Mitsilegas, *EU Criminal Law* (n 113) 198–201; L Surano, 'L'action extérieure d'Eurojust' in M Dony (ed), *La dimension externe de l'espace de liberté, de sécurité et de justice au*

mentioned that the Unit has the possibility to post liaison magistrates to third States, even though this has not happened yet.[301]

4.2.1 The Eurojust Regulation in a Limbo

Pursuant to Article 85 TFEU, the Council and the Parliament are empowered to adopt a regulation on Eurojust, determining the structure, operation, field of action, and tasks of the agency. This provision opens new scenarios for the future, because it seems to allow Eurojust to *initiate* prosecutions and to directly *solve conflicts of jurisdiction*.[302] On its basis, in July 2013 the Commission issued a Proposal for a Regulation on Eurojust, which has been discussed for a couple of years, before the negotiations stopped.[303]

The overall objective of the Proposal was to modernise the legal framework of the Unit and, insofar as the nature of Eurojust allows it, to streamline its functioning and structure in line with the Lisbon Treaty and the 2012 Common Approach on EU decentralised Agencies.[304] As far as the competence of the body is concerned, Annex 1 to the Eurojust Draft Regulation specifies that 'environmental crime' includes ship-source pollution. As for Europol, this does not add anything to the existing status quo, especially bearing in mind that Eurojust dealt with a known case of ship-source pollution already in 2003.[305]

The draft Regulation is oriented towards the restructuring of the agency so as to alleviate the administrative burden from national members, who can then focus on their operational tasks. In this context, it proposes a new governance

---

lendemain de Lisbonne et de Stockholm: un bilan à mi-parcours (Éditions de l'Université de Bruxelles 2012) 210–219.

301 Article 27a Eurojust Decision. See 'GENVAL final report' (n 273) 49–50.

302 According to Article 85(1) TFEU, the tasks that could be bestowed upon Eurojust with the new regulation are: '(a) the *initiation* of criminal investigations [...] (c) the strengthening of judicial cooperation, including by *resolution of conflicts of jurisdiction* [...]' (emphasis added). On this provision see more in A Weyembergh, 'The development of Eurojust: potential and limitations of Article 85 TFEU' (2011) 2 *New Journal of European Criminal Law* 75; R Sicurella, 'Article 85' in G Grasso, R Sicurella and V Scalia, 'Articles 82–86 of the Treaty on the Functioning of the European Union and Environmental Crime'. Study in the framework of the EFFACE research project (University of Catania 2015).

303 'Proposal for a Regulation of the European Parliament and of the Council on the European Union Agency for Criminal Justice Cooperation (Eurojust)' COM(2013) 535 final, 17 July 2013.

304 'Joint Statement of the European Parliament, the Council of the EU and the European Commission on decentralised agencies' (2012) <https://europa.eu/european-union/about-eu/agencies/overhaul_en> accessed 18 September 2016.

305 See section 6.1.

structure, with the introduction of an Executive Board which will take care of the administrative and organisation issues which are nowadays dealt with by the College. Another change involves the status and powers of national members, since the draft Regulation explicitly sets out the operational powers that all national members must have, powers which have been further aligned in order to improve Eurojust's effectiveness. Moreover, the proposal provides for increased involvement of the European Parliament and the national parliaments in the evaluation of Eurojust's activities. Similarly, the rules on information exchange and data protection have been strengthened. Finally, as it is provided in the Europol Regulation, Eurojust should no longer be able to negotiate international agreements with third countries or international organisations, but only to conclude working arrangements with them.

The extent to which the reforms on the tasks of Eurojust correspond to the potential of Article 85 TFEU is fairly limited. The Commission chose to retain the status quo and not address the clauses of this provision that would allow for binding decisions from Eurojust vis-à-vis national authorities. A limited improvement can be found in Article 2 of the Proposal—which confirms the current objectives of the agency—because it refers to any 'information collected by Eurojust itself' and to the possibility for Eurojust to act 'on its own initiative'. Therefore, it seems that, on the one hand, the strategic work of Eurojust will be improved and that, on the other, the proactive role of the agency is enhanced. Especially the possibility for Eurojust to act on its own initiative is definitely to be welcomed, since it could address (at least partially) the problem of the scarce willingness of Member States to involve Eurojust in their cases;[306] however, no further interpretation of this clause is provided.

The draft Regulation confirms the division of tasks carried out by Eurojust as a College and through its national members, whose powers are now listed in just one provision.[307] The proposal contained other, quite limited, improvements to the status quo, but most of them have been watered down in the General Approach adopted by the Council in February 2015.

Overall, the Council endorsed the alternative model of governance for Eurojust, which is designed to allow the College to focus primarily on its operational tasks by designating the preparations of all managerial matters to the new Executive Board, and made interventions in numerous respects. During the negotiations with the Council, the potential offered by Article 85(1) TFEU was discussed. It was pointed out that the Article could be further explored

306 See more *infra*, section 4.5.

307 Article 8 Eurojust Draft Regulation (the last version available can be found in Council doc 6643/15, 27 February 2015).

(and exploited), for example with regard to an enhanced role of Eurojust in respect either of the initiation of criminal investigations or of the resolution of conflicts of jurisdictions. Eventually, the calls for binding decisions from Eurojust did not materialise.

In sum, assuming that the last version of the Eurojust Draft Regulation will be adopted, the powers of Eurojust will not change in comparison with the current ones and the balance between EU law and national criminal law in the field will remain the same.[308] However, one of the current weaknesses of the present situation should be overcome, namely the discrepancies among Member States with regard to the powers of national members: in light of its direct applicability pursuant to Article 288(2) TFEU, the Regulation should lead to overcome the current patchy situation.

However, at the time of writing, it is not clear if and when the negotiations on the draft Regulation will resume and the text is lingered in limbo since the first months of 2015.

4.3 *Europol: Structure and Operational Activities*

Whereas Eurojust has a collegial structure, Europol is organised in a hierarchical way, since it is headed by the Executive Director.[309] The other main organ of Europol, basically its decision-making body,[310] is the Management Board, composed of one representative of each Member State and of the Commission.[311]

However, also within Europol, each Member State has its own Representative, the so-called 'Liaison Bureau'.[312] This Bureau is composed of the

308 V Mitsilegas, *EU Criminal Law After Lisbon* (n 221) 94–103.

309 Article 16 Europol Regulation.

310 G De Amicis, 'I soggetti della cooperazione giudiziaria' in RE Kostoris (ed), *Manuale di procedura penale europea* (Giuffrè 2014) 179.

311 Article 10 Europol Regulation. In addition, Article 7(9) Europol Regulation provides that the heads of the national units (HENUs) shall meet 'on a regular basis, in particular to discuss and resolve problems that occur in the context of their operational cooperation with Europol'. On the ENUs see immediately *infra* in the text.

312 As for Eurojust, this work intends to present only the main features of Europol. For a broader analysis of this agency and its functioning see, among the others, E Marotta, 'Role and Action of EUROPOL in combating organised crime' in F Longo (ed), *The European Union and the Challenge of Transnational Organised Crime. Towards a Common Police and Judicial Approach* (Giuffrè 2002) 109–115; J Storbeck, 'The European Union and Enlargement: Challenge and Opportunity for Europol in the Fight Against International Crime' (2003) 8 *European Foreign Affairs Review* 283; A Nunzi, 'European Police Office—EUROPOL' (2006) 77 *Revue internationale de droit penal* 285; M Den Boer

Europol Liaison Officers (ELOs),[313] who are seconded at Europol from the Europol National Units (ENUs), ie those national offices located in each Member State acting as the *trait d'union* between the agency and the national authorities. In the Europol Council Decision, the ENUs were thought to be the *only* national office empowered to exchange information with Europol, even though Member States could 'allow direct contacts between designated competent authorities and Europol';[314] nevertheless, this provision has not received an appropriate follow-up in practice.[315] In the Europol Regulation, this scenario has been maintained: the Member States retain the right to allow direct contacts between national authorities and Europol, but the ENUs are still conceived as the main liaison body.[316]

While Eurojust mainly carries out its activities through the kingpins of the Unit's structure, ie the national Desks, this is not the case of the Liaison Bureaux at Europol. Of course, they are extremely useful to allow national authorities to get in contact with Europol and to exchange information with it,[317] but Europol's core mission (operational analysis) is mostly achieved through the work of the *analysts*, who elaborate the data provided from national law enforcement authorities.

The main tasks of Europol are 'to collect, store, process, analyse and exchange information, including criminal intelligence'.[318] This information is

---

and W Bruggeman, 'Shifting Gear: Europol in the Contemporary Policing Era' (2007) 22 *Politique européenne* 77; H Brady, 'Europol and the European Criminal Intelligence Model: A non-state Response to Organized Crime' (2008) 2 *Policing* 103; S Puntscher Riekmann, 'Security, Freedom and Accountability' in E Guild and F Geyer (eds), *Security versus Justice? Police and Judicial Cooperation in the European Union* (Ashgate 2008) 19–34; V Mitsilegas, *EU Criminal Law* (n 113) 161–187; V Amici, 'Europol et la nouvelle décision du Conseil: entre opportunités et contraintes' [2010] *Revue du Droit de l'Union Européenne* 77; A De Moor and G Vermeulen, 'The Europol Council Decision: Transforming Europol into an Agency of the European Union' (n 266); S Peers (n 272) 930–934; A Klip (n 272) 435–445; M Busuioc and M Groenleer, 'Beyond Design: The Evolution of Europol and Eurojust (2013) 14 *Perspectives on European Politics and Society* 285; S Hufnagel, *Police Cooperation Across Borders* (n 293) 80–86; G De Amicis, 'I soggetti della cooperazione giudiziaria' (n 310) 184–207; S Gless, 'Europol' (n 271) 457–479.

313 Article 8 Europol Regulation.

314 Article 8(2) Europol Council Decision.

315 E Disley, B Irving, W Hughes and B Patruni, 'Evaluation of the implementation of the Europol Council Decision' (n 250) 52.

316 Article 7 Europol Regulation.

317 Usually, information is exchanged via SIENA (Secure Information Exchange Network Application), which is managed by Europol itself.

318 Article 4(1)(a) Europol Regulation.

then crosschecked with the existing data already stored in Europol's databases. In that regard, the activity of Europol can help to establish links among existing cases, to discover relevant information that can be used during national investigations, to identify the precise location of people, goods or companies, and so on.

The detailed analysis of the different databases existing within Europol would exceed the purposes of this work. However, what is necessary to remind is that, at the bottom line, the agency can deal with and analyse data, including *personal* ones, concerning ongoing investigations. More precisely, until the Europol Decision is in force, this can happen if such data is stored in the so-called analysis working files (AWFs).[319] The internal organisation of Europol is recently changed and there are just two AWFs (one devoted to organised crime and the other to terrorism), inside which analysts work in smaller groups called *focal points* or *target groups*. As explained by Drewer and Ellermann, '[a] Focal Point is an area within an AWF which focuses on a certain phenomenon from a commodity based, thematic or regional angle. It allows Europol to provide *analysis*, prioritise resources, ensure purpose limitation and maintain focus on expertise', whereas 'a Target Group is an *operational* project with a dedicated Europol team to support an international criminal investigation or criminal intelligence operation against a *specific target*'.[320]

Therefore, the most far-reaching analysis of Europol can be done on the basis of data stored in focal points or target groups. Other data can also be collected within the Europol Information System (EIS),[321] which contains less sensitive information than the AWFs: e.g., the latter can store information on victims and witnesses of the crimes under investigation, which cannot be recorded in the EIS. Consequently, access to the information in the AWFs is much more strictly regulated and limited than access to the EIS.[322]

When the Regulation enters into force, the internal structure of the agency should change and the existing fragmentation should be abandoned. The main idea behind the new piece of legislation is that, once the information is sent

---

319 See Article 14 Europol Council Decision.

320 D Drewer and J Ellermann, 'Europol's data protection framework as an asset in the fight against cybercrime' (2012) 13 *ERA Forum* 390 (also available at <https://www.europol.europa.eu/content/publication/europols-data-protection-framework-asset-fight-against-cybercrime-1838> accessed 18 September 2016). Emphasis added. In the same article the authors provide more details on the concept of AWF within Europol.

321 See Articles 11–13 Europol Council Decision.

322 See E Disley, B Irving, W Hughes and B Patruni, 'Evaluation of the implementation of the Europol Council Decision' (n 250) 83.

to Europol, the body is empowered to process and analyse it without the current restrictions linked to the AWFs, focal points, and target groups. Also recital No 24 of the Europol Regulation seems to suggest such a shift in the organisation of Europol: '[...] Europol should be able to swiftly detect links between investigations and common modi operandi across different criminal groups, to check cross-matches of data and to have a clear overview of trends, while guaranteeing a high level of protection of personal data for individuals'. Similarly, the Explanatory Memorandum to the Commission Proposal for a Regulation on Europol mentioned that the processing architecture of the agency will be redesigned: rather than pre-defined databases or systems, the agency will adopt a new 'privacy by design approach'.[323] This approach 'would allow Europol to link and make analyses of relevant data, reduce delays in identifying trends and patterns and *reduce multiple storage of data*'.[324]

Of course, it remains to be evaluated how the new Regulation will be implemented in practice. In that regard, one can wonder whether the fact that the processing of data with the purposes of operational analysis needs to be performed by means of 'operational analysis projects'[325] will actually lead to a change in the current, fragmented scenario. However, a simplification of the existing structure would be an important step forward, which could help to easily crosscheck the information inside Europol's databases and which could therefore enhance the fight against each form of crime falling within the competence of the agency. It goes without saying that serious concerns on data protection issues arise, even though the Regulation itself contains different provisions on the matter.[326]

Moreover, as Eurojust, Europol can (only) *request* the national competent authorities to begin an investigation and it can also take part to JITs,[327] in the frame of whose activities it can process the relevant information with the consent and under the responsibility of the Member State that provided the information.

323 'Explanatory Memorandum to the Proposal for a Regulation of the European Parliament and of the Council on the European Union Agency for Law Enforcement Cooperation and Training (Europol) and repealing Decisions 2009/371/JHA and 2005/681/JHA' COM(2013) 173 final, 27 March 2013, 8.

324 Ibid. Emphasis added.

325 Article 18(3) Europol Regulation.

326 See especially Articles 28ff Europol Regulation. For further details on issues concerning data protection within Europol see V Mitsilegas, *EU Criminal Law* (n 113) 175ff; A Klip (n 272) 440–444.

327 Respectively, Articles 6 and 5 Europol Regulation.

Finally, Europol was expressly empowered by the Europol Council Decision to sign *agreements* with other EU bodies, as well as with third States and organisations.[328] The latter agreements were usually divided into 'strategic' and 'operational', the main difference being that only the latter allowed the exchange of *personal* data (under the further conditions provided for in Article 24 Europol Council Decision), whereas the former did not consent to transfer any kind of information which was not merely strategical.[329] In addition, Europol was allowed to deal with data coming from private parties and private persons, once the requisites listed in Article 25 Europol Council Decision were met.

With the new Regulation, the scenario is changed. Article 23 Europol Regulation lays down the common provisions for the relations of Europol with all the partners (EU bodies, third States, international organisations, and private parties). Europol is still authorised to receive and process personal data coming from its partners and to transfer information to them: all the details and the prerequisites can be found in Articles 23–27 Europol Regulation. What is changed is that the agency will no longer be able to negotiate *international agreements* with third countries or international organisations: in the aftermath of the Treaty of Lisbon, the power to conclude international agreements sits only with the Council, according to the procedure set out in Article 218 TFEU. Europol is only empowered to conclude *working arrangements* with its partners:[330] such arrangements are quite different—and much less far-reaching—than the proper international agreements which Europol could have signed before the Regulation. These agreements remain valid, but the Commission shall assess the provisions contained in the cooperation agreements by 14 June 2021; if appropriate, it can submit a recommendation to the Council for a decision authorising the opening of negotiations for the conclusion of an international agreement.[331]

4.4 *The 'Non-operational' Tasks of the Agencies and the Policy Cycle*

Eurojust and Europol are in an ideal position to collect and spread *knowledge* both on cross-border criminality and on the best ways to curb it.

---

328 Respectively, Articles 22 and 23 Europol Council Decision.

329 At the time of writing (September 2016), Europol has signed 12 *strategic* agreements and 16 *operational* agreements: see more at <https://www.europol.europa.eu/content/mega-menu/partners-1835> accessed 18 September 2016.

330 Article 23(4) Europol Regulation.

331 Article 25(4) Europol Regulation.

For instance, Europol issues documents known as 'Threat Assessments', intended to offer an evaluation on the diffusion and on the main peculiarities of a given crime, as well as on the needs to effectively contrast it. The most known Threat Assessment is probably the annual OCTA (EU Organised Crime Threat Assessment, which has recently become SOCTA, ie Serious and Organised Crime Threat Assessment), but also the IOCTA (Internet Organised Crime Threat Assessment, published in 2014 and 2015) and the Assessment on Italian Organised Crime (issued in 2013) could be mentioned.[332] Another relevant document is the TE-SAT (European Union Terrorism Situation and Trend Report), annually drafted by Europol since 2007 with the contributions of Members States, third countries, Eurojust, and other partner organisations.

Furthermore, in 2010 a *scanning, analysis, and notification* (SCAN) team had been established inside Europol, with the aim to provide 'national competent authorities and policy-makers at national and EU level with *early warning notifications* on new organised crime threats'.[333] Such notifications were usually brief documents knowns as 'OC-SCAN Threat Notices', disseminated among national authorities. Some of these notices regarded environmental crimes, as it is discussed below. However, at the time of writing, two years and a half have passed since the last Threat Notice has been published on the Europol website.[334]

Also Eurojust plays a similar 'strategic' role, e.g. through the strategic or tactical meetings periodically organised to allow national authorities to discuss some pressing problems in the field. As argued by Groenleer, these meetings have a further strategic function 'in that they are intended to *promote Eurojust*, demonstrating its added value to national authorities and therewith attracting more case referrals'.[335] Eurojust's strategic activity—in line with the composition and the aim of the Unit—is mainly concerned with *legal* issues in the fight against cross-border crimes. This is confirmed by the drafting of documents such as the Memorandum on Terrorism Financing and the Terrorism Conviction Monitor or by the significant contribution of the Unit

---

332 These documents are available at <https://www.europol.europa.eu/content/page/strategic_analysis_reports> accessed 18 September 2016.

333 'Europol Review 2013' (2014) <https://www.europol.europa.eu/category/publication-category/key-publications/europol-review> accessed 18 September 2016, 14. Emphasis added.

334 See <https://www.europol.europa.eu/latest_publications/39> accessed 18 September 2016.

335 M Groenleer (n 267) 318. Emphasis added.

to the 'European Handbook on how to issue a European Arrest Warrant'.[336] Sometimes, the two agencies pool their expertise, as it happened with the JITs Manual, drafted at the end of a joint project of Europol and Eurojust.[337]

The peculiar position of these bodies as central coordinators in the field of criminal justice allows them to play three other roles, which can fall within a broader understanding of 'non-operational' functions. First, they are 'trust promoter[s]':[338] gathering national authorities coming from the 28 Member States in the very same building should foster the *mutual trust* among them. Second, Eurojust and Europol are in an ideal position to *monitor* the functioning of the instruments of cooperation.[339] For instance, the Member States that are unable to respect the time limits for the execution of an EAW have the duty to report such a delay to Eurojust, pursuant to Article 17(7) EAW Framework Decision.

Third, as a further consequence of their peculiar role and expertise, it would not be unreasonable to envisage that Europol and Eurojust could (or even should) play a sort of '*lobbying/advising*' role on the EU institutions, when the latter are called to legislate on matters related to the judicial or police cooperation. The knowledge of Eurojust and Europol is precious and first-hand, and it would be undesirable not to take advantage of it. In that regard, however, Eurojust and Europol bear a significant difference.

As far as the former is concerned, its role in 'policy development and strategy making'[340] has been quite limited, even though—for instance—Article 32 Eurojust Council Decision expressly states that the Commission or the Council

336 'Revised version of the European handbook on how to issue a European Arrest Warrant', Council doc 17195/1/10, 17 December 2010.

337 'Joint Investigation Teams Manual', Council doc 15790/1/11, 4 November 2011.

338 J Vlastník, 'Eurojust—A Cornerstone of the Federal Criminal Justice System in the EU?' in E Guild and F Geyer (eds), *Security versus Justice? Police and Judicial Cooperation in the European Union* (Ashgate 2008) 38ff. Likewise, it has been stated that the vision of the Unit is to 'develop and enhance judicial cooperation, coordination and *mutual trust* in the European Union in the fight against organised serious cross-border crime' (Eurojust, 'Multi-Annual Strategy 2016–2018' (2015) <http://www.eurojust.europa.eu/doclibrary/corporate/corporatepublications/Eurojust%20Multi-Annual%20Strategy%202016-2018/Eurojust-MASP-2016-2018_EN.pdf> accessed 18 September 2016, 2; emphasis added). See also M Groenleer (n 267) 294 (on Europol) and 328ff (on Eurojust).

339 The 'monitoring function' of Eurojust is discussed by J Monar, 'Eurojust's present and future role at the frontline of European Union criminal justice cooperation' (2013) 14 *ERA Forum* 187, 193–194.

340 P Jeney (n 272) 80.

may seek the opinion of Eurojust on all draft instruments related to the field of judicial and police cooperation in criminal matters.[341]

On the contrary, the impact of Europol on EU policy has recently become of extreme relevance. The reference is meant to the so-called 'EU policy cycle for organised and serious international crime', which has been adopted by the EU 'in order to tackle the most important criminal threats in a coherent and methodological manner through optimum cooperation between the relevant services of the Member States, EU Institutions and EU Agencies as well as relevant third countries and organisations'.[342]

A first, limited policy cycle covered the years between 2011 and 2013, whereas in 2013 the fully-fledged policy cycle for the period 2014–2017 was adopted.[343] The functioning of the Policy Cycle is clearly represented by the following image, available on the Europol website:

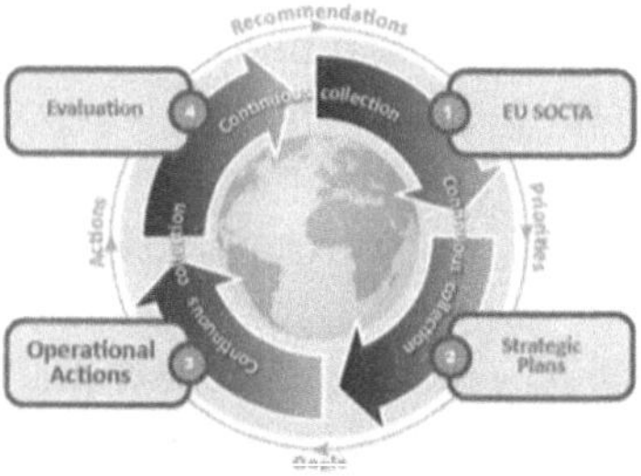

FIGURE 1
The EU policy cycle.
SOURCE: <HTTPS://WWW.EUROPOL.EUROPA.EU/CONTENT/EU-POLICY-CYCLE-EMPACT> ACCESSED 18 SEPTEMBER 2016.

341 Ibid 80–81. A more relevant role of Eurojust in that regard is advocated also by F Spiezia, 'Le linee evolutive della cooperazione giudiziaria penale in ambito europeo' (n 272) 252–254, whereas Coninsx underlines the involvement of the Unit in the adoption of the Council Framework Decision 2008/919/JHA of 28 November 2008 amending Framework Decision 2002/475/JHA on combating terrorism [2008] OJ L330/21 (M Coninsx, 'Strengthening interstate cooperation: the Eurojust experience' in AM Salinas De Frías, K Samuel and N White (eds), *Counter-Terrorism. International Law and Practice* (OUP 2012) 983–984).

342 'Council conclusions on the creation and implementation of a EU policy cycle for organised and serious international crime', Justice and Home Affairs Council meeting, 8–9 November 2010.

343 'Council conclusions on setting the EU's priorities for the fight against serious and organised crime between 2014 and 2017', Justice and Home Affairs Council meeting, 6–7 June 2013.

The first step of the 2013–2017 cycle is represented by the 2013 Europol SOCTA, which identified the main criminal threats in Europe;[344] on the basis of this Assessment, the Council set the *priorities* of the EU in the field.[345] For each of them, Strategic Plans have been elaborated; they imply Operational Actions Plans (OAPs), which should lead to a more effective reaction against the crimes identified as priorities. At the end of the cycle, the activities carried out will be evaluated, in order to the further setting of new priorities for the next cycle. In line with the above-mentioned multidisciplinary approach, the Council also invites the Member States to use alternative and complementary approaches in the fight against serious and organised crime.[346]

In this Cycle, an important coordinating and monitoring role is to be played by COSI, ie the Standing Committee on Internal Security, established with the aim to 'ensure that operational cooperation on internal security is promoted and strengthened within the Union'.[347]

Once briefly pointed out the functioning of the Policy Cycle, the question to be addressed concerns the destiny of those crimes *not* regarded as *priorities*, such as *environmental crime*, which has been not defined in the 2013 EU SOCTA as a 'key threat', but rather as an 'emerging threat'.[348] The Council has aligned its position to that of Europol, and in the conclusions setting the priorities for the period 2014–2017, there is only one generic reference to environmental crime.[349] The consequences of this choice are discussed below, but before it seems appropriate to add a final remark with regard to Europol and Eurojust.

4.5 *Theory vs Practice: The Exchange of Information and the Evolving Role of EU Agencies*

In the previous sections, we have described the operational and non-operational facets of Eurojust and Europol. Such a difference is helpful to have a systematic

344 Europol, 'EU Serious and Organised Crime Threat Assessment' (2013) <https://www.europol.europa.eu/content/eu-serious-and-organised-crime-threat-assessment-socta> accessed 18 September 2016.

345 'Council conclusions on setting the EU's priorities' (n 343).

346 Ibid 5. In the first Policy Cycle, the Council explicitly mentioned the need of a multidisciplinary approach to fight the prioritised threats ('Council conclusions on the creation and implementation of a EU policy cycle' (n 342) 5).

347 Article 71 TFEU. See 'Council conclusions on setting the EU's priorities' (n 343) 4.

348 Europol, 'EU Serious and Organised Crime Threat Assessment' (n 344) 39.

349 'The Council [...] noting that all actors involved must retain a margin of flexibility to address unexpected or emerging threats to EU internal security, in particular regarding *environmental crime* and energy fraud [...]' ('Council conclusions on setting the EU's priorities' (n 343) 3, emphasis added).

overview of their functioning; however, it is evident that the two aspects are actually sides of the same coin, not least because they necessarily rely on the same prerequisite in order to be successful, namely the willingness of national authorities to *share their information and their cases* with the EU bodies. It is a well-known problem that domestic police and judicial bodies are often reluctant to send the data at their disposal to Eurojust and Europol.[350] Probably, this is *the* problem par excellence of the judicial and police cooperation in the EU, so that it comes as no surprise that Member States are constantly urged to share their information with EU agencies on a more regular basis. Just to mention an example, one of the paragraphs of the 2016 European Agenda on Security is entitled 'improving information exchange'.[351] As far as environmental crime is concerned, the Commission has underlined this issue in the document accompanying the recent EU Action Plan against Wildlife Trafficking.[352]

Even though national authorities '*shall* exchange with Eurojust any information necessary for the performance of its tasks'[353] and the Member States—via the ENUs or national authorities, when allowed to do so—*shall* 'supply Europol with the information necessary for it to fulfil its objectives',[354] these provisions are largely disregarded in practice.[355] One of the possible reasons of this problematic status quo is that, in the day-to-day activities of national prosecutors, they usually have not time, incentives, and resources enough to embark upon complex investigations on transnational cases.[356] Another reason is linked to a problem shared by Europol and Eurojust: being all in all 'young' institutions, they are still not very known at national level, or at least

350 See, among the many, A De Moor and G Vermeulen, 'The Europol Council Decision: Transforming Europol into an Agency of the European Union' (n 266); M Groenleer (n 267) 296ff; A Klip (n 272) 441.

351 'Communication from the Commission to the European Parliament, the European Council and the Council delivering on the European Agenda on Security to fight against terrorism and pave the way towards an effective and genuine Security Union' COM(2016) 230 final, 20 April 2016.

352 See the 'Commission Staff Working Document accompanying the Communication on the EU Action Plan against Wildlife Trafficking' (n 45) 50.

353 Article 13(1) Eurojust Council Decision. Emphasis added.

354 Article 7(6)(a) Europol Regulation. Previously, Article 8(4)(a) Europol Council Decision was phrased in a similar way.

355 See, respectively on Eurojust and Europol, 'GENVAL final report' (n 273) 33–35 and E Disley, B Irving, W Hughes and B Patruni, 'Evaluation of the implementation of the Europol Council Decision' (n 250) 47–65.

356 M Groenleer (n 267) 327.

their added value is not always exactly perceived. The Europol Regulation now faces directly this issue, tasking the ENUs with the duty to 'raise awareness of Europol's activities'.[357]

In that regard, it is even more evident that operational and non-operational activities are inextricably linked, and enhance each other. It is obvious that the more national authorities resort to Eurojust and Europol, the more these bodies are able not only to carry out their operational tasks but also to collect useful information in view of further diffusion of knowledge in the field and to make domestic authorities aware of the support they can provide. The other way round, similarly, if Eurojust and Europol manage to gain adequate expertise in the fight against cross-border crimes and if they succeed in rising adequate awareness on the added value of the cooperation through EU instruments and bodies, the possibilities of their involvement in the coordination of national investigations grow accordingly.

In that regard, the boundaries between 'operational' and 'strategic' tasks are still valid in theory, but in practice they become quite blurred. This is especially true with regard to Europol, whose strategic activities lie at the core of its mission. Moreover, as shown, the actions to be taken under the umbrella of the Policy Cycle are based on the outcomes of the 2013 EU SOCTA, which is issued by Europol. Therefore, it is clear that the role played by this agency in terms of policy making is extremely relevant and that operational and strategic activities support and fuel each other: the knowledge and the cases of Europol lead the agency to detect the most urging threats, and consequently the Council to identify the priorities in the fight against organised and international crimes. Comparing the key threats identified by Europol in the EU SOCTA 2013 with the priorities of the Council, it emerges that the latter has entirely aligned its position to that of Europol; it added just one priority that was not mentioned in the SOCTA, ie 'to reduce the risk of firearms to the citizen including combating illicit trafficking in firearms'.[358]

However, not only the difference between operational and non-operational facets of the two bodies seems to be often lame, but also the difference between 'coercive' measures of national authorities and the activities carried out by the agencies has recently been called into question.

---

357 Article 7(6)(c) Europol Regulation. It remains to be evaluated whether and how this symbolical statement will be implemented in practice; for sure, it shows that the European legislator has become aware of one of the most relevant obstacles for the effective functioning of police cooperation.

358 'Council conclusions on setting the EU's priorities' (n 343) 4.

It is clear that Eurojust is not a prosecutor's office, despite being composed mainly by prosecutors; similarly, although most of its members are police officers, Europol is a not police authority, least of all it is a European FBI. In other words, their very nature seems to be that of 'service providers'.[359] However, in some instances their operational functions cannot always be clearly distinguished from the proper coercive powers of national authorities.

For instance, in view of the above-mentioned powers of Europol both to *request* national authorities to initiate or coordinate investigations and to *take part* to the JITs, it can be argued that the line between assisting and operating may become rather blurred.[360] Bearing in mind that Eurojust has the same powers[361] and that its national members in limited cases can exercise the powers they have as national prosecutors, a similar consideration seems to be valid also with regard to the Unit.

Gless likewise submits that 'gathering and processing information, as Europol does, generate "knowledge" and produces "evidence", which by *their very essence* are *no different* from a traditional house search conducted by a police unit using its operational power'.[362] Similarly, it has been argued that

> [...] although Europol does not have the competence to conduct any operations on its own, its tools and activities are of great importance for operational measures in Member States. Not only can its staff take part in national and joint investigations, but, more importantly, if Europol does its job correctly, *the information collected and analysed will set off operational measures in Member States*.[363]

359 See the intervention of N Pensaert at the tenth ECLAN Conference, 'The Needed Balances of EU Criminal Law: Past, Present and Future', held in Bruxelles, 25–26 April 2016. For a similar expression see also A Mégie, 'L'institutionnalisation d'un pouvoir judiciaire européen incertain en quête de lègitimité : l'unité de coopération Eurojust' (2007) 23 *Politique européenne* 57, 60.

360 V Mitsilegas, *EU Criminal Law* (n 113) 186.

361 The power of Eurojust, acting through its national members or as a College, to ask national authorities to undertake an investigation or prosecution of specific acts is enshrined, respectively, in Articles 6(1)(a)(i) and 7(1)(a)(i) Eurojust Council Decision. Eurojust national members can participate in the JITs pursuant to Article 9f Eurojust Council Decision.

362 S Gless (n 271) 464. Emphasis added.

363 A Jonsson Cornell, 'EU Police Cooperation Post-Lisbon' in M Bergström and A Jonsson Cornell (eds), *European Police and Criminal Law Co-operation* (Hart 2014) 154. Emphasis added.

These conclusions on the blurring of the mentioned boundaries—still theoretically useful—are even more valid when the role of Eurojust and Europol in the fight against transnational environmental crime is analysed.

5 Europol and Transnational Environmental Crime

The analysis of the role of Europol in the fight against transnational environmental crime will separately take into account the 'operational' and the 'non-operational' activities of the agency. As already pointed out, whereas the former encompasses the so-called 'operational analysis' and the coordination of national investigations, the latter refers to the strategic work carried out by Europol.

For the time being, there is not a unit, a focal point or a target group specifically dedicated to environmental crime within Europol. The activities of the agency in this field are carried out by a couple of Europol officers working within the department dealing with frauds.[364] At least at a symbolical level, this seems to confirm that environmental crime is often conceived as an economic crime.

5.1 *The 'Non-operational' Activities of Europol in the Field of Environmental Crime*

Europol is committed to collect and share knowledge on environmental crimes and on the best instruments and strategies to cope with them. Apart from the organisation of, and participation to, meetings and conferences, such as the 2012 'Awareness Conference on Fake and Illicit Pesticides',[365] Europol has issued different strategic documents concerning environmental crime. For instance, in 2010 Europol released a report where some scenarios of the possible future involvement of OCGs in energy supply were discussed.[366] As we can read in this document, such a report was 'not a threat assessment and [was] not

364 Interview with W Gowitzke, Seconded National Expert at Europol, working in the fraud unit of Europol and dealing with environmental crime (Europol, The Hague, 21 April 2016; further clarifications have been provided in subsequent email exchanges).

365 'Report and Conclusions' of the Europol-OHIM Awareness Conference on Fake and Illicit Pesticides (n 35). As we can read in the report, Eurojust took also part to the conference and outlined its 'growing role in dealing with environmental crime and how it is placed to hold coordination meetings to support specific action days' (ibid 5).

366 Europol, 'Organised crime & energy supply. Scenarios to 2020' (2010) <https://www.europol.europa.eu/content/publication/organised-crime-energy-supply-scenarios-2020-1505> accessed 18 September 2016.

intended to provide specific recommendations for operational responses',[367] it rather was a basis to trigger and facilitate further reflections on the issue, in line with those increasing 'concerns about global warming and other environmental threats [which] have brought increased public attention to energy issues in general'.[368]

In 2011, Europol issued four OC-SCAN Threat Notices related to environmental crime.[369] They all have the same structure: one-page documents, which contain, in the first part, the main findings on a given threat, and some recommendations to national authorities, in the second one.

Three of these OC-SCAN Threat Notices concern general issues, ie trafficking in endangered species, use of improvised illegal waste disposal sites, and trade in counterfeit and illegal pesticides in Europe.[370] They all underline the involvement of OCGs in these activities, because of the expected high economic incomes. The recommendations to national authorities concern both operational aspects (such as the resort to controlled deliveries as an instrument to disrupt OCGs or the launching of cross-border investigations) and strategic aspects, such as the need to undertake a tactical analysis on the use of internet by the OCGs trafficking in endangered species. The same pattern has been adopted also by the fourth OC-SCAN Threat Notice, issued in June 2011 and concerning a specific case of an Irish OCG involved in the illegal trade of rhino horns.[371]

In the same year, a privileged partner of Europol in this matter was established, ie EnviCrimeNet (Environmental Crime Network), an informal network of national law enforcement officers with expertise in the field of environmental criminality. EnviCrimeNet has been conceived as a network without proper operational powers, as it can be inferred from the Council Resolution

---

367 Ibid 3.

368 Ibid.

369 On the OC-SCANs in general see section 4.4.

370 Respectively: Europol, 'OC-SCAN Policy Brief for Threat Notice: 006–2010. Trafficking in Endangered Species by Organised Crime Groups' (March 2011); Europol, 'OC-SCAN Policy Brief for Threat Notice: 2521–88. Use of improvised illegal waste disposal sites by criminals and OC Groups in the EU' (June 2011); Europol, 'OC-SCAN Policy Brief for Threat Notice: 2521–93. Growth in the trade in counterfeit and other illegal pesticides across Europe' (November 2011). All the Europol OC-SCANs are available at <https://www.europol.europa.eu/latest_publications/39> accessed 18 September. On the illegal trade in pesticides see EnviCrimeNet, 'Report on Environmental Crime' (n 3) 36–41.

371 Europol, 'OC-SCAN Policy Brief for Threat Notice: 2521–86. Involvement of an Irish mobile OCG in the illegal trade in rhino horn' (June 2011) <https://www.europol.europa.eu/latest_publications/39> accessed 18 September 2016.

on its creation, where it is defined as 'an appropriate platform and forum for exchanging *non-operational information and experiences* with a view to combating effectively and efficiently environment-related cross-border crime'.[372] Its Annual General Meetings represent important occasions 'to discuss best practices, latest developments and challenges posed by environmental crime'.[373] Europol supports this Network and helps to coordinate its activities, as it emerges from the mentioned Council Resolution.[374]

A relevant example of the cooperation between Europol and EnviCrimeNet is represented by the Intelligence Project on Environmental Crime (IPEC), carried out jointly by them between 2014 and 2015. Before dealing with this Project, it must be reminded that after the adoption of the Policy Cycle 2014–2017, since environmental crime had been recognised as an *emerging threat* that requires 'intensified monitoring',[375] a Threat Assessment devoted only to this form of criminality was issued by Europol in 2013 (hereinafter '2013 Threat Assessment').

Drafted on the basis of information provided by the Member States and by the Europol's partners, this document mainly deals with the above-mentioned forms of illegal trafficking (in waste and in endangered species) and gives some interesting information on them.[376] For example, confirming and expanding what had already been pointed out in the mentioned OC-SCANs, it underlines that these kinds of trafficking are driven by *economic* reasons and are usually

372 Council Resolution on the creation of an informal network for countering environmental crime—"EnviCrimeNet", Council doc 10291/11, 20 May 2011. Emphasis added. With similar purposes, also the European Network of Prosecutors for the Environment and the European Union Forum of Judges for the Environment have been set up. On the latter, see L Lavrysen, 'The European Union Forum of Judges for the Environment' in M Faure, P De Smedt and A Stas (eds), *Environmental Enforcement Networks. Concepts, Implementation and Effectiveness* (Edward Elgar 2015) 276–288.

373 <https://www.europol.europa.eu/latest_news/environmental-crime-experts-meet-milan> accessed 18 September 2016.

374 'The Council of the European Union [...] [convinced] that "EnviCrimeNet" [...] will benefit from the analytical skills and know-how of Europol [...]' (Council Resolution on the creation of an informal network for countering environmental crime—"EnviCrimeNet" (n 372) 3); '[welcomes] the creation of an informal network for countering environmental crime called "EnviCrimeNet", supported by Europol [...]' (ibid 4); '[invites] "EnviCrimeNet" to fully benefit from the Europol Platform for Expert (EPE) [...], [invites] Europol to help to coordinate the activities of "EnviCrimeNet" in the fight against environmental crime' (ibid 5).

375 Europol, 'Threat Assessment 2013. Environmental Crime in the EU' (n 29) 4.

376 The 2013 Threat Assessment briefly deals also with illegal, unreported and unregulated fishing and illegal sand mining (ibid 16).

not adequately investigated or punished by the competent national authorities. Being 'high profit-low risk' activities, they become particularly attractive for OCGs, even though sometimes also legitimate companies are involved.

Moreover, the 2013 Threat Assessment explains the reasons why these forms of trafficking affect the EU. The issue seems particularly contentious in the case of wildlife trafficking, which could be perceived as a threat that does not regard directly (or at least seriously) Europe. However, the document shows that 'the EU is both a destination and source region'[377] for this form of trafficking. This conclusion is confirmed in the EU Action Plan against Wildlife Trafficking, in which it is stated that the EU is also a transit region.[378]

However, the 2013 Threat Assessment was perceived to have left some *gaps* in describing the current scenario concerning environmental crime at the EU level. Therefore, after the request of the COSI to EnviCrimeNet 'to report about their activities and to provide a scan in relation to environmental crime in the EU by the end of 2014',[379] the above-mentioned IPEC Project was launched in May 2014. The aim was 'to gain a better knowledge on the types of environmental crimes impacting on EU Member States [...], their extent, and the obstacles which exist to fight these crimes'.[380]

In the frame of this Project, Europol and EnviCrimeNet collected information on environmental crime in different ways: review of the existing literature, interviews with the practitioners, and participation in conferences and meetings of experts. In addition, a questionnaire was sent to national authorities of the Member States and of some non-EU organisations and jurisdictions. The Project ended up in the drafting and issuing of two Reports. Whereas the second mainly represents a literature review of articles, studies, and other materials, the first provides the results of the interviews and the main findings of the Project.

The latter report was presented at COSI in December 2014, where the conclusion was the following: 'the Delegations acknowledged the *growing importance* of environmental crime in the EU, which was identified as an emerging threat in the EU SOCTA. Europol was invited to take the reports into account

377 Ibid 14.

378 See the 'Commission Staff Working Document accompanying the Communication on the EU Action Plan against Wildlife Trafficking' (n 45) 19–20. This Document recalls the 2013 Threat Assessment and it adds further data on the impact of the phenomenon at stake on the EU (ibid 15–27).

379 EnviCrimeNet and Europol, 'Intelligence Project on Environmental Crime' (n 146) 4.

380 Ibid 1.

when preparing *the 2015 Interim SOCTA*'.[381] The 2015 Interim SOCTA is the document, drafted by Europol, which was meant to report on the status of the Policy Cycle after more than one year from its launching. However, even after its adoption (March 2015), nothing is changed in practice with regard to the role of Europol (and Eurojust) in the fight against environmental crime,[382] insofar as the Council decided to confirm the priorities previously set and not to add environmental crime to them.[383]

The 2013 Threat Assessment and the IPEC Report, as well as the cooperation with EnviCrimeNet, are clear examples of the 'non-operational' activities of Europol in the field. They are aimed at raising awareness on the matter at stake, and the same goal is pursued by Europol by keeping continuous contacts with other partners in the field, such as Interpol or Eurojust.[384]

Europol also strives to facilitate the growth of the existing knowledge on environmental crime through the development and the maintenance of a secure online platform, the Europol Platform for Experts (EPE). This is an online environment thought to share 'best practices, documentation, innovation, knowledge and *non-personal data* on crime'.[385] The access to the EPE can be granted only by invitation of Europol or ENUs and it is open to law enforcement officers and experts in the field. Some sections of this platform are devoted to environmental crime. Therefore, it is one of the instruments that Europol can use to raise awareness and increase knowledge on the matter. The EPE has also been used by Europol with the aim to reinforce the multidisciplinary approach to organised crime.[386]

---

381 'Summary of discussion of the meeting of 11 December 2014', Council doc 16163/14, 19 December 2014, 5. Emphasis added.

382 Interview with W Gowitzke, Europol (n 364).

383 'On the basis of this *interim* SOCTA, COSI decided that the EU *crime priorities* which were agreed on in 2013 should *remain valid* for the second part of the 2014–2017 Policy Cycle' ('Report to the European Parliament and national Parliaments on the proceedings of the Standing Committee on operational cooperation on internal security for the period July 2014-December 2015', Council doc 7033/16, 11 March 2016, 4; emphasis added).

384 Interview with W Gowitzke, Europol (n 364).

385 <https://www.europol.europa.eu/content/page/europol-platform-experts-1851> accessed 18 September 2016. Emphasis added. See also E Disley, B Irving, W Hughes and B Patruni, 'Evaluation of the implementation of the Europol Council Decision' (n 250) 100.

386 'The EPE Administrative Approach tool was created in May 2012 [...]. It promotes the important role of administrative authorities as part of a multidisciplinary approach which is increasingly being used by Member States to combat organised crime. [...] This electronic tool can help to put people in touch, spread awareness internationally and

Another online tool at the disposal of national authorities, but only focused on wildlife crime, is the so-called EU-TWIX (European Union Trade in Wildlife Information eXchange). It consists of two main components: a mailing list and a seizures database accessible via a secured website. EU-TWIX is an initiative of the Belgian Federal Police, Belgian CITES Management Authority, Belgian Customs, and TRAFFIC.[387] This tool aims at facilitating the exchange of information and international cooperation between wildlife law enforcement and management agencies in Europe. The EU-TWIX database contains information on seizures and offences reported by the EU Member States and, in addition, it 'has a section with information on technical, scientific, economic and other fields to help with the identification, valuation, disposal, etc. of seized or confiscated specimens'.[388]

Over 900 wildlife law officials are currently connected to EU-TWIX (police, judges' and prosecutors' offices, veterinary inspection services, etc), and approximately 40 % of the total is represented by customs officials. All the 28 EU Member States take part to it, as well as eight other non-EU countries (Albania, Macedonia, Montenegro, Norway, Serbia, Switzerland, Turkey, and the Ukraine), even though only the data shared by the former are included in the database; however, the information from non-EU States is planned to be integrated in the near future. Also international and regional organisations and bodies take part to EU-TWIX, including Eurojust and Europol. Since funds to support the functioning of the tool need to be raised on a yearly basis, the long-term continuation of the project remains a concern. Over the years, EU-TWIX has been funded on several occasions, and is funded at present, by the European Commission, as well as by many EU Member States, Norway, and Switzerland.[389]

Bearing in mind the above-mentioned inherent complexity of wildlife trafficking legislation, which often criminalises the purchase and the selling of

---

find answers to questions and problems as well as to reduce research costs and save time' ('Activity Report on the Administrative Approach to Prevent and Fight Organised Crime' (n 236) 5).

387 TRAFFIC, the wildlife trade monitoring network, is an NGO with the mission 'to ensure that trade in wild plants and animals is not a threat to the conservation of nature' (<http://www.traffic.org/overview/> accessed 18 September 2016).

388 <http://www.eu-twix.org/> accessed 18 September 2016. For further information on the history, functioning, and added value of EU-TWIX see V Sacré, 'EU-TWIX: ten years of information exchange and cooperation between wildlife law enforcement officials in Europe' in L Elliott and WH Schaedla, *Handbook of Transnational Environmental Crime* (Edward Elgar 2016) 478–488.

389 Interview with V Sacré, EU-TWIX Project Manager (19 September 2016, email interview).

certain protected species, the practical importance of this instrument is clear-cut. For instance, if the police of an EU country carries out a seizure on a suspect transaction in animals or plants and needs to know something more on the found samples, it could ask through EU-TWIX all the necessary information and, generally, it gets a quick and precise reply. Even though personal information cannot be exchanged through EU-TWIX, TRAFFIC (which administrates the system on behalf of European agencies) does not plan to change this situation, since other formal channels for sharing this kind of data already exists, such as SIENA.[390]

In light of the foregoing, it comes as no surprise that the feedback received from the users of EU-TWIX is extremely positive, as it also emerges from the fact that since its establishment the number of officials connected to it have increased from 150 to more than 900.[391] Moreover, in February 2016, the AFRICA-TWIX tool was also launched in central Africa, in four pilot countries, namely Cameroon, Congo, Gabon, and the Democratic Republic of Congo. As explained by the current EU-TWIX Project Manager,

> TRAFFIC, including EU-TWIX staff, facilitated contact-making between all relevant agencies and has been/is responsible for the creation and further development of the tool. TRAFFIC has been confirmed by participating states as the organisation to manage the tool on their behalf. [...] AFRICA-TWIX is modelled after EU-TWIX and contains the two same, main, functional components: the mailing list and the database. However, the AFRICA-TWIX system has been adjusted to the needs of central African agencies, for example in terms of the resources made available to them via the website or the fields contained in the database.[392]

As mentioned, Europol is part to EU-TWIX and it has contributed to, and used information from, EU-TWIX on regular occasions in the past. For instance, it used this tool in relation to the phenomenon of rhino thefts in European museums, on which Europol issued the fourth of the above-mentioned OC-SCANS. In that case, the agency used the EU-TWIX mailing list to gather information

390 Ibid.

391 Ibid.

392 Ibid. Likewise, 'Impel has recently developed a communication system to exchange information and facilitate cooperation between enforcement officials, national authorities and (inter)national and regional organisations of stakeholders in relation to protected bird species' (ibid). For more information on this system see <http://www.impel-esix.eu/> accessed 18 September 2016.

on thefts or attempted thefts. For the time being, eight Europol representatives are connected to EU-TWIX and EU-TWIX staff are in regular contact with two of them.[393]

Against this backdrop, it can be concluded that the 'non-operational' side of the activities of Europol concerning TEC is remarkable. On the contrary, its operational activities are more limited, as it is argued below.

5.2 *Operational Activities: Limited Analysis, Increasing Cooperation*

It has already been reminded that, as far as environmental crime is concerned, there is not a specific focal point, target group, or dedicated unit inside Europol. It implies that, for the time being, Europol cannot carry out its operational analysis with regard to this phenomenon. This status quo will probably not change in the near future, since environmental crime is not a priority according to the Policy Cycle; therefore, bluntly put, it does not seem realistic that *additional resources* will be earmarked for the fight against it.[394]

Nevertheless, the establishment of a focal point on environmental crime has been suggested several times over the years. For instance, in the frame of the consultation launched by the Commission in 2014 on the EU Approach against Wildlife Trafficking,[395] Eurojust submitted a contribution where it stated that 'the opening of a *Focal Point* at Europol on environmental crime (including wildlife crime) would clarify trends, links with other crime areas, allow for precise threat assessments and *ultimately also support coordination of investigation/prosecutions at judicial level*'.[396] In the summary of the responses to this consultation, it is possible to read that the setting up of a focal point or at least of a dedicated task force within Europol was considered an important step by five Member States and several NGOs.[397] In 2011, also the Council invited 'Europol to consider the establishment of a dedicated *focal point* for environmental crime as part of the possible upcoming implementation of the revised AWF concept'.[398]

---

393 Interview with V Sacré, EU-TWIX (n 389).

394 Interview with W Gowitzke, Europol (n 364).

395 'Communication from the Commission to the Council and the European Parliament on the EU Approach against Wildlife Trafficking' (n 186).

396 'Eurojust's contribution to the Commission Communication on the EU approach against wildlife trafficking', Annex 4 to the Eurojust, 'Strategic Project on Environmental Crime. Report' (n 29) 94. Emphasis added.

397 'Commission Staff Working Document. Summary of the Responses to the Stakeholder Consultation on the EU Approach against Wildlife Trafficking' SWD(2014) 347 final, 26 November 2014, 11.

398 Council Resolution on the creation of an informal network for countering environmental crime—"EnviCrimeNet" (n 372) 5. Emphasis added.

However, inside Europol there is a perception that, for the moment, there is not a real need to establish similar structures, insofar as the national authorities send to the agency a very limited number of contributions concerning environmental crime. As mentioned, the focal point is based on the work of the analysts. If a focal point had to be created without additional resources, this would imply that analysts from other focal points should be moved to the new one; however, the fact that environmental crime is not a priority and that the contributions from national authorities are limited does not justify similar reallocations. Plus, when a focal point is created, the Member States obviously have a legitimate expectation that it delivers its analytical work, with the risk that further additional resources would then be necessary.[399]

In other words, there seems to be a perception that there are no sufficient reasons to alter the status quo, even though the risk of triggering a vicious circle is self-evident: why should national authorities send their cases on environmental crime to Europol, if they know that they cannot obtain an in-depth analysis of the relevant information?

For the sake of completeness, however, one last remark is necessary. Should information concerning environmental crime be sent to Europol, the absence of a specific focal point or target group does not prevent Europol from storing that information in the so-called 'general nature and strategic type' (GNST) Resource focal point. As we can read in a 2012 Europol document, the purpose of this focal point is 'to determine the scale, significance and consequences of so far *non-prioritised criminal phenomena* as well as the ability of Member States to contribute related information and intelligence in order to ensure responsible, meaningful and transparent resource allocation'.[400]

The activities that can be carried out within this focal point are more limited than the usual ones. It *cannot* carry out *operational analysis* but it only cross-checks the provided pieces of information with the already existing ones in the Europol databases, and then informs accordingly the Member States of the identified links.[401] Moreover, 'trends and patterns across different commodities and criminal groups can be detected'.[402] The GNST Resource focal point is allowed to keep the data shared by national authorities for a shorter

399 Interview with W Gowitzke, Europol (n 364). A similar problem has been underlined also in the interview with L Görts, National Member for Sweden at Eurojust and Eurojust Contact Point for Environmental Crime (Eurojust, The Hague, 22 April 2016).

400 Europol, 'New AWF Concept Guide for MS and Third Parties' (2012) <http://www.statewatch.org/news/2013/jan/europol-awf-new-concept.pdf> accessed 18 September 2016, 37. Emphasis added.

401 Ibid. See also ibid 39.

402 Ibid 37.

period than other focal points, namely 18 months; this term 'will provide analysts with the opportunity to collate sufficient data during 12 months, so that in the course of the following 6 months they are in a position to detect trends and patterns'.[403] After 18 months, if the information cannot be transferred to another focal point or target group and it does not seem appropriate to establish a new focal point or a target group, that information must be deleted.[404]

As far as environmental crime is concerned, GNST focal point could represent an important resource. Since this crime is not prioritised at the EU level and no dedicated focal points or target groups exist within Europol, information that national authorities want to share with the agency can be stored in the GNST focal point for 18 months. There are no doubts that this would be possible since environmental crime falls within Europol's competence.

However, once the 18 months are over, it seems that Europol cannot continue to process this data, unless this is transferred to an already existing focal point or a target group, which should therefore deal with crimes closely linked with environmental ones.[405] If this is not the case, it does not seem realistic that a new focal point can be established with regard to environmental crime in the next future. Two of the four criteria to be taken into account in the assessment on the need to open a new focal point or target group at the end of the 18 months, indeed, are 'the volume and quality of the information already exchanged' and 'whether the topic concerns a priority on EU level':[406] as mentioned, the information already exchanged on the matter is very limited and environmental crime is *not* a priority according to the Policy Cycle. Therefore, it seems highly realistic that, after those 18 months, the possible pieces of information on environmental crime transmitted by the national authorities to Europol will be destroyed, unless they can be stored in an existing focal point.

Finally, it remains to be evaluated whether the new system of processing data provided by the Europol Regulation will lead to the abolishment of focal points, target groups, and AWFs, so that the absence of a specific focal point on environmental crime would not be an obstacle anymore for this agency to carry out its fully-fledged operational analysis on this phenomenon. If, as

403 Ibid 21.

404 Ibid. See also ibid 39.

405 On the possibility for Europol to provide operational analysis on environmental crimes in the frame of focal points dealing with other crimes see more in the next section.

406 Europol, 'New AWF Concept Guide for MS and Third Parties' (n 400) 39. The other two criteria are the number of Member States affected and 'the existence of sufficient elements (identity of certain suspects; minimal knowledge of the Modus Operandi etc) to organize international police cooperation' (ibid).

it seems realistic, the setting of the priorities will continue to influence the allocation of resources, the change of Europol's structure will *not* be followed by relevant improvements in the fight against environmental crime, unless the Council decides to include it among the priority crimes.

In addition to the operational analysis, the 'operational side' of Europol's activities now encompasses also the cooperation tasks of the agency. Quite interestingly, already before the adoption of the Regulation and the formal acknowledgment of this power, Europol had been involved in, and helped to coordinate, two relevant operations concerning environmental crime.

The most recent one, which is also a good example of the *external* action of Europol in the field, is the so-called 'COBRA III' operation, which came to an end in June 2015. Organised by the ASEAN-WEN (Association of Southeast Asian Nations Wildlife Enforcement Network) and the Lusaka Agreement Task Force (LAFT),[407] its aim was to detect possible cases of transnational wildlife crime. In March and in May 2015, in all the 62 involved countries (among them, 25 EU Member States), some 'action weeks' were carried out: during those days the police and the other competent enforcement authorities carried out checks and inspections, mainly at the borders and at the airports, in order to detect possible ongoing trafficking of protected species. Globally, the outcomes of the operation were relevant, with seizures of 12 tonnes of elephant ivory and of 119 rhino horns, but also in the EU the results were quite satisfactory (139,7 kilos of corals and 5067,9 kilos of wood were seized, for instance).[408] For the time being, however, there are no reliable feedbacks on the opening of investigations in the EU Member States after these operations.[409]

For the purpose of this work, it is interesting to highlight the role played by Europol in 'COBRA III', more precisely by those—admittedly not many—people working on environmental crime within the agency. As mentioned, the operations on the ground were carried out by domestic authorities; moreover,

407 These bodies were among the organisers of operations 'Cobra' (2013) and 'Cobra II' (2014), in which the EU did not take part. For more information, see respectively <https://cites.org/eng/news/pr/2013/20130218_operation-cobra.php> accessed 18 September 2016 and <https://cites.org/eng/news/sundry/2014/20140210_operation_cobra_ii.php> accessed 18 September 2016. On the LAFT more in general see EB Kasimbazi, 'The Lusaka Agreement Task Force as a mechanism for enforcement against wildlife crime' in M Faure, P De Smedt and A Stas (eds), *Environmental Enforcement Networks. Concepts, Implementation and Effectiveness* (Edward Elgar 2015) 239–262.

408 <https://www.europol.europa.eu/content/operation-cobra-iii> accessed 18 September 2016.

409 Interview with W Gowitzke, Europol (n 364).

no personal data were transmitted to Europol in view of future *operational* analysis, given the absence of an *ad hoc* focal point. In this sense, the potential of the role of Europol in the cooperation of national authorities was unfortunately halved, since it could not go as far as to include the operational analysis of data collected during the action weeks.

Nevertheless, Europol was empowered to coordinate the operations at the EU level. It implied, first, a number of contacts with ASEAN-WEN and LAFT to agree on the details of the operations. Then, Europol had to liaise with all the 28 Member States checking for their availability to participate to the project. During the action weeks of 'COBRA III', moreover, Europol was the hub where information on ongoing operations in Europe was collected, since national authorities of the EU Member States were required to report regularly on the outcomes of their activities. Even though not all of them complied scrupulously with this request, Europol was still able to monitor the operations and to give reliable information at the end of 'COBRA III'. The results were also shared via EU-TWIX. Therefore, this was an important occasion for the agency to gather further *strategic* data, which could be elaborated and disseminated among national authorities, with the aim of increasing the knowledge of this under-investigated area.

In a sense, also Eurojust was involved in COBRA III, since it was kept informed of the outcomes of the operations when they were ongoing. Unfortunately, it could not play a more relevant role since there were hardly any European cross-border cases investigated and none of them was referred to Eurojust.[410]

The other case in which Europol coordinated the actions in the field of environmental crime dates back to 2014: the so-called operation 'Waste Trafficking', carried out by the Environmental Protection Unit of the Italian force *Carabinieri* in collaboration with Europol.[411] Unlike 'COBRA III', this operation intended to contrast illegal *waste* trafficking and concerned only the EU, where 14 Member States decided to participate.[412] As we can read in the final report, the core of this operation has been represented by another *action week* that took place in November 2014, during which the police forces of the involved countries made 'random checks on sites and/or input/output waste movements from/to those sites coming from third countries'.[413] During the action week, a *coordination*

410 Ibid.

411 Eurojust was not called to carry out any peculiar task or activity in this operation.

412 See Report of the 'European action against the involvement of Organized Crime and Mafia-related crime in Waste Trafficking' (n 39) 67.

413 Ibid 66.

centre was set up at Europol. The results of the operations were successful and it appears that they triggered 58 investigations at the national level.[414]

Unlike 'COBRA III', 'Waste Trafficking' was coordinated by the Europol's Focal Point on Italian Organised Crime (ITOC).[415] As mentioned, when a focal point—which is part of one of the two AWFs—is dedicated to a given crime, it means that Europol is in a position to exercise its full operational powers, ie to proceed with an operational analysis of information shared by national authorities in the frame of ongoing investigations. Therefore, it comes as no surprise that during the 'Waste Trafficking' operation, 'all participating Member States were invited to submit their results, when relevant, through SIENA to Europol's *Analysis Work File* on Serious and Organised Crime (SOC)'.[416] In this sense, Europol was in the condition to exercise its full operational potential in the frame of 'Waste Trafficking'.

In other words, due to the absence of a focal point on the matter, Europol is not allowed to analyse personal data on ongoing investigations concerning environmental crime, *unless* similar information is dealt with by focal points devoted to some *other forms of crime* which encompass, are connected to, or even overlap with environmental crime. In the 'Waste Trafficking' operation, as mentioned, it was the case of Italian organised crime. Something similar, for example, could happen with the illicit trafficking in *counterfeit pesticides*, which is usually considered as falling within the broader concept of 'environmental crime'. Because inside Europol there is a focal point devoted to the contrast of counterfeiting more in general,[417] the agency could carry out its usual tasks of analysis and elaboration of data, if national authorities decide to share their information with Europol.[418]

Finally, in light of the success of 'Waste Trafficking', the Italian *Carabinieri* have launched another Project, which is still ongoing at the time of writing, 'TECUM' (Tackling Environmental Crime through Standardized Methodologies). For the moment, Europol is not expected to play any peculiar role in this regard.[419]

---

414 Ibid 69.

415 Ibid.

416 Ibid 67. Emphasis added.

417 D Drewer and J Ellermann (n 320) 392.

418 Interview with W Gowitzke, Europol (n 364).

419 Ibid. Further information on the project are available at <http://www.tecumproject.eu/> accessed 18 September 2016.

5.3 *Europol and the Fight against Transnational Environmental Crime: An Assessment*

Against this backdrop, the current role of Europol in the fight against transnational environmental crime can be represented with the following diagram.

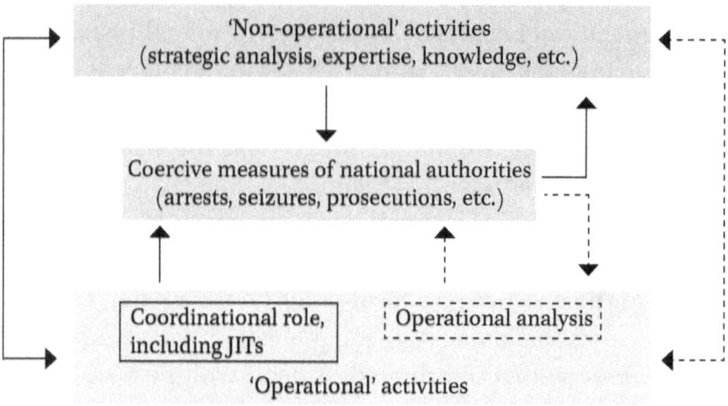

FIGURE 2 *The role of Europol against transnational environmental crime.*

The *operational* role of Europol in the fight against environmental crime is somehow halved. The agency has already shown a great commitment in the coordination of operations in this field, such as during the 'Waste Trafficking' and 'COBRA III' projects. In the latter one, Europol has coordinated the activities of law enforcement agencies acting in 25 EU Member States and has liaised with international partners. This is a meaningful example of the importance that the EU becomes a global actor in the fight against transnational crime. As shown, both the operations have benefitted from the *previous strategic knowledge* collected by Europol and, in the meanwhile, they have provided *further strategic data* to be elaborated by the agency. In theory, Europol could also coordinate national investigations in the frame of Joint Investigation Teams,[420] but this has never happened in the field of environmental crime up to now.

Despite these significant achievements, however, looking at the *core* of the operational functions of Europol, ie the analysis of data and information with the aim to support national investigations, the absence of a focal point or a target group on environmental crime represents a serious obstacle for the agency to provide its services in this field. Nevertheless, there is a leeway that already allows Europol to carry out operational analysis with regard to environmental

420 Article 4(1)(c)(ii) Europol Regulation.

crimes, namely to deal with them in the frame of focal points or target groups devoted to other forms of crime, which either are connected to environmental crime (such as organised criminality) or actually overlap with it (such as trafficking in pesticides). Apart from that, limited analysis can also be carried out in the frame of the GNST focal point.

The issue of the overlapping of environmental crime with other illegal activities has been already dealt with in this work. It has been shown that when national authorities deal with this phenomenon in the frame of organised crime activity, they are better equipped to fight environmental crime. Therefore, it seems that the same pattern applies inside Europol. As a consequence, along with the already mentioned scarce willingness of the Member States to share their information with the agency, the fact that Europol can already deal with environmental crimes—even though in some circumstances and indirectly—makes the creation of a specific focal point dedicated to the crime at stake less urgent.

The establishment of a focal point could have positive effects on the use of JITs, because when Europol is involved in their frame, this usually happens through its focal points.[421] However, since other focal points devoted to crimes encompassing or overlapping with environmental crime already exist, the absence of such a dedicated focal point does not imply a total ban on Europol's participation to JITs concerning the criminal phenomena at issue: not even in that regard, therefore, there is a pressing need to alter the existing situation.[422]

Such a scenario could improve thanks to the expected changes to be introduced by the new Regulation when it will become effective (May 2017): the current fragmentation of Europol's databases could be finally overcome and no more limits should be put on the analysis of data sent to Europol. However, since environmental crime remains outside the priorities set by the Council, the possibilities that—in practice—things will change seem quite limited. If the choice of priorities is reflected in the allocation of resources, one can understand the reason of this scepticism.

As the diagram shows, however, it is undeniable that, should Europol be in a position to provide its full 'operational services', its analysis and elaboration of data would be beneficial: i) first and foremost, for the adoption of the coercive measures by national authorities, which could in turn provide further data to analyse; ii) for the coordination role of Europol, since it would allow the agency

421 Interview with V Jamin, Head of the JITs Network Secretariat (1 June 2016, Skype interview).

422 Ibid.

to have a better and more complete overview of the ongoing national investigations, which could then be coordinated at the European level; and iii) for the strategic activities of Europol, because the operational analysis would provide more data which can then be used for 'non-operational' purposes; similarly, and vice versa, such an operational analysis would draw on the strategic information already at the disposal of Europol to better elaborate the information transmitted by national authorities.

One of the other reasons why there is not a strong pressure to extend the operational functions of the agency to environmental crime is the fact that the strategic side of its activities is deemed to be already sufficient, to a certain extent, to answer the needs of the practitioners. Europol is strongly engaged in different *non-operational activities*, ranging from the release of strategic documents to the participation to conferences, meetings, and research projects. It also keeps contacts with the relevant partners, especially EnviCrimeNet, Interpol, and Eurojust. Such activities generate useful information that can be used by national authorities when they undertake their 'coercive' measures (e.g. information on the *modus operandi* of OCGs, the routes they follow, etc). With the same aim to support national investigations and the cooperation among domestic law enforcement authorities, Europol manages the SIENA platform. It is also part of EU-TWIX and it offers an online platform to provide useful information (EPE).

Therefore, even though the 'operational' role of Europol is not fully-fledged, it is undeniable that the agency strives to collect and spread *knowledge* both on the peculiarities of environmental criminality and on the best ways to cope with it ('non-operational'). When national authorities deal with environmental crimes, they could draw on such a knowledge to better exercise their ('coercive') powers and they could also be coordinated by Europol ('operational'). In other words, gathering information can lead to concrete actions that allow to obtain further data, which can be analysed and used for subsequent activities. In a similar context, it seems that the above-mentioned tasks of Europol can be regarded as 'non-operational' only in theory, whereas in practice they really have a significant impact on the 'coercive' actions of national authorities.

Such a virtuous circle is perfectly described in the 'Waste Trafficking' final report:

> [...] as a first step, the operation was conceived precisely in order to *share the investigative experience* aiming to *raise awareness* regarding the illicit waste trafficking phenomenon, by giving all participating Member States some *common guidelines* in order to:—*recognise* environmental crime (and in particular its most concerning branch, the illicit waste

> trafficking) which is often linked to organised crime;—*acquire a better picture* of illicit waste trafficking in Europe; [...]—*exchange best practices*;—establish an *operational contact*.[423]

Likewise, the spin-off project 'TECUM' aims at analysing the results and the outcomes of the operation 'Waste Trafficking', in order to gain further *knowledge* on the crime at stake, on which basis specific *training* will be provided to the involved law enforcement authorities. Once this phase will be over, new *actions* on the ground will be carried out.[424]

A similar scenario is also engraved in the above-mentioned Eurojust's contribution to the Commission Communication on the EU approach against Wildlife Trafficking, where the agency underlines that

> even if other crimes, "easier" to investigate and prosecute, were discovered during a wildlife crime investigation, they could only be so if there was *sufficient intelligence gathered in the first place* on the wildlife crime itself, which brings back the question of an effective and systematic collection and analysis of intelligence in this particular field.[425]

Therefore, adequate strategic analysis seems the first, necessary step to achieve significant goals in the fight against transnational environmental crime.

This become even blatant if one takes into account another (indirect) effect of the non-operational activities of Europol. Thanks to similar activities, indeed, Europol can give its contribution to the creation of a *network* of experts and practitioners in the field.

This latter implicit aim of Europol's action is deemed to be of extreme importance for an effective fight against cross-border crime (including environmental one), since most of the times the biggest problem authorities face in police (and judicial) cooperation is to identify the right person to get in touch with. Therefore, if national law enforcement officers dealing with environmental crime know who to contact in another country and are aware of the fact that within Europol there is a person dedicated to this phenomenon who can help them to get in touch with each other, they can proceed smoothly in

---

423 Report of the 'European action against the involvement of Organized Crime and Mafia-related crime in Waste Trafficking' (n 39) 65–66. Emphasis added.

424 See <http://www.tecumproject.eu/> accessed 18 September 2016.

425 'Eurojust's contribution to the Commission Communication on the EU approach against wildlife trafficking' (n 396) 96. Emphasis added.

cases of cross-border environmental crime.[426] In this sense, it can be argued that a typical non-operational activity, as should be labelled that of striving to establish a network of people operating in this field, gives actually a fundamental support to national authorities dealing with investigations on environmental crime.[427]

It emerges that the theoretical dividing line between operational and non-operational tasks is quite blurred in practice. They substantiate each other and they definitely run together towards the same end, namely the effective fight against transnational criminal phenomena. Likewise, the basic principle according to which Europol is not allowed to carry out coercive measures is still valid in theory, but it would be a mistake to consider that Europol's (operational and strategic) support is not fundamental, in some instances, to the effectiveness of national investigations.

6 Eurojust and Transnational Environmental Crime

Unlike Europol, Eurojust has already assumed certain *operational* tasks with regard to environmental crime. Therefore, it seems more appropriate to begin with them, before dealing with the strategic role played by the Unit.

6.1 *Eurojust and the Coordination of National Authorities: Limited Cases vs Great Potential*

The number of cases of environmental crime dealt with by Eurojust is extremely low: 3 in 2012 (out of an overall number of 1533 cases), 8 in 2013 (total 1576), 5 both in 2014 (total 1804) and in 2015 (total 2214).[428] However, the *potential* added value of Eurojust in the matter at issue emerges straightforwardly from the public information available on three of these cases.

---

426 Interview with W Gowitzke, Europol (n 364).

427 Ibid.

428 These numbers are based on the statistics provided in the Annual Reports of Eurojust for the years 2012, 2013, 2014, and 2015, available at <http://www.eurojust.europa.eu/doclibrary/corporate/Pages/annual-reports.aspx> accessed 18 September 2016. In the Commission Staff Working Document accompanying the EU Action Plan on Wildlife Trafficking, it is stated that 'between 1 January 2004 and 1 December 2015, [Eurojust] dealt with a *total of 49 cases* of environmental crime, of which five involved illicit trafficking of endangered animal species and two illicit trafficking of endangered plant species and varieties' ('Commission Staff Working Document accompanying the Communication on the EU Action Plan against Wildlife Trafficking' (n 45) 49, emphasis added).

Beginning with the most recent, an illegal trafficking in wild bird eggs affecting UK, Finland and Sweden was discovered in 2013 (the 'Bird-Egg case'). Eurojust assisted the authorities of the latter two countries in setting up and *funding* a JIT.[429] This intervention has been defined by one of the Finnish prosecutors involved as '*invaluable* in coordinating communication'[430] between them and the Swedish and Scottish counterparts, even though it seems that the coordination of Eurojust should have taken place in an *earlier* stage of the investigations. Likewise, another of the prosecutors involved in that case said:

> [i]nternational communication and coordination *at the beginning* of the investigation may have achieved wide-ranging results. For example, Eurojust has a Liaison Prosecutor from the USA. Using Eurojust to facilitate contact between the UK, Sweden and out counterparts in the USA may have assisted in the coordinated engagement of all States at the same time.[431]

These words show that there is room for improvement in the use of Eurojust, which can give its best support if it is involved by national authorities from the early stages of the investigations.[432] In fact, if contacted in a late moment, Eurojust can play a limited role: for instance, if its intervention is requested just before the expiring of the time limitation for national investigations, Eurojust could not have enough time to coordinate the operations. Similarly, another problem usually faced by the Unit is linked with the different domestic rules on the discovery of investigative elements. If the investigations are in an advanced stage in a Member State, in which the discovery has already taken place, it becomes quite problematic to coordinate the actions with the authorities of other countries where the investigations are still under secrecy. In these cases, Eurojust cannot overcome national diversities, even though it could try to find the best way to solve potential problematic issues.

---

429 On the financial support of Eurojust to the establishment of the JIT it was commented by the Swedish National Member that 'the benefits here are clearly demonstrated in this case when we see that the JIT funding enabled Sweden to hire the *services of an expert*, an ornithologist' ('The Bird-Egg case' (2013) 10 *Eurojust News* 16, emphasis added).

430 Ibid 15. Emphasis added.

431 Ibid. Emphasis added.

432 The same need with regard to the involvement of Europol in national investigations has been underlined by S Chin and W Veening, 'Actors and Institutions Relevant to Fighting Environmental Crime'. Study in the frame of the EFFACE Project (Institute for Environmental Security 2015) 32.

Moreover, the Bird-Egg case raises another question. Within the Policy Cycle, could the choice of regarding environmental crime as a mere 'emerging threat' have an impact on the possible financing of JITs? Some authors have argued that *putting* environmental crime *in the list of priorities* 'would also *increase the probability* that *JITs* set up for combating environmental crimes are eligible for funding by the grants from Eurojust'.[433] This is submitted pursuant to Annex IV of the 2015 Eurojust Annual Work Programme, where one of the criteria to be taken into account in the awarding of grants for the setting up of a JIT is the inclusion of the crime to investigate among the priorities decided by the Council.[434] The 2016 Eurojust Annual Work Programme has upheld this provision.[435] However, on the basis of the experience of the JITs funding, there is no reason to believe that the status quo prevents Eurojust from supporting the establishment of JITs in the field of environmental crime, since the inclusion among the priorities of the Council is only one of the six criteria provided for in the Annual Work Programmes.[436]

Nevertheless, apart from the one in the Bird-Egg case, no other JITs have been set up via Eurojust to investigate environmental crimes up to now. Since the awareness on the usefulness of such a tool is growing, it cannot be excluded that in the future the situation will improve.[437] After all, it is not a case that, in many documents and studies on the matter, the need to establish more JITs is continuously restated.[438]

In addition, a growing number of JITs involving third countries—but concerning other crimes—have been set up in the last years through Eurojust:[439] this could be of extreme relevance for those—admittedly many—environmental crimes having an intrinsic cross-border dimension. However, a similar hope for the future could be curtailed by the fact that third States involved up

433 K Klaas and S Sina (n 160) 4. Emphasis added.

434 Ibid 7. See Eurojust, 'Annual Work Programme 2015' (2014) <http://eurojust.europa.eu/doclibrary/budget-finance/Pages/work-programmes.aspx> accessed 18 September 2016, 30.

435 Eurojust, 'Annual Work Programme 2016' (2015) <http://eurojust.europa.eu/doclibrary/budget-finance/Pages/work-programmes.aspx> accessed 18 September 2016, 33.

436 Interview with V Jamin, JITs Network Secretariat (n 421).

437 Ibid.

438 See, among the many, Eurojust, 'Strategic Project on Environmental Crime. Report' (n 29) 34; S Chin and W Veening, 'Actors and Institutions Relevant to Fighting Environmental Crime' (n 432) 36; T Fajardo del Castillo, 'Organised Crime and Environmental Crime' (n 50) 17 and 35–36; K Klaas and S Sina (n 160) *passim*.

439 See Eurojust, 'Annual Report 2015' (n 267) 16.

to now are mainly the neighbouring ones (e.g., Norway or Switzerland),[440] so that it seems unrealistic that the most serious forms of worldwide trafficking in waste or in endangered species could be comprehensively tackled with such an instrument.

Another case in which Eurojust was called to exercise its operational powers was the 'Manure' one (2012). It concerned the illegal trading in manure, which led to a tax evasion in the Netherlands of about 8–9 millions of euros. This case involved other four countries and Eurojust managed to set up a *coordination meeting* among national competent authorities, so that they could discuss the problems occurred during the procedures of mutual assistance. They also agreed to organise an *action day* and the operations thereof were monitored at Eurojust by a coordination centre. The involvement of Eurojust turned out to be relevant, insofar as '*several seizures* of illegally obtained assets and administrative documents were made. *Witnesses* were heard in order to collect evidence'.[441]

The third interesting case dates back to 2003 and it is unfortunately famous: the 'Prestige case', named after the oil tanker which sank in the Galician waters in 2002, causing impressive damages to the environment. The main problem arising from the investigations was related to the *choice of jurisdiction*: where have the captain and the other persons allegedly responsible of the disaster had to be prosecuted? France or Spain? In this case, Eurojust managed to gather the competent authorities together in a couple of meetings: the first one mainly aimed at the exchange of the necessary expertise to deal with such a complicate matter, whereas the second one faced the issue of jurisdiction. More in detail, the latter meeting was intended to 'explore the possibility and draw on legal expertise to decide if it was possible, and if so how, to centralize the ongoing prosecutions into a single proceeding, to be led by one of the countries'.[442]

---

440 Interview with V Jamin, JITs Network Secretariat (n 421). According to the interviewee, this is due to the fact that JITs inevitably rely on common (or at least similar) legal standards of the participating countries, so that it could be difficult to find a common understanding with non-European countries when some sensitive topics come into consideration (such as data protection).

441 'Report of the Strategic Meeting towards an enhanced coordination of environmental crime prosecutions across the EU: The role of Eurojust', Council doc 8101/14, 24 March 2014, 9–10. Emphasis added. For other details on the Manure case see also 'The Manure Case' (2013) 10 *Eurojust News* 16.

442 Eurojust, 'Annual Report 2003' (2004) <http://www.eurojust.europa.eu/doclibrary/corporate/Pages/annual-reports.aspx> accessed 18 September 2016, 29. For some remarks on

At the end, Eurojust suggested that Spain was in a better position to initiate the proceedings, and all the involved authorities accepted this recommendation. The adequate protection of the French victims was a sensitive topic, but as a result of the cooperation of the two countries those victims were treated 'as if they were Spanish victims. The French Public Prosecutor participated in the oral proceedings, sitting beside the Spanish prosecutor, and hearing the statements of some French victims'.[443] The conclusion of Eurojust was mainly driven by pragmatic reasons, which were welcome by national authorities. As argued by Pozdnakova, the

> main factors in Eurojust's decision were as follows: first, more evidence had been gathered in Spain due to the direct contact from the start of the investigation between the Spanish authorities and the ship and crew; and second, more injured parties were situated in Spain than in France, with some of the French victims already having joined the judicial procedure in Spain.[444]

Therefore, in that case Eurojust found a reasonable balance between the needs to deliver justice in an effective way and the rights of the individuals concerned: the defendants avoided to be judged twice for the same facts and the interests of the victims were adequately taken into account.

The three described cases show that Eurojust can have a real added value in the fight against transnational crime. In light of these good experiences, it is surprising that the involvement of Eurojust has been so limited up to now. The possible reasons of this status quo are discussed in the Report of the Strategic Project on environmental crime, issued by Eurojust at the end of 2014 ('2014

the allocation of jurisdiction in the case concerning the shipwreck of the tanker 'Erika' (1999) see N Giovannini, L Melica, E Cukani and others, 'Addressing Environmental Crimes and Marine Pollution in the EU Legal guidelines and case studies' (Droit au Droit 2013) <http://www.dadinternational.org/images/PDF/Guide-Web.pdf> accessed 18 September 2016, 26–30.

443 'The Prestige case' (2013) 10 *Eurojust News* 14. Nevertheless, the case did not lead to any significant conviction: 'The three judges of the Galician High Court concluded that establishing criminal responsibility was impossible. Captain Apostolos Mangouras, Chief Engineer Nikolaos Argyropoulos and the former head of Spain's Merchant Navy, Jose Luis Lopez, were found not guilty of crimes against the environment. Lopez was the only government official charged in the case. Mangouras, 78, was found guilty of a lesser charge of disobedience and given a nine-month suspended sentence. (Source: Reuters International)' (Ibid 15).

444 A Pozdnakova, *Criminal Jurisdiction over Perpetrators of Ship-Source Pollution. International Law, State Practice and EU Harmonisation* (Martinus Nijhoff Publishers 2013) 157.

Eurojust Report'),[445] which represents one of the best examples of the *strategic* role played by the Unit in the field.

6.2 *The Growing 'Non-operational' Role of Eurojust in the Field of Environmental Crime*

As the 2013 Threat Assessment of Europol, the 2014 Eurojust Report mainly deals with trafficking in waste and in endangered species. Based on the evaluation of national legislation, on a questionnaire sent to the Member States, and on the outcomes of a *strategic meeting* on environmental crime held at the Eurojust's premises in 2013,[446] the 2014 Eurojust Report offers an interesting overview of the main peculiarities of the mentioned phenomena and of the difficulties faced by national authorities in the investigations and in the prosecutions thereof.

In a nutshell, the Report confirms the scenario described throughout this work: domestic legislations on the matter are usually complex and extremely technical, on the one hand, and they provide for too lenient sanctions, on the other hand. The situation is even worsened not only by the problems faced by the competent authorities in gathering evidence, but also by the insufficient and unsatisfactory status of the cooperation among national bodies, and between them and the supranational ones. This picture, coupled with the fact that in many circumstances these forms of trafficking have been carried out by OCGs, is definitely alarming.[447]

Another interesting facet of the non-operational tasks of Eurojust in the field at stake is represented by the establishment of a *Contact Point on Environmental Crime*. Appointed in July 2014, the Contact Point is one of the Eurojust National Members and has a merely *strategic* role, since the cases of environmental crime will continue to be dealt with by national Desks. This figure is thought to have someone inside Eurojust who pays peculiar attention to this field and its developments, as well as to facilitate possible approaches from the externals for the purposes of fighting environmental crime.[448] As it has been stated in the 2015 Eurojust Annual Report, the Contact Point 'follows up on environmental crime matters and shares expertise and best practice with practitioners and external stakeholders'.[449]

---

445 Eurojust, 'Strategic Project on Environmental Crime. Report' (n 29).

446 See 'Report of the Strategic Meeting towards an enhanced coordination of environmental crime prosecutions across the EU: The role of Eurojust' (n 441).

447 See Eurojust, 'Strategic Project on Environmental Crime. Report' (n 29) 10–20.

448 Interview with L Görts, Eurojust (n 399).

449 Eurojust, 'Annual Report 2015' (n 267) 44.

In addition, he aims to raise awareness on the role Eurojust could play in the matter and regularly reports to the Eurojust's College and to the Financial and Economic Crime Team of the Unit (FECT).[450] Composed of members of the national Desks, each Eurojust's team is devoted to a specific form of criminality or to some thematic issues concerning judicial cooperation. The teams do not handle operational cases, since they mainly represent a platform—inside Eurojust—to discuss on some forms of crimes, on possible activities to be undertaken by the Unit to raise awareness, etc. The inclusion of environmental crime within the FECT is highly symptomatic of the already mentioned economic drivers which lead the criminals (especially organised groups) to engage with similar activities. As mentioned, also within Europol environmental crime is dealt with by some officials within the unit dedicated to frauds.

The role of the Contact Point is quite similar to that played by the small group of persons inside Europol working on environmental crime. For instance, he keeps contacts with other actors in the field, such as Europol itself, EnviCrimeNet, ENPE (European Network of Prosecutors for the Environment), and the CITES Enforcement Group within DG ENVI.[451] However, whereas Europol is generally open towards the private sector (NGOs, sometimes banks, etc), Eurojust is more hesitant to liaise with it. As a body aimed at facilitating investigations and prosecutions, its partners are mainly represented by law enforcement authorities.[452]

Another partner of Eurojust is the European Union Network for the Implementation and Enforcement of Environmental Law (IMPEL). It is composed of members of environmental authorities of the EU Member States and other European countries, and one of its recent projects has been regarded as particularly useful by Eurojust, namely the so-called 'IMPEL-TFS Prosecutors Project'.[453] Among the others, it aimed at establishing a *database of decisions* on illicit shipment of waste. Even though this matter is regulated at the EU level,[454] the legislations of the Member States still bear significant differences, so that the idea of collecting decisions concerning this issue and making them

450 Eurojust, 'Strategic Project on Environmental Crime. Report' (n 29) 9.

451 Ibid; interview with L Görts, Eurojust (n 399). The Enforcement Group is based in Brussels and it has a monitoring and advisory role on the legislation on wildlife trade.

452 Interview with L Görts, Eurojust (n 399); interview with W Gowitzke, Europol (n 364). See also, for Europol, E Disley, B Irving, W Hughes and B Patruni, 'Evaluation of the implementation of the Europol Council Decision' (n 250) 116ff.

453 Interview with L Görts, Eurojust (n 399).

454 See above n 137.

available to all the interested practitioners should answer the 'need for a systematic exchange of information and practices among countries'.[455]

More in detail, the relevance of such project is shown by some practical examples given during the 2013 strategic meeting on environmental crime: 'an English appellate court made references to a Dutch case concerning the definition of "transport" and a court in Göteborg, Sweden, used the Dutch experience as a tool to establish an appropriate penalty in a case concerning the illegal shipment of waste'.[456] Eurojust welcomes similar initiatives and it already issues reports aiming at collecting information on cases and legislations, such as the above-mentioned Terrorism Conviction Monitor. However, for the time being, it does *not* seem *realistic* that in the near future something similar could be arranged with regard to environmental crime.[457] Even though the number of cases dealt with by Eurojust has steadily increased over the years, the resources of the Unit have not grown accordingly. Consequently, choices have to be made: bearing in mind that 'Eurojust regularly aligns its priority crime areas with the Council Conclusions setting up the priorities for the fight against serious and organized crime',[458] measures against environmental crime do not seem in pole position to receive an extra-funding.

Another example of the non-operational role of the Unit in the fight against environmental crime is represented by the already mentioned contribution sent by Eurojust to the Commission Communication on the EU approach against Wildlife Trafficking. The Commission launched a consultation on this matter and Eurojust replied to 'provide a practitioner's point of view'.[459] In this contribution, the Unit confirms its limited involvement in cases of environmental crime; moreover, it states that a good step forward would be represented by the 'upgrading' of environmental crime from an emerging threat to an EU priority. However, Eurojust cannot avoid acknowledging that the real, preliminary obstacle for an effective EU action in the field is the lack of an

455 Intervention of R De Rijck, responsible of the project at stake, during the mentioned 2013 Eurojust Strategic Meeting on environmental crime ('Report of the Strategic Meeting towards an enhanced coordination of environmental crime prosecutions across the EU: The role of Eurojust' (n 441) 5).

456 Ibid.

457 Interview with L Görts, Eurojust (n 399).

458 M Coninsx, 'Eurojust' (n 267) 447.

459 'Eurojust's contribution to the Commission Communication on the EU approach against wildlife trafficking' (n 396) 90.

adequate awareness of the Member States on the seriousness of the offence at stake.[460]

Moreover, as mentioned before, since it emerges that one of the most recurring problems of the judicial cooperation is the lack of knowledge on who to contact (and how) in another country, it comes as no surprise that Eurojust is committed to establish a *list of contact points* 'within the national prosecution services of the Member States with expertise in the field of environmental crime'.[461] At the time of writing, the list has not been finalised, but Eurojust and the Contact Point on Environmental Crime are working on it.[462]

Finally, Eurojust is an active observer in EU-TWIX, which the agency could use to identify European-wide cases in which it could play a role. Two representatives from Eurojust are currently connected to the system.[463]

6.3 *Eurojust and the Fight against Transnational Environmental Crime: An Assessment*

On the basis of the previous considerations, the role of Eurojust in the field at issue can be represented with the following diagram.

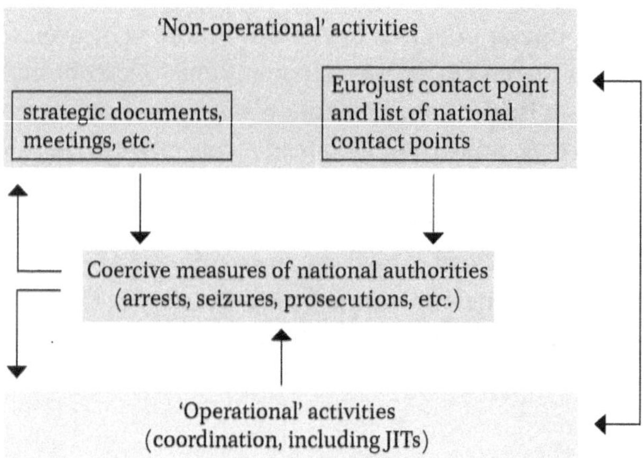

FIGURE 3 *The role of Eurojust against transnational environmental crime.*

460 Ibid 93.

461 Eurojust, 'Annual Report 2015' (n 267) 44.

462 Interview with L Görts, Eurojust (n 399). On the importance to build networks of prosecutors and investigators throughout Europe and on the role of Eurojust in that regard see M Groenleer (n 267) 318.

463 Interview with V Sacré, EU-TWIX (n 389).

It is emerged that Europol and Eurojust share some similarities and bear some differences as far as their operational role is concerned. Unlike Europol, Eurojust's operational role is already fully-fledged: transnational environmental crimes could be dealt with by the Unit, which could offer its services to national authorities dealing with these offences. However, although often envisaged and suggested,[464] the involvement of this body in the fight against transnational environmental crime is unfortunately still limited. Public information is available only on few cases, which show that when national authorities resort to the Unit its intervention is highly appreciated. In the three above-mentioned cases, Eurojust has supported domestic authorities in identifying the authorities in a better position to launch an investigation or a prosecution, in coordinating arrests and seizures, in providing the necessary strategic information, etc. In other words, Eurojust has proven to be ideally placed to solve all the main concerns related to investigations and prosecutions of transnational environmental crimes.

Furthermore, even though a JIT has been set up and funded through Eurojust, the use of Joint Investigation Teams to deal with environmental crimes is still extremely rare. This issue has been addressed also in the 2014 Eurojust Report. As commented by an expert in the field, to set up a JIT three requirements should be necessary: i) an investigation on cross-border crimes, preferably a long-term one, since it seems that national authorities are more inclined to request the establishment of a JIT in such cases, rather than when the investigations are limited in time; ii) adequate awareness on the seriousness of environmental crime and on the involvement of OCGs; and iii) knowledge of the advantages of JITs and of the ways to set them up.[465] The conclusions of the 2014 Eurojust Report lead to think that none of these three conditions is met and actually the same Report states that 'the establishment of joint investigations teams [...] in the three environmental crime types mentioned above [trafficking in waste and in protected species and surface water pollution] is not very well developed'.[466]

---

464 See, among the many, Eurojust, 'Strategic Project on Environmental Crime. Report' (n 29); I Fouchard and L Neyret, '35 Propositions pour mieux sanctionner les crimes contre l'environnement. Rapport de synthèse' in L Neyret (ed), *Des écocrimes à l'écocide. Le droit pénal au secours de l'environnement* (Bruylant 2015) 430–431; M Faure, N Philipsen, T Fajardo del Castillo and others, 'Conclusions and Recommendations'. Study in the framework of the EFFACE Research Project (2016) 24–25.

465 Interview with V Jamin, JITs Network Secretariat (n 421).

466 Eurojust, 'Strategic Project on Environmental Crime. Report' (n 29) 34.

The limited knowledge of the instruments of judicial cooperation available at the EU level, including Eurojust itself, was confirmed by one of the prosecutors involved in the 'Bird-Egg case': he submitted that 'knowing what I do now allows me to better inform my colleagues, and knowing how Eurojust can assist in a more coordinated approach will surely lead to better results'.[467] These words confirm that national authorities still have a scarce *knowledge* of Eurojust's mission and services, but when they have the opportunity to get in touch with Eurojust, they usually realise the importance of its services and are then more inclined to resort to it in future cases.[468] Such a lack of awareness allows to infer that, as for Europol, also the involvement of Eurojust in the coordination of national investigations on environmental crime is hampered by 'external' factors which do not necessarily relate to the nature of the phenomenon itself but rather include the limited acquaintance of domestic authorities with the Unit or their limited willingness to share their information with Eurojust.[469]

Another reason is the

> *lack of an un-ambiguous definition of environmental crime* at the European and the international level, e.g. whether it is fundamentally transnational, and in particular what kind of offences have to be considered environmental crimes. One of the reasons for the very low number of cases of environmental crime registered by Eurojust [...] is the limited ability of national law enforcement authorities to recognize what constitutes environmental crime and to report it as such, and also to properly address and deal with initiatives/requests for judicial cooperation in this field.[470]

---

467 'The Bird-Egg case' (2013) 10 *Eurojust News* 16.

468 Similarly, see S Chin and W Veening, 'Actors and Institutions Relevant to Fighting Environmental Crime' (n 432) 36.

469 Interview with W Gowitzke, Europol (n 364).

470 M Faure, C Gerstetter, S Sina and GM Vagliasindi, 'Instruments, Actors and Institutions in the Fight Against Environmental Crime'. Study in the framework of the EFFACE research project (Ecologic Institute 2015) 64. Emphasis added. As far as Europol is concerned, similar difficulties arising from the lack of an harmonised definition of organised crime in the EU are pointed out in A De Moor and G Vermeulen, 'The Europol Council Decision: Transforming Europol into an Agency of the European Union' (n 266) 1098–1099; E Disley, B Irving, W Hughes and B Patruni, 'Evaluation of the implementation of the Europol Council Decision' (n 250) 71.

The same goes for the similarly problematic notion of 'organised crime'. The concepts of 'environmental crime' and 'organised crime' at the EU level have been discussed in the previous sections; it is now possible to add that clarity as to what constitutes environmental crime or organised crime is key towards achieving *legal certainty* with regard to the mandate of Eurojust (and Europol), as well as fundamental to avoid these bodies to struggle with different understanding and regulations of the phenomena at stake.[471] As shown at the beginning of this work, however, this status quo does not seem on the way to be modified in the short term.

In sum, despite the positive experiences of the past, Eurojust is not often involved by national authorities who carry out investigations and launch prosecutions concerning transnational environmental crimes. It has been demonstrated that Europol shares the same problem.[472]

In order to enhance its possible involvement in cases of environmental crimes and to raise adequate awareness, Eurojust—as Europol—is strongly committed in many strategic activities.[473] Among them, the establishment of the list of national contact points is extremely important for its operational impact: according to the 2015 Eurojust Annual Report, in fact, this list is aimed at increasing 'the *operational* capacities of competent authorities in cross-border cases involving environmental offences'.[474]

In addition, Eurojust can provide national authorities with relevant *strategic* knowledge on how to proceed with investigations on cross-border crimes, as it happened in the first of the two meetings organised in the Prestige case:

> [t]he purpose of the first meeting was to assist the magistrates in gathering *experience* about how to manage such a case, in which hundreds of victims have suffered loss. Colleagues leading similar investigations such as the shipwreck of *"Erika"* investigated in the Court of Paris and *"Mar Egeo"* investigated in the Court of La Corunna were invited to share their experience.[475]

471 V Mitsilegas, 'The Council Framework Decision on the Fight against Organised Crime' (n 38) 20. See also F Calderoni (n 200) 1384.

472 See, among the many, K Klaas and S Sina (n 160) *passim*; M Faure, C Gerstetter, S Sina and GM Vagliasindi, 'Instruments, Actors and Institutions in the Fight Against Environmental Crime' (n 471) 64–65.

473 Interview with L Görts, Eurojust (n 399).

474 Eurojust, 'Annual Report 2015' (n 267) 44. Emphasis added.

475 Eurojust, 'Annual Report 2003' (n 442) 29. Emphasis added.

In conclusion, the same virtuous circle described with regard to Europol's activities can be triggered by Eurojust. Its operational role has turned out to be—even though in a limited number of cases—of substantial importance for the national investigations and prosecutions on environmental crime, meanwhile providing the Unit with further strategic information to elaborate on and helping it to spread the knowledge of the agency itself. In turn, Eurojust has shown an increasing commitment to engage with 'non-operational activities', such as the Strategic Project and the appointment of a Contact Point on Environmental Crime. Both the coordination tasks of the Unit and the national investigations heavily draw on these activities.

In such a scenario of intertwined powers, services, information, and instruments it does not seem inappropriate to argue that, in practice, the contribution of Eurojust can be sometimes *necessary* to allow national authorities to carry out their 'coercive' activities, as the three mentioned cases have proven. Against this backdrop, drawing a clear line between operational and non-operational tasks of the Unit, as well as between its activities and the 'coercive' ones of national authorities, is not always so straightforward as it could seem at first sight.

7 Europol, Eurojust and Environmental Crime: To the Future and Beyond, Waiting for the European Public Prosecutor's Office

After the analysis of the current role of Eurojust and Europol in the fight against environmental crime, it is now appropriate to mention the expected challenges for the future. This is done by taking into account two issues: the EU Action Plan against Wildlife Trafficking and the (possible) establishment of the European Public Prosecutor's Office.

7.1 *The EU Action Plan against Wildlife Trafficking: The Need for More Europol and Eurojust*

The Commission adopted the EU Action Plan against Wildlife Trafficking in February 2016 and the Council expressed its support to this initiative in June 2016.[476] Aimed at reinforcing the position of the EU in the eradication of wildlife trafficking, the Plan is expected to cover the five-year period between 2016 and 2020 and it is based on three priorities. Each *priority* encompasses

476 'Communication from the Commission. EU Action Plan Against Wildlife Trafficking' (n 45); 'Outcome of the Council meeting. Environment', 20 June 2016, Council doc 10444/16, 21–25.

different *objectives*, which are composed of multiple *actions*. Whereas the first and the third priority concern the strengthening, respectively, of *preventive* actions and of global *partnership* in the field, the second one is formulated as 'implementing and enforcing existing rules and combating *organised wildlife crime* more effectively'.[477] Within the frame of this priority, therefore, Eurojust and Europol can be called to play an important role, even though for the time being nothing is significantly changed in theirs tasks on the matter.[478]

Nevertheless, a closer look to the Action Plan allows to draw some considerations.

First, the Action Plan seems consistent with the previous strategic projects in the field, which had identified trafficking in endangered species as a crime with a main economic nature that raises (or should raise) the concerns of national authorities, not least because of the increasing involvement of OCGs.[479] Similar considerations on the nature and on the impact of wildlife crime underpin the whole Action Plan. On a more general level, it is interesting to note that one of the main drivers for this ambitious EU project is the acknowledgment of the increasing involvement of OCGs in such activities, as well as the alarming links between wildlife crime and terrorism, with the former sometimes providing the economic resources for the latter. It is not surprising, therefore, that the very first paragraph of the document with which the Council has welcomed the Plan reads as follows:

> [t]he Council of the European Union, [noting] with deep concern that wildlife trafficking has become one of the world's most profitable *organised criminal activities*; that it is facilitated by corruption and weak governance structures; that in some regions it threatens national security and fuels conflicts by providing funding to militia and *terrorist groups* [...].[480]

Second, also the Action Plan highlights that one of the main reasons of the current deficiencies in the fight against wildlife crime is the lack both of *resources* and of *awareness* on the seriousness of the phenomenon. As far as the latter is concerned, the very *first* action of the Plan is to 'increase support

477 'Communication from the Commission. EU Action Plan Against Wildlife Trafficking' (n 45) 5. Emphasis added.

478 Interview with W Gowitzke, Europol (n 364); interview with L Görts, Eurojust (n 399).

479 See more in the 'Commission Staff Working Document accompanying the Communication on the EU Action Plan against Wildlife Trafficking' (n 73) 28–33.

480 'Outcome of the Council meeting. Environment' (n 476) 21. Emphasis added.

for awareness-raising [...]'.[481] As for the economic side, one of the expected results of the Plan is to earmark *more resources* for Eurojust and Europol for an appropriate work on the matter.[482] If this Plan will really lead to allocate more resources to the two bodies, it will be interesting to assess how they will be used.

Third, according to their different nature and tasks, the involvement of Eurojust and Europol is regulated in a different way. The former is only mentioned, along with Europol, in Action 13 ('improve *cooperation* among Member States on cases of cross-border wildlife trafficking'), which is expected to result in three outcomes. The first, concerning the destination of more resources, has just been mentioned. The other two regard an increased involvement of Eurojust in *JITs* as well as in '*joint operations* involving cross-border cooperation carried out by EU Member States (facilitated by Europol)'.[483]

Therefore, on the one hand, the Action Plan aligns itself with all those documents and studies supporting the usefulness of establishing JITs in the fight against cross-border environmental crime.[484] However, for the time being, nothing has changed in that regard and JITs are still very rare in this field.[485] On the other hand, even though the joint operations (such as 'COBRA III' or 'Waste Trafficking') will continue to be facilitated by Europol,[486] the Action Plan seems to request that also Eurojust should be involved. In the previous experiences, as mentioned, the Unit has not been called to play any peculiar role, so that it remains to be seen what will change in practice.

As far as Europol is concerned, the Action Plan supports the role of the agency in the stepping up of *international cooperation* in the field, and in that regard it is expected that joint meetings will be held 'involving Europol, the EU Wildlife Trade Enforcement Group and relevant regional enforcement networks (e.g. ASEAN-WEN and Lusaka Agreement Task Force) and the INECE'.[487]

481 'Communication from the Commission. EU Action Plan Against Wildlife Trafficking' (n 45) 8.

482 Ibid 11.

483 Ibid 12. Emphasis added.

484 See above n 438.

485 Interview with V Jamin, JITs Network Secretariat (n 421).

486 The role of Europol as facilitator of similar actions is also supported in Action 24, one of whose expected results is that 'Member States, *assisted by Europol*, participate in joint international law enforcement operations' ('Communication from the Commission. EU Action Plan Against Wildlife Trafficking' (n 45) 16, emphasis added).

487 'Communication from the Commission. EU Action Plan Against Wildlife Trafficking' (n 45), Action 24, 16. INECE stands for International Network for Environmental Compliance and Enforcement and is 'a partnership of government and non-government

Especially in light of the mentioned COBRA III operations, Europol has already established a link with ASEAN-WEN and the Lusaka Agreement Task Force, so that it seems that the Action Plan only aims at supporting the agency in keeping such relations alive. More in general, a similar provision of the Action Plan confirms the paramount importance of networks and contacts to make the cooperation in the fight against TEC smoother and more effective.

In line with this, the Council has called on the Member States and the Commission to

> improve cooperation, coordination, communication and data sharing between their implementation and enforcement agencies, as well as with agencies in third countries and other wildlife enforcement networks, including through the promotion of existing tools such as the EU-Twix database [...].[488]

The Action Plan also suggests an enhancement of the competences of Europol with regard to *strategic* analysis; for instance, it is provided that the agency shall cooperate with the Commission and the Member States on a 'common risk-based assessment of EU-wide priorities agreed at the EU Wildlife Trade Enforcement Group'.[489] However, the practical effects of the Action Plan in that regard seem to be at least unclear, since Europol works on the basis of the Policy Cycle and of the SOCTA, where wildlife crime is not even regarded as an emerging threat. It is to be reminded, indeed, that the *text* of the SOCTA briefly deals with both trafficking in waste and trafficking in endangered species, but in its *conclusions*, among the 'emerging threats', the SOCTA only mentions 'environmental crime: [i]llicit waste trafficking'.[490]

According to the Plan, the forthcoming SOCTAs shall include an assessment of the 'wildlife trafficking threat'.[491] Since, as shown, the 2013 SOCTA already has a very limited assessment on wildlife trafficking, it seems that the Action Plan envisages that something more is necessary from the side of Europol in that regard. However, despite its ambitious goals, the Action Plan quite strikingly

enforcement and compliance practitioners from more than 150 countries' (<http://inece.org> accessed 18 September 2016).

488 'Outcome of the Council meeting. Environment' (n 476) 24.

489 'Communication from the Commission. EU Action Plan Against Wildlife Trafficking' (n 45), Action 12, 11.

490 Europol, 'EU Serious and Organised Threat Assessment' (n 344) 39.

491 'Communication from the Commission. EU Action Plan Against Wildlife Trafficking' (n 45), Action 20, 14.

does not urge to consider wildlife crime as a priority crime in the Policy Cycle. Likewise, the Council has devoted only a mild statement to the matter, inviting 'Europol to consider the wildlife crime threats when preparing its next EU Serious and Organised Crime Threat Assessment'.[492]

Continuing with the brief analysis of the Action Plan, it is worth mentioning also Action 16, which aims to '*improve knowledge* base on checks, investigations, prosecutions and judicial proceedings against wildlife trafficking'.[493] One of the expected results of this action should be the establishment of a '*database* containing case law on wildlife trafficking from Member States established at ENPE to facilitate knowledge-sharing'.[494] As discussed in section 6.2, such an instrument is perceived as particularly useful by national judicial authorities.

Another expected result of the same Action 16 should be that Member States will send '*systematic information* to Europol about *all* cases with organised crime and/or cross-border implications'.[495] On this note, it can be reminded that the Council has also expressly invited the 'Member States to *provide relevant information* on wildlife crime to Europol, including through the SOCTA questionnaire'.[496] In light of the above-mentioned reluctance of national authorities to share their cases with the EU agencies, it is difficult not to be sceptical on the practical effectiveness of such invitations and expected results. Moreover, it is quite surprising that the Action Plan is silent on the need that national authorities send systematic information also to *Eurojust*, since the Unit shares with Europol the same problem of being limitedly involved by national authorities dealing with cross-border cases.

In conclusion, the EU Action Plan, on the one hand, seems to consider the EU as already equipped with a useful toolbox to fight wildlife trafficking, even though the use of such a toolbox should become much more regular and systematic (JITs, joint operations, more funding to Europol and Eurojust). On the other hand, the Action Plan has missed the opportunity to take a firm stand with regard to some of the detected gaps in the field, strikingly at odds with the ambitious goals of the Plan itself.

---

492 'Outcome of the Council meeting. Environment' (n 476) 25.

493 'Communication from the Commission. EU Action Plan Against Wildlife Trafficking' (n 45), Action 16, 13. Emphasis added.

494 Ibid. Emphasis added.

495 Ibid. Emphasis added.

496 'Outcome of the Council meeting. Environment' (n 476) 25. Emphasis added.

7.2 *The European Public Prosecutor's Office and Its Possible Competence on Environmental Crimes*

If it will be established, the European Public Prosecutor's Office (EPPO) will be the *European body* empowered to investigate and prosecute *crimes affecting the financial interests of the EU*. Being the first European agency to be given *direct* powers in the sensitive field of criminal law, the EPPO represents a Copernican revolution in the history of EU (criminal) law.

After years of political and academic debate, the Treaty of Lisbon finally provided the legal basis for the establishment of this body.[497] Article 86 TFEU allows the Council—with the previous consent of the European Parliament—to set up the EPPO by means of regulations. Article 86(1) TFEU also states that, in the absence of unanimity in the Council, the EPPO can be set up with the procedure of enhanced cooperation, if nine Member States agree.

Pursuant to Article 86 TFEU, in July 2013 the Commission issued a Proposal for a Council Regulation on the establishment of the EPPO and the negotiations are still ongoing.[498] After three years of discussions in the Council,

---

497 Because the possible establishment of a European Public Prosecutor's Office has been discussed since the mid-nineties, the literature is enormous: for a list of the main works until 2011 see A Damaskou, 'The European Public Prosecutor's Office. A Ground-Breaking New Institution of the EU Legal Order' (2015) 6 *New Journal of European Criminal Law* 126, 126–127. Among the subsequent ones see K Ligeti (ed), *Toward a Prosecutor for the European Union*, vol 1 (Hart 2012); G Grasso, G Illuminati, R Sicurella and S Allegrezza (eds), *Le sfide dell'attuazione di una Procura europea: definizione di regole e loro impatto sugli ordinamenti interni* (Giuffrè 2013); L Hamran and E Szabova, 'European Public Prosecutor's Office—Cui Bono?' (2013) 4 *New Journal of European Criminal Law* 40; K Ligeti and M Simonato, 'The European Public Prosecutor's Office: Towards a Truly Prosecution Service?' (2013) 4 *New Journal of European Criminal Law* 7; S Manacorda, 'Le droit pénal de l'Union à l'heure de la Charte et du Parquet européen' [2013] *Revue de science criminelle et de droit pénal comparé* 927; M Wade, 'A European public prosecutor: potential and pitfalls' (2013) 59 *Crime, Law and Social Change* 439; P Asp (ed), *The European Public Prosecutor's Office—Legal and Criminal Policy Perspectives* (Stiftelsen Skrifter utgivna av Juridiska fakulteten vid Stockholms universitet 2015); LH Erkelens, AWH Meij and M Pawlik (eds), *The European Public Prosecutor's Office. An extended arm or a Two-Headed dragon?* (Springer-Verlag 2015); K Ligeti, 'The European Public Prosecutor's Office' in V Mitsilegas, M Bergström and T Konstadinides (eds), *Research Handbook on EU Criminal Law* (Edward Elgar 2016) 480–504.

498 'Proposal for a Council Regulation on the establishment of the European Public Prosecutor's Office' COM(2013) 534 final, 17 July 2013. See, for instance, L Bachmaier Winter, 'The Potential Contribution of a European Public Prosecutor in Light of the Proposal for a Regulation of 17 July 2013' (2015) 23 *European Journal of Crime, Criminal Law and Criminal Justice* 121.

a consolidated text of the Draft Regulation has been released in July 2016 ('EPPO Draft Regulation').[499]

The in-depth analysis of the EPPO Draft Regulation falls beyond the scope of this work. Just a few details are given, before evaluating which role the EPPO could play in the field of environmental crime.

Even though the original Proposal has been significantly amended over the years, some features of the EPPO have remained unchanged, such as the fact that the *trial* following the investigations led by the EPPO will take place before *domestic* courts. Moreover, the European Public Prosecutor's Office will be strongly embedded in national prosecution offices, insofar as it is thought to be composed not only by the European Chief Prosecutor and his deputies, operating at the *central level* (say, in Brussels or in The Hague), but also by the European Delegated Prosecutors (EDPs), who are and remain national prosecutors. In practice, the latter will carry out the investigations, whereas the central office will mainly coordinate their activities. In other words, the national prosecutors chosen as EDPs will have a 'double hat': when they 'wear' the European one, they follow the instructions of the Central Office, but when they switch to the 'national hat' they come back to their regular activities, roles, and accountability.

According to the EPPO Draft Regulation, and quite differently from the original proposal, the Central Office now 'consists of the College, the Permanent Chambers, the European Chief Prosecutor, his/her deputies, the European Prosecutors [...]'.[500] After the pressure of the French and German Ministers of Justice, the hierarchical structure originally provided in the Commission proposal has been abandoned and such a collegiate, multilayered and admittedly complex model has been adopted.

The EPPO Draft Regulation lists different rules concerning the powers of the EPPO to initiate and conduct the investigations, to evoke a case of its competence if it has been opened by a national authority, to adopt the investigations measures listed in the Draft Regulation and those available according to national law, to adopt measures in the frame of cross-border investigations, and to prosecute before national courts.[501] Many other sensitive issues are dealt with in the Draft Regulation, such as the admission of the evidence collected during the investigations before the domestic courts, the dismissal of

---

499 'Proposal for a Regulation on the establishment of the European Public Prosecutor's Office—Consolidated text: update of the provisional version', Council doc 11350/1/16, 28 July 2016.

500 Article 7(3) EPPO Draft Regulation.

501 Respectively, Articles 22, 23, 22a, 25, 26, and 30 EPPO Draft Regulation.

the case, and the rights of the suspects and the accused persons, as well as the judicial review of the acts of the EPPO.[502]

For the purpose of this work, it needs to be underscored that the competence of the EPPO has been limited to the *crimes affecting the financial interests of the EU* (ie mainly frauds and related offences, such as corruption and money laundering). More precisely, these crimes will be defined in a Directive, which is still under negotiations in the Council.[503] This seems one of the features that this body will definitely have, should it be established sooner or later.

Nevertheless, because the EPPO will also be competent for those crimes which are '*inextricably linked*' to frauds,[504] it cannot be excluded that it could be called to investigate environmental crimes, should such a link occur in a given case.[505] One can therefore wonder when this could happen in practice. This implies to understand, first of all, what is the meaning of offences 'inextricably linked' to crimes affecting the financial interests of the EU.

In that regard, recital No. 49 of the Draft Regulation states that the notion of 'inextricably linked offences'

> should be considered in light of the jurisprudence of the Court of Justice of the European Union. Such may be the case, for example, for offences which have been committed for the main purpose of *creating the conditions* to commit the offence affecting the financial interests of the Union, such as offences strictly aimed at ensuring the material or legal means to commit the offence affecting the financial interests of the Union, or *to ensure the profit or product thereof*.[506]

Probably it is the latter case that could turn out to be more common, such as in those cases where the money obtained through frauds are used in the frame

502 Respectively, Articles 31, 33, 35, and 36 EPPO Draft Regulation.

503 Article 17(1) EPPO Draft Regulation. The Proposal for such a Directive was issued by the Commission in 2012 ('Proposal for a Directive of the European Parliament and of the Council on the fight against fraud to the Union's financial interests by means of criminal law', Council doc 12683/12, 17 July 2012).

504 See Article 17(2) EPPO Draft Regulation. Emphasis added. See also Article 20 EPPO Draft Regulation, which lays down the further conditions for the exercise of this ancillary competence of the EPPO.

505 See R Sicurella, 'Article 86' in G Grasso, R Sicurella and V Scalia, 'Articles 82–86 of the Treaty on the Functioning of the European Union and Environmental Crime'. Study in the framework of the EFFACE research project (University of Catania 2015) 43; V Mitsilegas, 'Contribution to conclusions and recommendations on environmental crime' (n 210) 5.

506 Recital No 49 of the EPPO Draft Regulation. Emphasis added.

of other crimes, including environmental ones (trafficking in waste or in protected species, for instance).

The European Council—acting unanimously—could decide to broaden the competence of the EPPO in order to include also 'serious crime having a cross-border dimension'.[507] In light of this possibility, the EPPO could be made competent, in the future, also for those forms of environmental crime that are cross-border in their nature, such as trafficking in waste and in protected species.[508] After all, as Europol was original competent only for drug-related crimes and subsequently its remit has been broadened, also the EPPO could begin to operate with a limited competence, which could be expanded when (and if) the body will have shown its expected added value.[509]

A similar extension would seem justified on the basis of many similarities between environmental crime and frauds to the detriment of the EU budget. First, they both attract OCGs for their nature of 'high profit/low risk' crimes.[510] Because of their common *economic* drivers, it is not a case that in some systems these offences are dealt with by the same prosecution office.[511]

Second, they often (could) have a cross-border nature:[512] a typical example of cross-border frauds to the detriment of the EU budget would be VAT carousel

---

507 Article 86(4) TFEU.

508 See GM Vagliasindi, 'Istituzione di una Procura europea e diritto penale sostanziale: l'eventuale estensione della competenza materiale della futura Procura alla criminalità ambientale' in G Grasso, G Illuminati, R Sicurella and S Allegrezza (eds), *Le sfide dell'attuazione di una Procura europea: definizione di regole e loro impatto sugli ordinamenti interni* (Giuffrè 2013) 206ff; R Sicurella, 'Article 86' (n 505) 46–47; V Mitsilegas, 'Contribution to conclusions and recommendations on environmental crime' (n 210) 5.

509 See A Klip (n 272) 460.

510 Whereas for environmental crime this has been argued several times in the text, for crimes against the EU budget see the 'Commission Staff Working Document. Impact Assessment Accompanying Proposal for a Council Regulation on the establishment of the European Public Prosecutor's Office' SWD(2013) 274 final, 17 July 2013, 7.

511 In The Netherlands, for instance, a specific branch of the Prosecution Service, the Functional Public Prosecutor's Office, is 'especially tasked to handle *fraud and environmental cases*' (W Geelhoed, 'Embedding the European Public Prosecutor's Office in Jurisdictions with a Wide Scope of Prosecutorial Discretion: the Dutch Example' in C Novak (ed), *The European Public Prosecutor's Office and National Authorities* (Wolters Kluwer-CEDAM 2016) 94).

512 'Commission Staff Working Document. Impact Assessment Accompanying Proposal for a Council Regulation on the establishment of the European Public Prosecutor's Office' (n 510) *passim*. However, some authors have rebutted that a significant part of the economic losses of the EU is actually due to the (small) frauds committed by national or local groups, within the national borders and for limited amounts of money: see, for instance,

frauds, but at the time of writing their inclusion within the competence of the EPPO is under discussion.[513] Third, both areas of crime are under-investigated and often not regarded as a priority by national prosecutors: environmental crime is usually perceived as a victimless crime, which then quite naturally is neglected by domestic authorities.[514] Similarly, for the offences against EU financial interests, it has been stated that 'there is a perceived tendency to put complex European fraud cases involving cross-border cooperation on offences affecting the EU's financial interest "at the bottom of the pile"'.[515]

Fourth, national legislations are not sufficiently harmonised with regard to environmental crimes and crimes against the EU budget, with possible drawbacks for the effective use of some instruments of judicial cooperation in the field.[516] Finally, also a legal and axiological similarity between the two areas of crime has been claimed, stating that the environment is 'a proper "supranational" legal interest'[517] that should fall within the competence of the (forthcoming) supranational prosecution body.

For all the above-mentioned reasons, it would not be inappropriate to make the EPPO, if and once set up, competent also for cross-border environmental crimes, even though it is unclear whether its competence could be extended pursuant to Article 86(4) TFEU if the EPPO will be established—as it seems realistic—through enhanced cooperation.[518]

W Tupman, 'Keeping under the radar: watch out for the "Smurfs"' (2010) 17 *Journal of Financial Crime* 152.

513 At the time of writing, the latest update available can be found in 'Proposal for a Directive of the European Parliament and of the Council on the fight against fraud to the Union's financial interests by means of criminal law—Progress report/Policy debate', Council doc 9804/16, 3 June 2016.

514 C Gerstetter, C Stefes, A Farmer and others, 'Environmental crime and the EU' (n 39) 37ff. On environmental crime as a 'victimless crime' see above, section 2.1.

515 'Commission Staff Working Document. Impact Assessment Accompanying Proposal for a Council Regulation on the establishment of the European Public Prosecutor's Office' (n 510) 19.

516 As far as environmental crime is concerned, see above sections 3.3 and 3.4. With regard to frauds, see for instance the 'Commission Staff Working Paper, Impact Assessment (Part I) Accompanying the document Proposal for a Directive of the European Parliament and of the Council on the fight against fraud to the Union's financial interests by means of criminal law' SWD(2012) 195 final, 11 July 2012, 48.

517 R Sicurella, 'Article 86' (n 505) 47.

518 This possibility has been denied by: K Ligeti, 'Introduction' in K Ligeti (ed) *Toward a Prosecutor for the European Union*, vol 1 (Hart 2012) 2; G Grasso, 'Relazione di sintesi' in G Grasso, G Illuminati, R Sicurella and S Allegrezza (eds), *Le sfide dell'attuazione di una Procura europea: definizione di regole e loro impatto sugli ordinamenti interni* (Giuffrè 2013)

Finally, should a case of transnational environmental crime be dealt with by the EPPO, the (probably) forthcoming agency could also cooperate with Europol and Eurojust in order to curb that crime in an effective way. The relations of the EPPO with Eurojust are deemed to be quite close, as the text of Article 86 TFEU itself makes clear: it states that the EPPO should be established 'from Eurojust'. Article 57 EPPO Draft Regulation is devoted to the cooperation among the two bodies. Apart from the technical and administrative provisions, it is interesting to note that the EPPO may associate Eurojust with its activities concerning cross-border cases, for example by sharing information (including personal data) on its investigations or by inviting 'Eurojust or its competent national member(s) to provide support in the transmission of its decisions or requests for mutual legal assistance to, and execution in, States members of Eurojust but not taking part in the establishment of the European Public Prosecutor's Office or *third countries*'.[519] Therefore, the EPPO Draft Regulation enhances the operational role of Eurojust and it underlines its importance as an instrument to liaise with third countries. This could be positive in cases of cross-border environmental crimes concerning also non-EU States, even though once again only the practice will show whether a fruitful cooperation with third countries can actually be launched.

As far as Europol is concerned, it is provided that this agency and the EPPO will conclude a working arrangement to regulate their cooperation. Moreover, the EPPO will have to be empowered both to request any relevant information held by Europol and concerning the crimes falling within the competence of the European Public Prosecutor's Office and to ask Europol to give its *analytical* support to a specific investigation carried out by the EPPO.[520] Should the EPPO be made competent for cross-border environmental crimes, therefore, it seems that Europol could not guarantee the latter analytical support, in light of the above-mentioned lack of any structure within the agency that can provide operational analysis with regard to environmental crimes (save the limited exceptions discussed before). On the contrary, it is clear that also the EPPO Draft Regulation acknowledges that the strategic information held by Europol can be of substantial importance for the adoption of coercive measures.

767–768. For further reflections on the issue see M Zwiers, *The European Public Prosecutor's Office. Analysis of a Multilevel Criminal Justice System* (Intersentia 2011) 391–393.

519 Article 57(2)(b) EPPO Draft Regulation. Emphasis added. Moreover, the EPPO should also have an indirect access to the Eurojust's case management system, on the basis of a hit/no-hit system (Article 57(3) EPPO Draft Regulation).

520 Article 58(2) EPPO Draft Regulation.

Even though these are only tentative conclusions, since the EPPO has not been established yet, it seems that in the medium (or even long) term it would be appropriate to broaden its competence to cover also transnational environmental crimes.[521]

8 Conclusion

Tackling transnational environmental crime remains a challenge for judicial and police authorities.

Although organised crime groups show an increasing involvement in this 'high profit-low risk' area of crime, the link between environmental and organised crime has not been addressed in detail at EU and international level.

The protection of the environment has been of fundamental importance in EU law since the 1970s. Nevertheless, the harmonisation of the substantive criminal law of EU Member States is limited, since the 2008 Directive on environmental crime and the 2009 Directive on ship-source pollution are formulated in a broad way which has challenged legal certainty and left a considerable degree of discretion to national legislators.

As a consequence, domestic legislations on the matter still bear significant differences, especially as far as the definition of, and the penalties for, those crimes are concerned. Such discrepancies could have negative outcomes both on the investigations concerning environmental criminality at the national level and on the smooth functioning of the procedures of judicial cooperation at the EU level. Not even the legal framework on organised crime seems to be satisfactory and it does not address adequately environmental crime and its economic dimension. The Treaty of Lisbon has laid the foundations for a renewed fight against transnational and organised environmental crime; however, for the time being, nothing is changed, apart from a growing interest on the multidisciplinary approach to these phenomena.

As far as the role of the EU agencies in the field is concerned, the abovementioned lack of clarity on what constitutes environmental and organised crime seems to be one of the reasons for their limited involvement. The common mission of Europol and Eurojust is to support national authorities dealing with transnational crimes, including environmental ones. Eurojust mainly aims to coordinate national prosecutors and to help them in facing the typical obstacles of cross-border investigations. A similar role can be played by

521 See also C Gerstetter, C Stefes, A Farmer and others, 'Environmental crime and the EU' (n 39) 43.

Europol with regard to police bodies, but the core of its tasks is represented by the operational analysis of information provided by domestic authorities (if and when they are willing to share it).

Apart from that, both agencies have a strong 'non-operational' role, since they strive to collect and spread knowledge on transnational crimes and on the most effective methods to curb them. Especially the strategic role of Europol is relevant, if one bears in mind that the priorities in the fight against serious and organised crime at the EU level are set on the basis of the SOCTA.

However, environmental crime has not been included among the priorities for the period 2014–2017. This choice implies that less resources are earmarked for the fight against this form of criminality. In light of the perceived low priority of this crime among national authorities and of all the other problems mentioned in the text (ranging from lack of resources and expertise to inadequate cooperation among the competent agencies and units at the national and supranational level), the fact that environmental crime is not regarded as a 'key threat' definitely does not help to tackle it in an effective way. For instance, this makes the establishment of a focal point, target group or even a dedicated unit within Europol highly unrealistic.

Overall, it seems that the operational role of Europol and Eurojust is quite limited in the field. On the one hand, Europol is not currently empowered to carry out operational analysis on data concerning investigations on environmental crimes *per se*, even though a leeway exits when they are connected (or even overlap) with other crimes for which a focal point or a target group already exists within Europol. In addition, limited analysis could be provided within the frame of the GNST Resource focal point. It is still to be evaluated whether the recently adopted Regulation will improve the situation when it will become effective (May 2017). However, Europol has already coordinated some operations concerning environmental crime, and especially the 'COBRA III' project has represented an important example of the possible external action of the EU in the field.

On the other hand, given its different structure and powers, Eurojust can already undertake operational activities concerning environmental crimes, but this has happened quite rarely in the past. Likewise, as far as the JITs established through Eurojust are concerned, only one Joint Investigation Team has been set up to coordinate national investigations on environmental crime up to now.

At the same time, the efforts of Eurojust and Europol to raise adequate awareness on the crimes at stake and on the best ways to cope with them are noteworthy. The two agencies are strongly committed to an unceasing *strategic* work, which actually helps to bridge the existing gaps in their operational activities. Europol and Eurojust also strive, directly or indirectly, to build a network of experts and practitioners working in the field, with the aim to address one of the recurring problems in the cross-border police and judicial cooperation, namely the lack of knowledge on who to contact (and how) in another country.

Since the operational activities of the two agencies strongly benefit from the strategic knowledge previously collected and elaborated by them, the boundaries between operational and non-operational activities are quite blurred in the field at stake. Moreover, since in some instances the services provided by Europol and Eurojust have been (and are recognised to be) of such an importance for the success of national ('coercive') measures, it has been similarly submitted that it is not very easy to draw a clear line between the powers and competences of national authorities and those of the EU agencies. Operations such as 'Waste Trafficking' demonstrate the benefits of a synergy between strategic, operational and coercive measures in tackling transnational environmental crime.

This approach has been confirmed in the recently adopted EU Action Plan against Wildlife Trafficking, which underlines the need for an enhanced role of Europol and Eurojust in the field. At the time of writing, however, it is not clear how the Plan will improve the current scenario and whether it will really have a positive effect on the involvement of EU agencies in the fight against wildlife crime. Similarly, it is not certain whether the European Public Prosecutor's Office will be finally established and, if so, whether it will be made competent also for environmental crime.

Bibliography

Articles, Books and Studies

Agnew DJ, Pearce J, Pramod G and others, 'Estimating the Worldwide Extent of Illegal Fishing' (2009) 4 PLoS ONE 1 (<http://journals.plos.org/plosone/article?id=10.1371/journal.pone.0004570> accessed 18 September 2016).

Albanese J, 'Deciphering the Linkages between Organized Crime and Transnational Crime' (2012) 66 *Journal of International Affairs* 1.

Amici V, 'Europol et la nouvelle décision du Conseil: entre opportunités et contraintes' [2010] *Revue du Droit de l'Union Européenne* 77.

Andreas P, 'Illicit Globalisation Myths and Misconceptions' in Mitsilegas V, Alldridge P and Cheliotis L (eds), *Globalisation, Criminal Law and Criminal Justice. Theoretical, Comparative and Transnational Perspectives* (Hart 2015) 45–64.

Asp P (ed), *The European Public Prosecutor's Office—Legal and Criminal Policy Perspectives* (Stiftelsen Skrifter utgivna av Juridiska fakulteten vid Stockholms universitet 2015).

Ayling J, 'What sustains Wildlife Crime? Rhino Horn Trading and the Resilience of Criminal Networks' (2013) 16 *Journal of International Wildlife Law & Policy* 57.

Bachmaier Winter L, 'The Potential Contribution of a European Public Prosecutor in Light of the Proposal for a Regulation of 17 July 2013' (2015) 23 *European Journal of Crime, Criminal Law and Criminal Justice* 121.

Banks D, Davies C, Gosling J and others, 'Environmental Crime. A threat to our future' (Environmental Investigation Agency 2008).

Beauvais P, 'Les limites de l'internationalisation du droit pénal de l'environnement' in Neyret L (ed), *Des écocrimes à l'écocide. Le droit pénal au secours de l'environnement* (Bruylant 2015) 3–18.

Bisschop L, 'Transnational environmental crime: exploring (un)charted territory' in Cools M, De Ruyver B, Easton M and others (eds), *EU Criminal Justice, Financial & Economic Crime: new perspectives* (Maklu 2011) 155–183.

Block L, 'EU Joint Investigation Teams; political ambitions and police practices' in Hufnagel S, Harfield C and Bronitt S, *Cross-Border Law Enforcement. Regional Law Enforcement Cooperation—European, Australian and Asia-Pacific Perspectives* (Routledge 2013) 87–108.

Boister N, '"Transnational Criminal Law"?' (2003) 14 *European Journal of International Law* 953.

Boister N, *An Introduction to Transnational Criminal Law* (OUP 2012).

Boister N, 'Further reflections on the concept of transnational criminal law' (2015) 6 *Transnational Legal Theory* 9.

Bouley T and Thompson S, 'Trafficking wildlife and transmitting disease: Bold threats in an era of Ebola' [2014] <http://blogs.worldbank.org/voices/trafficking-wildlife-and-transmitting-disease-bold-threats-era-ebola> accessed 18 September 2016.

Brady H, 'Europol and the European Criminal Intelligence Model: A non-state Response to Organized Crime' (2008) 2 *Policing* 103.

Bruinsma G, 'Criminology and Transnational Crime' in G Bruinsma (ed), *Histories of Transnational Crime* (Springer 2015) 1–8.

Busuioc M, *European Agencies. Law and Practices of Accountability* (OUP 2013).

Busuioc M and Groenleer M, 'Beyond Design: The Evolution of Europol and Eurojust (2013) 14 *Perspectives on European Politics and Society* 285.

Cabrejo le Roux A, Reitano T and Shaw M, *Tightening the Net: Toward a Global Legal Framework on Transnational Organized Environmental Crime* (WWF-Global Initiative Against Transnational Organized Crime 2015) <http://d2ouvy59podg6k.cloudfront.net/downloads/tightening_the_net__1.pdf> accessed 18 September 2016.

Calderoni F, 'A definition that does not work: The impact of the EU Framework Decision on the fight against organized crime' (2012) 49 *Common Market Law Review* 1365.

Cardwell PJ, French D and Hall M, 'Tackling environmental crime in the European Union: the case of the missing victim?' (2011) 23 *Environmental Law and Management* 113.

Chin S and Veening W, 'Actors and Institutions Relevant to Fighting Environmental Crime'. Study in the frame of the EFFACE Project (Institute for Environmental Security 2015).

Chin S, Veening W and Gerstetter C, 'EFFACE Policy Brief 1: Limitations and challenges of the criminal justice system in addressing environmental crime' (2014).

Cleary Yeager P and Simpson SS, 'Environmental Crime' in Tonry M (ed), *The Oxford Handbook of Crime and Public Policy* (OUP 2009) 325–355.

Coninsx M, 'Strengthening interstate cooperation: the Eurojust experience' in Salinas De Frías AM, Samuel K and White N (eds), *Counter-Terrorism. International Law and Practice* (OUP 2012) 965–989.

Coninsx M, 'Eurojust' in Mitsilegas V, Bergström M and Konstadinides T (eds), *Research Handbook on EU Criminal Law* (Edward Elgar 2016) 441–456.

D'Alisa G, Falcone PM, Germani AR and others, 'Victims in the "Land of Fires": case study on the consequences of buried and burnt waste in Campania, Italy'. Case study compiled as part of the EFFACE project (University of Rome "La Sapienza" 2015).

Damaskou A, 'The European Public Prosecutor's Office. A Ground-Breaking New Institution of the EU Legal Order' (2015) 6 *New Journal of European Criminal Law* 126.

De Amicis G, 'Eurojust' in Grasso G and Sicurella R (eds), *Lezioni di diritto penale europeo* (Giuffrè 2007) 467–536.

De Amicis G, 'I soggetti della cooperazione giudiziaria' in Kostoris RE (ed), *Manuale di procedura penale europea* (Giuffrè 2014).

De Buck B, 'Joint Investigation Teams: The participation of Europol officials' (2007) 8 *ERA Forum* 253.

De Coning E, 'Transnational Organized Crime in the Fishing Industry. Focus on: Trafficking in Persons, Smuggling of Migrants, Illicit Drugs Trafficking' (UNODC 2011).

De Moor A and Vermeulen G, 'The Europol Council Decision: Transforming Europol into an Agency of the European Union' (2010) 47 *Common Market Law Review* 1089.

De Sadeleer N, 'Principle of subsidiarity and the EU Environmental Policy' (2012) 9 *Journal of European Environment and Planning Law* 63.

De Sadeleer N, *EU Environmental Law and the Internal Market* (OUP 2014).

Den Boer M and Bruggeman W, 'Shifting Gear: Europol in the Contemporary Policing Era' (2007) 22 *Politique européenne* 77.

Di Nicola A, Gounev P, Levi M and others, 'Study on paving the way for future policy initiatives in the field of fight against organised crime: the effectiveness of specific criminal law measures targeting organised crime. Final report' (Rand 2015) <http://www.rand.org/randeurope/research/projects/organised-crime.html> accessed 18 September 2016.

Disley E, Irving B, Hughes W and Patruni B, 'Evaluation of the implementation of the Europol Council Decision and of Europol's activities'. Report for Europol Management Board (Rand Europe 2012) <https://www.europol.europa.eu/content/publication/evaluation-implementation-europol-council-decision-and-europol%E2%80%99s-activities-1677> accessed 18 September 2016.

Drewer D and Ellermann J, 'Europol's data protection framework as an asset in the fight against cybercrime' (2012) 13 *ERA Forum* 381 (also available at <https://www.europol.europa.eu/content/publication/europols-data-protection-framework-asset-fight-against-cybercrime-1838> accessed 18 September 2016).

Elliott L, 'Fighting Transnational Environmental Crime' (2012) 66 *Journal of International Affairs* 87.

Elliott L and Schaedla WH, 'Transnational environmental crime: excavating the complexities—an introduction' in Elliott L and Schaedla WH (eds), *Handbook of Transnational Environmental Crime* (Edward Elgar 2016) 3–23.

Elliott L and Schaedla WH (eds), *Handbook of Transnational Environmental Crime* (Edward Elgar 2016).

Environmental Investigation Agency, 'In Cold Blood. Combating organised wildlife crime' (2014) <https://eia-international.org/wp-content/uploads/EIA-In-Cold-Blood-FINAL.pdf> accessed 18 September 2016.

Erkelens LH, Meij AWH and Pawlik M (eds), *The European Public Prosecutor's Office. An extended arm or a Two-Headed dragon?* (Springer-Verlag 2015).

Fajardo del Castillo T, 'Revisiting the External Dimension of the Environmental Policy. Some Challenges Ahead' (2010) 7 *Journal of European Environmental Law* 365.

Fajardo del Castillo T, 'EU Environmental Law and Environmental Crime: An Introduction'. Study in the framework of the EFFACE research project (University of Granada 2015).

Fajardo del Castillo T, 'Organised Crime and Environmental Crime: Analysis of EU Legal Instruments'. Study in the framework of the EFFACE Research Project (University of Granada 2015).

Farmer A, Germani AR and Sollund R, 'Conclusions of the EFFACE Case studies' (2015).

Faure M, 'Environmental Crimes' in De Geest G (ed), *Encyclopedia of Law and Economics*, vol 3 (2nd edn, Edward Elgar 2009) 320–345.

Faure M, 'Vague notions in environmental criminal law (part 1)' (2010) 18 *Environmental Liability, Law Practice and Policy* 119.

Faure M and Heine G, *Criminal Enforcement of Environmental Law in the European Union* (Kluwer Law International 2005).

Faure M, Gerstetter C, Sina S and Vagliasindi GM, 'Instruments, Actors and Institutions in the Fight Against Environmental Crime'. Study in the framework of the EFFACE research project (Ecologic Institute 2015).

Faure M, Philipsen N, Fajardo del Castillo F and others, 'Conclusions and Recommendations'. Study in the framework of the EFFACE Research Project (2016).

Felson M, 'Routine Activities and Transnational Crime' in Natarajan M (ed), *International Crime and Justice* (Cambridge University Press 2010) 11–18.

Fichera M, 'Organised crime: development and challenges for an enlarged European Union' in Eckes C and Konstadinides T (eds), *Crime within the Area of Freedom, Security and Justice. A European Public Order* (Cambridge University Press 2011) 159–191.

Fijnaut C, 'Transnational Crime and the Role of the United Nations in Its Containment through International Cooperation: A Challenge for the 21st Century' (2000) 8 *European Journal of Crime, Criminal Law and Criminal Justice* 119.

Fijnaut C, 'The globalisation of police and judicial cooperation: drivers, substance and organisational arrangements, political complications' in Hufnagel S, Harfield C and Bronitt S, *Cross-Border Law Enforcement. Regional Law Enforcement Cooperation—European, Australian and Asia-Pacific Perspectives* (Routledge 2013) 1–16.

Finckenauer J, 'Organized Crime' in Tonry M (ed), *The Oxford Handbook of Crime and Public Policy* (OUP 2009) 304–324.

Fletcher M, Lööf R and Gilmore B, *EU Criminal Law and Justice* (Edward Elgar 2008).

Flore D, 'Eurojust ou Ministère public européen : un choix de politique criminelle' [2000] *Agon* 9.

Fouchard I and Neyret L, '35 Propositions pour mieux sanctionner les crimes contre l'environnement. Rapport de synthèse' in Neyret L (ed), *Des écocrimes à l'écocide. Le droit pénal au secours de l'environnement* (Bruylant 2015) 305–441.

Frank V, 'Consequences of the *Prestige* Sinking for European and International Law' (2005) 20 *The International Journal of Marine and Coastal Law* 1.

Geelhoed W, 'Embedding the European Public Prosecutor's Office in Jurisdictions with a Wide Scope of Prosecutorial Discretion: the Dutch Example' in Novak C (ed), *The European Public Prosecutor's Office and National Authorities* (Wolters Kluwer-CEDAM 2016) 87–102.

Gerstetter C, Stefes C, Farmer A and others, 'Environmental crime and the EU Synthesis of the Research Project "European Action to Fight Environmental Crime" (EFFACE)' (2016).

Giardi G, 'Fighiting the European Ecomafia. Organised Trafficking in Waste and the Need for a Criminal Law Response from the EU' (2015) 6 *New Journal of European Criminal Law* 229.

Gibbs C, McGarrell EF and Sullivan B, 'Intelligence-led policing and transnational environmental crime: A process evaluation' (2015) 12 *European Journal of Criminology* 242.

Giovannini N, Melica L, Cukani E and others, 'Addressing Environmental Crimes and Marine Pollution in the EU Legal guidelines and case studies' (Droit au Droit 2013) <http://www.dadinternational.org/images/PDF/Guide-Web.pdf> accessed 18 September 2016.

Giovannini N, Melica L, Giannotta M and Zingoni M, 'Compendium of International and EU Law Instruments' (Droit au Droit 2013) <http://www.dadinternational.org/images/PDF/DRD-Compendium.pdf> accessed 18 September 2016.

Gless S, 'Europol' in Mitsilegas V, Bergström M and Konstadinides T (eds), *Research Handbook on EU Criminal Law* (Edward Elgar 2016) 457–479.

Gless S and Vervaele JAE, 'Law Should Govern: Aspiring General Principles for Transnational Criminal Justice' (2013) 9 *Utrecht Law Review* 1.

Goldsmith A, 'Organized crime' in Marmo M and Chazal N, *Transnational Crime & Criminal Justice* (SAGE 2016) 113–135.

Goncalves MP, Panjer M, Greenberg TS and Magrath WB, *Justice for Forests. Improving Criminal Justice Efforts to Combat Illegal Logging* (World Bank Study 2012) <http://elibrary.worldbank.org/doi/abs/10.1596/978-0-8213-8978-2> accessed 18 September 2016.

Gouritin A and De Hert P, 'Directive 2008/99/EC: A new start for criminal law in the European Community?' [2009] *Environmental Law Network International Review* 22.

Grasso G, 'Il Trattato di Lisbona e le nuove competenze penali dell'Unione europea' in *Studi in onore di Mario Romano* (Jovene 2011) 2307–2350.

Grasso G, 'Relazione di sintesi' in Grasso G, Illuminati G, Sicurella R and Allegrezza S (eds), *Le sfide dell'attuazione di una Procura europea: definizione di regole e loro impatto sugli ordinamenti interni* (Giuffrè 2013) 715–768.

Grasso G, 'Article 83' in Grasso G, Sicurella R and Scalia V, 'Articles 82–86 of the Treaty on the Functioning of the European Union and Environmental Crime'. Study in the framework of the EFFACE research project (University of Catania 2015) 19–32.

Grasso G, Illuminati G, Sicurella R and Allegrezza S (eds), *Le sfide dell'attuazione di una Procura europea: definizione di regole e loro impatto sugli ordinamenti interni* (Giuffrè 2013).

Groenleer M, *The Autonomy of the European Union Agencies* (Eburon 2009).

Gualtieri C, 'Joint Investigation Teams' (2007) 8 *ERA Forum* 233.

Haken J, 'Transnational Crime In The Developing World' (Global Financial Integrity 2011).

Hamran L and Szabova E, 'European Public Prosecutor's Office—Cui Bono?' (2013) 4 *New Journal of European Criminal Law* 40.

Harding C and Banach-Gutierrez JB, 'The Emergent EU Criminal Policy: Identifying the Species' (2012) 37 *European Law Review* 758.

Helmberg M, 'Eurojust and Joint Investigation Teams: How Eurojust can support JITs' (2007) 8 *ERA Forum* 245.

Hufnagel S, *Police Cooperation Across Borders: Comparative Perspectives on Law Enforcement within the EU and Australia* (Ashgate 2013).

Hufnagel S, 'Organized crime' in Mitsilegas V, Bergström M and Konstadinides T (eds), *Research Handbook on EU Criminal Law* (Edward Elgar 2016) 355–375.

Illes A, Newman S, Watkins E and others, 'Understanding the damages of environmental crime. Review of the availability of data'. Study in the framework of the EFFACE research project (2014).

Jeney P, 'The future of Eurojust'. Study for the LIBE Committee (2012) <http://www.europarl.europa.eu/RegData/etudes/etudes/join/2012/462451/IPOL-LIBE_ET(2012)462451_EN.pdf> accessed 18 September 2016.

Jonsson Cornell A, 'EU Police Cooperation Post-Lisbon' in Bergström M and Jonsson Cornell A (eds), *European Police and Criminal Law Co-operation* (Hart 2014) 147–161.

Kasimbazi EB, 'The Lusaka Agreement Task Force as a mechanism for enforcement against wildlife crime' in Faure M, De Smedt P and Stas A (eds), *Environmental Enforcement Networks. Concepts, Implementation and Effectiveness* (Edward Elgar 2015) 239–262.

Klaas K and Sina S, 'Contribution to conclusions and recommendations on environmental crime: Functioning of enforcement institutions and cooperation between them (MS/EU level)'. Study in the frame of the EFFACE Project (2016).

Klip A, *European Criminal Law. An Integrative Approach* (2nd edn, Intersentia 2012).

Krämer L, *EU Environmental Law* (7th edn, Sweet & Maxwell 2012).

Lavrysen L, 'The European Union Forum of Judges for the Environment' in Faure M, De Smedt P and Stas A (eds), *Environmental Enforcement Networks. Concepts, Implementation and Effectiveness* (Edward Elgar 2015) 276–288.

Lee M, *EU Environmental Law, Governance and Decision-Making* (2nd edn, Hart 2014).

Levi M, Innes M, Reuter P and others, 'The Economic, Financial & Social Impacts of Organised Crime in the EU'. Study for the European Parliament (2013) <http://www.europarl.europa.eu/RegData/etudes/etudes/join/2013/493018/IPOL-JOIN_ET(2013)493018_EN.pdf> accessed 18 September 2016.

Liddick D, 'The dimension of a transnational crime problem: the case of iuu fishing' (2014) 17 *Trends in Organized Crime* 290.

Ligeti K, 'Introduction' in Ligeti K (ed) *Toward a Prosecutor for the European Union*, vol 1 (Hart 2012) 1–6.

Ligeti K, 'The European Public Prosecutor's Office' in Mitsilegas V, Bergström M and Konstadinides T (eds) *Research Handbook on EU Criminal Law* (Edward Elgar 2016) 480–504.

Ligeti K (ed), *Toward a Prosecutor for the European Union*, vol 1 (Hart 2012).

Ligeti K and Simonato M, 'The European Public Prosecutor's Office: Towards a Truly Prosecution Service?' (2013) 4 *New Journal of European Criminal Law* 7.

Lo Voi F and Giuffrida F, 'The Dual Role of Eurojust in the Fight Against Transnational Crime: An Overview' (2014) 1 *The European Review of Organised Crime* 129.

Lotti L, 'Complessità degli illeciti ambientali ed evoluzione di metodi e strategie di accertamento' in Romano B (ed), *I reati ambientali alla luce del Diritto dell'Unione Europea* (CEDAM 2013) 89–111.

Luna M and Veening W, 'EFFACE Policy Brief 2: Organised Environmental Crime' (2014).

Manacorda S, 'Le droit pénal de l'Union à l'heure de la Charte et du Parquet européen' [2013] *Revue de science criminelle et de droit pénal comparé* 927.

Marguery T, 'Eurojust II: Un tiens vaut mieux que deux tu l'auras?' in Besselink L, Pennings F and Prechal S (eds), *The Eclipse of the Legality Principle in the European Union* (Kluwer Law International 2011) 249–272.

Marmo M and Chazal N, *Transnational Crime & Criminal Justice* (SAGE 2016).

Marotta E, 'Role and Action of EUROPOL in combating organised crime' in Longo F (ed), *The European Union and the Challenge of Transnational Organised Crime. Towards a Common Police and Judicial Approach* (Giuffrè 2002) 109–115.

Meeus R, 'Fill in the Gaps: EU Sanctioning Requirements to Improve Member State Enforcement of EU Environmental Law' (2010) 7 *Journal for European Environmental & Planning Law* 135.

Mégie A, 'L'institutionnalisation d'un pouvoir judiciaire européen incertain en quête de lègitimité : l'unité de coopération Eurojust' (2007) 23 *Politique européenne* 57.

Mégret F, 'The Problem of an International Criminal Law of the Environment' (2011) 36 *Columbia Journal of Environmental Law* 195.

Michalowski R and Kramer R, 'Transnational Environmental Crime' in Reichel P and Albanese J (eds), *Handbook of Transnational Crime and Justice* (2nd edn, SAGE 2014) 189–212.

Mitsilegas V, 'Defining organised crime in the European Union: the limits of European criminal law in an area of "freedom, security and justice"' (2001) 26 *European Law Review* 565.

Mitsilegas V, *EU Criminal Law* (Hart 2009).

Mitsilegas V, 'The third wave of third pillar law: which direction for EU criminal justice?' (2009) 34 *European Law Review* 523.

Mitsilegas V, 'The Council Framework Decision on the Fight against Organised Crime: What can be done to strengthen EU legislation in the field?'. Note for the European Parliament (2011) <http://www.europarl.europa.eu/document/activities/cont/201206/20120627ATT47779/20120627ATT47779EN.pdf> accessed 18 September 2016.

Mitsilegas V, 'The European Union and the Global Governance of Crime' in Mitsilegas V, Alldridge P and Cheliotis L (eds), *Globalisation, Criminal Law and*

Criminal Justice. Theoretical, Comparative and Transnational Perspectives (Hart 2015) 153–198.

Mitsilegas V, 'Contribution to conclusions and recommendations on environmental crime: Harmonisation of substantive environmental criminal law at EU level'. Study in the framework of the EFFACE research project (Queen Mary University of London 2016).

Mitsilegas V, *EU Criminal Law after Lisbon. Rights, Trust and the Transformation of Justice in Europe* (Hart 2016).

Mitsilegas V, 'Mutual recognition, mutual trust and fundamental rights after Lisbon' in Mitsilegas V, Bergström M and Konstadinides T (eds), *Research Handbook on EU Criminal Law* (Edward Elgar 2016) 148–167.

Mitsilegas V and Vavoula N, 'The Evolving EU Anti-Money Laundering Regime. Challenges for Fundamental Rights and the Rule of Law' (2016) 23 *Maastricht Journal of European and Comparative Law* 261.

Mitsilegas V, Fitzmaurice M and Fasoli E, 'The relationship between EU criminal law and environmental law' in Mitsilegas V, Bergström M and Konstadinides T (eds), *Research Handbook on EU Criminal Law* (Edward Elgar 2016) 272–293.

Mitsilegas V, Monar J and Rees W, *The European Union and Internal Security* (Palgrave Macmillan 2003).

Monar J, 'Eurojust's present and future role at the frontline of European Union criminal justice cooperation' (2013) 14 *ERA Forum* 187.

Morgera E (ed), *The External Environmental Policy of the European Union. EU and International Law Perspectives* (Cambridge University Press 2012).

Nellemann C, Henriksen R, Kreilhuber A and others (eds), 'The Rise of Environmental Crime—A Growing Threat To Natural Resources, Peace, Development And Security. A UNEP-INTERPOL Rapid Response Assessment' (United Nations Environment Programme and RHIPTO Rapid Response–Norwegian Center for Global Analyses, 2016) <http://unep.org/documents/itw/environmental_crimes.pdf> accessed 18 September 2016.

Nunzi A, 'European Police Office—EUROPOL' (2006) 77 *Revue internationale de droit penal* 285.

Orlando E, 'The evolution of EU Policy and Law in the Environmental Field: Achievements and Current Challenges' (2013) Transworld Working Paper 21 <http://www.iai.it/sites/default/files/TW_WP_21.pdf> accessed 18 September 2016.

Patrone I, 'Conflicts of jurisdiction and judicial cooperation instruments: Eurojust's role' (2013) 14 *ERA Forum* 215.

Peers S, *EU Justice and Home Affairs Law* (3rd edn, OUP 2011).

Pereira R, *Environmental Criminal Liability and Enforcement in European and International Law* (Brill 2015).

Petit Leclair S, 'Justice et sécurité en Europe: Eurojust ou la création d'un parquet européen' [2012] *Cahiers de la sécurité* 39.

Pires SF and Moreto WD, 'Preventing Wildlife Crimes: Solutions That Can Overcome the "Tragedy of the Commons"' (2011) 17 *European journal on criminal policy and research* 101.

Pirjatanniemi E, 'Desperately Seeking Reason—New Directions for European Environmental Criminal Law' (2009) 54 *Scandinavian Studies in Law* 409.

Plachta M, 'Joint Investigation Teams. A New Form of International Cooperation in Criminal Matters' (2005) 13 *European Journal of Crime, Criminal Law, and Criminal Justice* 284.

Pozdnakova A, *Criminal Jurisdiction over Perpetrators of Ship-Source Pollution. International Law, State Practice and EU Harmonisation* (Martinus Nijhoff Publishers 2013).

Puntscher Riekmann S, 'Security, Freedom and Accountability' in Guild E and Geyer F (eds), *Security versus Justice? Police and Judicial Cooperation in the European Union* (Ashgate 2008) 19–34.

Rijken C and Vermeulen G, *Joint Investigations Teams in Europe: from theory to practice* (TMC Asser Press 2006).

Rodopoulos I, 'Les activités criminelles organisées en matière environnementale: quelque réflexion en vue d'une réponse pénale internationale' in Neyret L (ed), *Des écocrimes à l'écocide. Le droit pénal au secours de l'environnement* (Bruylant 2015) 165–182.

Roth MP, 'Historical Overview of Transnational Crime' in Reichel P and Albanese J (eds), *Handbook of Transnational Crime and Justice* (2nd edn, SAGE 2014) 5–22.

Sacré V, 'EU-TWIX: ten years of information exchange and cooperation between wildlife law enforcement officials in Europe' in Elliott L and Schaedla WH, *Handbook of Transnational Environmental Crime* (Edward Elgar 2016) 478–488.

Salazar L, 'European judicial cooperation in the fight against environmental crime' in 'Summary of the EFFACE Workshop "Environmental Crime and the Criminal Justice System"' (Catania, 23 June 2014).

Saunders J and Hein J, 'EUTR, CITES and money laundering: A case study on the challenges to coordinated enforcement in tackling illegal logging'. A study for the EFFACE project (Chatham House 2015).

Schalken T and Fronk M, 'On Joint Investigation Teams, Europol and Supervision of Their Joint Actions' (2002) 10 *European Journal of Crime, Criminal Law, and Criminal Justice* 70.

Schneider J, 'Endangered Species Markets. A Focus for Criminology?' in Natarajan M (ed), *International Crime and Justice* (Cambridge University Press 2010) 208–209.

Sheptycki JWE, 'Transnational Crime and Transnational Policing' (2007) 1 *Sociology Compass* 485.

Shover N and Scroggins J, 'Organizational crime' in Tonry M (ed), *The Oxford Handbook of Crime and Public Policy* (OUP 2009) 273–303.

Sicurella R, '«Prove tecniche» per una metodologia dell'esercizio delle nuove competenze concorrenti dell'Unione europea in materia penale' in Grasso G, Picotti L and Sicurella R (eds), *L'evoluzione del diritto penale nei settori d'interesse europeo* (Giuffrè 2011) 3–65.

Sicurella R, 'Article 85' in Grasso G, Sicurella R and Scalia V, 'Articles 82–86 of the Treaty on the Functioning of the European Union and Environmental Crime'. Study in the framework of the EFFACE research project (University of Catania 2015).

Sicurella R, 'Article 86' in Grasso G, Sicurella R and Scalia V, 'Articles 82–86 of the Treaty on the Functioning of the European Union and Environmental Crime'. Study in the framework of the EFFACE research project (University of Catania 2015).

Sollund R and Maher J, 'The Illegal wildlife trade. A case study report on the illegal wildlife trade in the United Kingdom, Norway, Colombia and Brazil'. A study compiled as part of the EFFACE project (University of Oslo and University of South Wales 2015).

Spapens ACM, Peters M and Van Daele D (eds), 'Administrative approaches to crime. Administrative measures based on regulatory legislation to prevent and tackle (serious and organized) crime. Legal possibilities and practical applications in 10 EU Member States' (2015) <http://ec.europa.eu/dgs/home-affairs/e-library/documents/policies/organized-crime-and-human-trafficking/crime-prevention/docs/final_report_eu_study_administrative_approaches_to_crime_en.pdf> accessed 18 September 2016.

Spapens T, 'Joint Investigation Teams in the European Union: Article 13 JITS and the Alternatives' (2011) 19 *European Journal of Crime, Criminal Law, and Criminal Justice* 239.

Spapens T and Huisman W, 'Tackling Cross-Border Environmental Crime. A "Wicked Problem"' in Spapens T, White R and Huisman W (eds), *Environmental Crime in Transnational Context* (Routledge 2016) 27–42.

Spapens T, White R and Huisman W (eds), *Environmental Crime in Transnational Context* (Routledge 2016).

Spiezia F, 'Le linee evolutive della cooperazione giudiziaria penale in ambito europeo' in Aprile E and Spiezia F, *Cooperazione giudiziaria penale nell'Unione europea prima e dopo il Trattato di Lisbona* (IPSOA 2009) 167–260.

Spiezia F, 'La cooperazione investigativa e giudiziaria nell'Unione Europea per il contrasto alla contraffazione ed al contrabbando. Un caso riuscito: la vicenda Gomorrah' in Camaldo L (ed), *La circolazione e il contrabbando di prodotti contraffatti o pericolosi. La tutela degli interessi finanziari dell'Unione Europea e la protezione dei consumatori* (Giappichelli 2013) 71–78.

Storbeck J, 'The European Union and Enlargement: Challenge and Opportunity for Europol in the Fight Against International Crime' (2003) 8 *European Foreign Affairs Review* 283.

Suominen A, 'The Past, Present and the Future of Eurojust' (2008) 15 *Maastricht Journal of European and Comparative Law* 217.

Surano L, 'L'action extérieure d'Eurojust' in M Dony (ed), *La dimension externe de l'espace de liberté, de sécurité et de justice au lendemain de Lisbonne et de Stockholm: un bilan à mi-parcours* (Éditions de l'Université de Bruxelles 2012) 210–219.

Thwaites NLC, 'Eurojust autre brique dans l'édifice de la coopération judiciaire en matière pénale ou solide mortier?' [2003] *Revue de science criminelle et de droit pénal comparé* 45.

Tupman W, 'Keeping under the radar: watch out for the "Smurfs"' (2010) 17 *Journal of Financial Crime* 152.

Vagliasindi GM, 'The European Harmonisation in the Sector of Protection of the Environment through Criminal Law: the Results achieved and Further Needs for Intervention' (2012) 3 *New Journal of European Criminal Law* 320.

Vagliasindi GM, 'Istituzione di una Procura europea e diritto penale sostanziale: l'eventuale estensione della competenza materiale della futura Procura alla criminalità ambientale' in Grasso G, Illuminati G, Sicurella R and Allegrezza S (eds), *Le sfide dell'attuazione di una Procura europea: definizione di regole e loro impatto sugli ordinamenti interni* (Giuffrè 2013) 189–211.

Vagliasindi GM, 'Directive 2008/99/EC on Environmental Crime and Directive 2009/123/EC on Ship-source Pollution'. Study in the framework of the EFFACE research project (University of Catania 2015).

Vagliasindi GM, 'Organised environmental crime' in Farmer A, Mitsilegas V, Faure M and others, 'Evaluation of the strengths, weaknesses, threats and opportunities associated with EU efforts to combat environmental crime'. Study in the framework of the EFFACE research project (2015) 87–103.

Vagliasindi GM, 'Contribution to conclusions and recommendations on environmental crime: Organised Environmental Crime'. Study in the framework of the EFFACE research project (University of Catania 2016).

Van Asch E, 'Countering transnational organized wildlife crime: regional and sub-regional initiatives, global responses and the need for more effective coordination' in Faure M, De Smedt P and Stas A (eds), *Environmental Enforcement Networks. Concepts, Implementation and Effectiveness* (Edward Elgar 2015) 187–222.

Van den Wyngaert C, 'Eurojust and the European Public Prosecutor's Office: Water and Fire?' in Walker N (ed), *Europe's Area of Freedom, Security and Justice* (OUP 2004) 201–240.

Van Dinh TT, 'Addressing Corruption in the Environmental Sector: How the United Nations Convention against Corruption Provides a Basis for Action' (2012) <http://www.unodc.org/documents/corruption/Publications/2012/Corruption_Environment_and_the_UNCAC.pdf> accessed 18 September 2016, 34–50.

Vervaele JAE, 'The Shaping and Reshaping of Eurojust and OLAF' [2008] *Eucrim* 180.

Vlastník J, 'Eurojust–A Cornerstone of the Federal Criminal Justice System in the EU?' in Guild E and Geyer F (eds), *Security versus Justice? Police and Judicial Cooperation in the European Union* (Ashgate 2008) 35–49.

Von Homeyer I, 'The Evolution of EU Environmental Governance' in J Scott (ed), *Environmental Protection: European Law and Governance* (OUP 2009) 1–26.

Von Lampe K, 'Transnational organized crime challenges for future research' (2012) 58 *Crime, Law and Social Change* 179.

Wade M, 'A European public prosecutor: potential and pitfalls' (2013) 59 *Crime, Law and Social Change* 439.

Wade M, 'General Principles of Transnationalised Criminal Justice? Exploratory Reflections' (2013) 9 *Utrecht Law Review* 165.

Watkins E, 'A case study on illegal localized pollution incidents in the EU'. A study compiled as part of the EFFACE project (IEEP 2015).

Wellsmith M, 'Wildlife Crime: The Problems of Enforcement' (2011) 17 *European journal on criminal policy and research* 125.

Weyembergh A, 'The development of Eurojust: potential and limitations of Article 85 TFEU' (2011) 2 *New Journal of European Criminal Law* 75.

Weyembergh A, 'Coordination and initiation of investigations prosecutions through Eurojust' (2013) 14 *ERA Forum* 177.

Weyembergh A., Armada I and Brière C, 'The inter-agency cooperation and future architecture of the EU criminal justice and law enforcement area'. Study for the LIBE Committee (2014) <http://www.europarl.europa.eu/thinktank/en/document.html?reference=IPOL_STU(2014)510000> accessed 18 September 2016.

White R, 'Transnational Environmental Crime' in Natarajan M (ed), *International Crime and Justice* (Cambridge University Press 2010) 193–199.

Wright G, 'Conceptualising and combating transnational environmental crime' (2011) 14 *Trends in organized crime* 332.

Xanthaki H, 'Eurojust: Fulfilled or Empty Promises in EU Criminal Law?' [2006] *European Journal of Law Reform* 175.

Zeitler HE, 'Environmental Criminal Law' (2006) 77 *Revue Internationale de Droit Pénal* 255.

Zwiers M, *The European Public Prosecutor's Office. Analysis of a Multilevel Criminal Justice System* (Intersentia 2011).

Council of Europe, EU, Interpol, and UN Documents

'A Multidisciplinary Approach to Organised Crime: Administrative Measures, Judicial Follow-up, and the Role of Eurojust—Copenhagen, 11–13 March 2012—Outcome report', Council doc 11298/12, 14 June 2012.

'Activity Report on the Administrative Approach to Prevent and Fight Organised Crime', Council doc 13498/13, 16 September 2013.

'Commission Staff Working Document. Impact Assessment Accompanying Proposal for a Council Regulation on the establishment of the European Public Prosecutor's Office' SWD(2013) 274 final, 17 July 2013.

'Commission Staff Working Document. Tables "State of play" and "Declarations". Accompanying the document Report from the Commission to the European Parliament and the Council on the implementation by the Member States of the Framework Decisions 2008/909/JHA, 2008/947/JHA and 2009/829/JHA on the mutual recognition of judicial decisions on custodial sentences or measures involving deprivation of liberty, on probation decisions and alternative sanctions and on supervision measures as an alternative to provisional detention' COM(2014) 57 final, SWD (2014) 34 final, 5 February 2014.

'Commission Staff Working Document. Summary of the Responses to the Stakeholder Consultation on the EU Approach against Wildlife Trafficking' SWD(2014) 347 final, 26 November 2014.

'Commission Staff Working Document accompanying the Communication on the EU Action Plan against Wildlife Trafficking' SWD(2016), 26 February 2016.

'Commission Staff Working Paper, Impact Assessment (Part I) Accompanying the document Proposal for a Directive of the European Parliament and of the Council on the fight against fraud to the Union's financial interests by means of criminal law' SWD(2012) 195 final, 11 July 2012.

'Communication from the Commission on the precautionary principle' COM(2000) 1 final, 2 February 2000.

'Communication from the Commission to the European Parliament and the Council. Proceeds of organized crime. Ensuring that "crime does not pay"' COM(2008) 766 final, 20 November 2008.

'Communication from the Commission to the Council and the European Parliament on the EU Approach against Wildlife Trafficking' COM(2014) 64 final, 7 February 2014.

'Communication from the Commission to the European Parliament, the Council, the European Economic and Social Committee and the Committee of the Regions. EU Action Plan Against Wildlife Trafficking' COM(2016) 87 final, 26 February 2016.

'Communication from the Commission to the European Parliament, the European Council and the Council delivering on the European Agenda on Security to fight against terrorism and pave the way towards an effective and genuine Security Union' COM(2016) 230 final, 20 April 2016.

'Complementary approaches and actions to prevent and combat organised crime. A collection of good practice examples from EU Member States', Council doc 10899/11, 30 March 2011 (document partially accessible to the public).

Conference of the Parties to the United Nations Convention against Transnational Organized Crime, 'Expert consultation on the use of the Convention for combating emerging forms of crime'. Vienna, 18–22 October 2010 (2010) CTOC/COP/2010/3.

Convention implementing the Schengen Agreement of 14 June 1985 between the Governments of the States of the Benelux Economic Union, the Federal Republic of Germany and the French Republic on the gradual abolition of checks at their common borders [2000] OJ L239/19.

Convention on the Protection of the Environment through Criminal Law, ETS No 172, Strasbourg, 4 November 1998.

Council Act of 26 July 1995 drawing up the Convention based on Article K.3 of the Treaty on European Union, on the establishment of a European Police Office (Europol Convention) [1995] OJ C316/1.

Council Act of 29 May 2000 establishing in accordance with Article 34 of the Treaty on European Union the Convention on Mutual Assistance in Criminal Matters between the Member States of the European Union [2000] OJ C197/1.

'Council conclusions on the creation and implementation of a EU policy cycle for organised and serious international crime', Justice and Home Affairs Council meeting, 8–9 November 2010.

'Council conclusions on setting the EU's priorities for the fight against serious and organised crime between 2014 and 2017', Justice and Home Affairs Council meeting, 6–7 June 2013.

'Council conclusions on the administrative approach to prevent and fight serious and organised crime', Council doc 9935/16, 9 June 2016.

Council Decision of 14 December 2000 setting up a Provisional Judicial Cooperation Unit [2000] OJ L324/2.

Council Decision 2002/187/JHA of 28 February 2002 setting up Eurojust with a view to reinforcing the fight against serious crime [2002] OJ L63/1.

Council Decision 2003/659/JHA of 18 June 2003 amending Decision 2002/187/JHA setting up Eurojust with a view to reinforcing the fight against serious crime [2003] OJ L245/44.

Council Decision 2008/976/JHA of 16 December 2008 on the European Judicial Network [2008] OJ L348/130.

Council Decision 2009/371/JHA of 6 April 2009 establishing the European Police Office (Europol) [2009] OJ L121/37.

Council Decision 2009/426/JHA of 16 December 2008 on the strengthening of Eurojust and amending Council Decision 2002/187/JHA setting up Eurojust with a view to reinforcing the fight against serious crime [2009] OJ L138/14.

Council Directive 75/439/EEC of 16 June 1975 on the disposal of waste oils [1975] OJ L194/23.

Council Directive 75/716/EEC of 24 November 1975 on the approximation of the laws of the Member States relating to the sulphur content of certain liquid fuels [1975] OJ L327/22.

Council Framework Decision 2002/465/JHA of 13 June 2002 on joint investigation teams [2002] OJ L162/1.

Council Framework Decision of 13 June 2002 on the European arrest warrant and the surrender procedures between Member States (2002/584/JHA) [2002] OJ L190/1.

Council Framework Decision 2003/80/JHA of 27 January 2003 on the protection of the environment through criminal law [2003] OJ L29/55.

Council Framework Decision 2003/577/JHA of 22 July 2003 on the execution in the European Union of orders freezing property or evidence [2003] OJ L196/45.

Council Framework Decision 2005/214/JHA of 24 February 2005 on the application of the principle of mutual recognition to financial penalties [2005] OJ L76/16.

Council Framework Decision 2005/667/JHA of 12 July 2005 to strengthen the criminal-law framework for the enforcement of the law against ship-source pollution [2005] OJ L255/164.

Council Framework Decision 2006/783/JHA of 6 October 2006 on the application of the principle of mutual recognition to confiscation orders [2006] OJ L328/59.

Council Framework Decision 2008/841/JHA of 24 October 2008 on the fight against organised crime [2008] OJ L300/42.

Council Framework Decision 2008/909/JHA of 27 November 2008 on the application of the principle of mutual recognition to judgments in criminal matters imposing custodial sentences or measures involving deprivation of liberty for the purpose of their enforcement in the European Union [2008] OJ L327/27.

Council Framework Decision 2008/919/JHA of 28 November 2008 amending Framework Decision 2002/475/JHA on combating terrorism [2008] OJ L330/21.

Council Framework Decision 2008/947/JHA of 27 November 2008 on the application of the principle of mutual recognition to judgments and probation decisions with a view to the supervision of probation measures and alternative sanctions [2008] OJ L337/102.

Council Framework Decision 2008/978/JHA of 18 December 2008 on the European evidence warrant for the purpose of obtaining objects, documents and data for use in proceedings in criminal matters [2008] OJ L350/72.

Council Framework Decision 2009/829/JHA of 23 October 2009 on the application, between Member States of the European Union, of the principle of mutual recognition to decisions on supervision measures as an alternative to provisional detention [2009] OJ L294/20.

Council Regulation (EEC) No 3626/82 of 3 December 1982 on the implementation in the Community of the Convention on international trade in endangered species of wild fauna and flora [1982] OJ L384/1.

Council Regulation (EC) No 338/97 of 9 December 1996 on the protection of species of wild fauna and flora by regulating trade therein [1997] OJ L61/1.

Council Resolution on the creation of an informal network for countering environmental crime—"EnviCrimeNet", Council doc 10291/11, 20 May 2011.

Decision No 1386/2013/EU of the European Parliament and of the Council of 20 November 2013 on a General Union Environment Action Programme to 2020 'Living well, within the limits of our planet' [2013] OJ L354/171.

'Declaration of the Council of the European Communities and of the representatives of the Governments of the Member States meeting in the Council of 22 November 1973 on the programme of action of the European Communities on the environment' [1973] OJ C112/1.

Directive 2005/35/EC of the European Parliament and of the Council of 7 September 2005 on ship-source pollution and on the introduction of penalties for infringements [2005] OJ L255/11.

Directive 2008/99/EC of the European Parliament and of the Council of 19 November 2008 on the protection of the environment through criminal law [2008] OJ L328/28.

Directive 2009/123/EC of the European Parliament and of the Council of 21 October 2009 amending Directive 2005/35/EC on ship-source pollution and on the introduction of penalties for infringements [2009] OJ L280/52.

Directive 2011/36/EU of the European Parliament and of the Council on preventing and combating trafficking in human beings and protecting its victims, and replacing Council Framework Decision 2002/629/JHA [2011] OJ L101/1.

Directive 2013/40/EU of the European Parliament and of the Council of 12 August 2013 on attacks against information systems and replacing Council Framework Decision 2005/222/JHA [2013] OJ L218/8.

Directive 2014/41/EU of the European Parliament and of the Council of 3 April 2014 regarding the European Investigation Order in criminal matters [2014] OJ L130/1.

Directive 2014/42/EU of the European Parliament and of the Council of 3 April 2014 on the freezing and confiscation of instrumentalities and proceeds of crime in the European Union [2014] OJ L127/39.

Directive (EU) 2015/849 of the European Parliament and of the Council of 20 May 2015 on the prevention of the use of the financial system for the purposes of money laundering or terrorist financing, amending Regulation (EU) No 648/2012 of the European Parliament and of the Council, and repealing Directive 2005/60/EC of the European Parliament and of the Council and Commission Directive 2006/70/EC [2015] OJ L141/73.

'Draft Council Conclusions on the fight against crimes committed by mobile (itinerant) criminal groups', Council doc 15875/10, 5 November 2010.

EnviCrimeNet, 'Report on Environmental Crime' (2016) <http://www.envicrimenet.eu/EN/reports> accessed 18 September 2016.

EnviCrimeNet and Europol, 'Intelligence Project on Environmental Crime. Report on Environmental Crime in Europe' (2015) <http://www.envicrimenet.eu/EN/reports> accessed 18 September 2016.

'EU Handbook—Part II. Complementary Approaches and Actions to Prevent and Disrupt Organised Crime', Council doc 17600/13, 12 December 2013 (document partially accessible to the public).

Eurojust, 'Annual Report 2003' (2004) <http://www.eurojust.europa.eu/doclibrary/corporate/Pages/annual-reports.aspx> accessed 18 September 2016.

Eurojust, 'Annual Report 2012' (2013) <http://www.eurojust.europa.eu/doclibrary/corporate/Pages/annual-reports.aspx> accessed 18 September 2016.

Eurojust, *Eurojust News 10* (2013) <http://www.eurojust.europa.eu/doclibrary/corporate/Pages/newsletter.aspx> accessed 18 September 2016.

Eurojust, 'Annual Report 2013' (2014) <http://www.eurojust.europa.eu/doclibrary/corporate/Pages/annual-reports.aspx> accessed 18 September 2016.

Eurojust, 'Annual Work Programme 2015' (2014) <http://eurojust.europa.eu/doclibrary/budget-finance/Pages/work-programmes.aspx> accessed 18 September 2016.

Eurojust, 'Strategic Project on Environmental Crime. Report' (2014) <http://www.eurojust.europa.eu/press/pressreleases/pages/2014/2014-11-21.aspx> accessed 18 September 2016.

Eurojust, 'Annual Report 2014' (2015) <http://www.eurojust.europa.eu/doclibrary/corporate/Pages/annual-reports.aspx> accessed 18 September 2016.

Eurojust, 'Annual Working Programme 2016' (2015) <http://eurojust.europa.eu/doclibrary/budget-finance/Pages/work-programmes.aspx> accessed 18 September 2016.

Eurojust, 'Multi-Annual Strategy 2016–2018' (2015) <http://www.eurojust.europa.eu/doclibrary/corporate/corporatepublications/Eurojust%20Multi-Annual%20Strategy%202016-2018/Eurojust-MASP-2016-2018_EN.pdf> accessed 18 September 2016.

Eurojust, 'Report of Eurojust's casework experience in the field of Prevention and Resolution of Conflicts of Jurisdiction' (2015) <http://www.eurojust.europa.eu/doclibrary/corporate/Pages/caseworkpublications.aspx> accessed 18 September 2016.

Eurojust, 'Annual Report 2015' (2016) <http://www.eurojust.europa.eu/doclibrary/corporate/Pages/annual-reports.aspx> accessed 18 September 2016.

European Convention on Mutual Assistance in Criminal Matters, ETS No 030, Strasbourg, 20 April 1959.

European Environment Agency, 'Movements of waste across the EU's internal and external borders' (2012) <http://www.eea.europa.eu/publications/movements-of-waste-EU-2012> accessed 18 September 2016.

European Parliament resolution of 25 October 2011 on organised crime in the European Union (2010/2309(INI)).

Europol, '2004 European Union Organised Crime Report' (2004) <https://www.europol.europa.eu/latest_publications/31?page=1> accessed 18 September 2016.

Europol, 'Organised crime & energy supply. Scenarios to 2020' (2010) <https://www.europol.europa.eu/content/publication/organised-crime-energy-supply-scenarios-2020-1505> accessed 18 September 2016.

Europol, 'OC-SCAN Policy Brief for Threat Notice: 006–2010. Trafficking in Endangered Species by Organised Crime Groups' (March 2011) <https://www.europol.europa.eu/latest_publications/39> accessed 18 September 2016.

Europol, 'OC-SCAN Policy Brief for Threat Notice: 2521–86. Involvement of an Irish mobile OCG in the illegal trade in rhino horn' (June 2011) <https://www.europol.europa.eu/latest_publications/39> accessed 18 September 2016.

Europol, 'OC-SCAN Policy Brief for Threat Notice: 2521–88. Use of improvised illegal waste disposal sites by criminals and OC Groups in the EU' (June 2011) <https://www.europol.europa.eu/latest_publications/39> accessed 18 September 2016.

Europol, 'OC-SCAN Policy Brief for Threat Notice: 2521–93. Growth in the trade in counterfeit and other illegal pesticides across Europe' (November 2011) <https://www.europol.europa.eu/latest_publications/39> accessed 18 September 2016.

Europol, 'New AWF Concept Guide for MS and Third Parties' (2012) <http://www.statewatch.org/news/2013/jan/europol-awf-new-concept.pdf> accessed 18 September 2016.

Europol, 'EU Serious and Organised Crime Threat Assessment' (2013) <https://www.europol.europa.eu/content/eu-serious-and-organised-crime-threat-assessment-socta> accessed 18 September 2016.

Europol, 'Europol Review 2013' (2014) <https://www.europol.europa.eu/category/publication-category/key-publications/europol-review> accessed 18 September 2016.

Europol, 'Threat Assessment. Italian Organised Crime' (2013) <https://www.europol.europa.eu/content/threat-assessment-italian-organised-crime> accessed 18 September 2016.

Europol, 'Threat Assessment 2013. Environmental Crime in the EU' (2013) <https://www.europol.europa.eu/content/threat-assessment-2013-environmental-crime-eu> accessed 18 September 2016.

'Explanations relating to the Charter of Fundamental Rights' [2007] OJ C303/17.

'Explanatory Memorandum to the Proposal for a Regulation of the European Parliament and of the Council on the European Union Agency for Law Enforcement Cooperation and Training (Europol) and repealing Decisions 2009/371/JHA and 2005/681/JHA' COM(2013) 173 final, 27 March 2013.

'Final report on the 6th round of mutual evaluations on "The practical implementation and operation of the Council Decision 2002/187/JHA of 28 February 2002 setting up Eurojust with a view to reinforcing the fight against serious crime and of the Council Decision 2008/976/JHA on the European Judicial Network in criminal matters"', Council doc 14536/2/14 REV 2, 2 December 2014.

'Guidelines for deciding which jurisdiction should prosecute'. Annex to the Eurojust 'Annual Report 2003' <http://www.eurojust.europa.eu/doclibrary/corporate/Pages/annual-reports.aspx> accessed 18 September 2016.

Interpol, 'Assessment on Illegal Bear Trade' (2014) <http://www.interpol.int/contentinterpol/search?SearchText=assessment+on+illegal+bear+trade&x=0&y=0> accessed 18 September 2016.

Joint Action 95/73/JHA of 10 March 1995 adopted by the Council on the basis of Article K.3 of the Treaty on European Union concerning the Europol Drugs Unit [1995] OJ L62/1.

Joint Action 98/428/JHA of 29 June 1998 adopted by the Council on the basis of Article K.3 of the Treaty on European Union, on the creation of a European Judicial Network [1998] OJ L191/4.

Joint Action of 21 December 1998 adopted by the Council on the basis of Article K.3 of the Treaty on European Union, on making it a criminal offence to participate in a criminal organisation in the Member States of the European Union (98/733/JHA) [1998] OJ L351/1.

'Joint Investigation Teams—Proposal for designation of national experts', Council doc 11037/05, 8 July 2005.

'Joint Investigation Teams Manual', Council doc 15790/1/11, 4 November 2011.

'Joint Statement of the European Parliament, the Council of the EU and the European Commission on decentralised agencies' (2012) <https://europa.eu/european-union/about-eu/agencies/overhaul_en>.

'Outcome of the Council meeting. Environment', 20 June 2016, Council doc 10444/16.

'Presidency Conclusions of the Tampere European Council', 15 and 16 October 1999 <http://www.europarl.europa.eu/summits/tam_en.htm> accessed 18 September 2016.

'Proposal for a Council Regulation on the establishment of the European Public Prosecutor's Office' COM(2013) 534 final, 17 July 2013.

'Proposal for a Directive of the European Parliament and of the Council on the fight against fraud to the Union's financial interests by means of criminal law', Council doc 12683/12, 17 July 2012.

'Proposal for a Directive of the European Parliament and of the Council on the fight against fraud to the Union's financial interests by means of criminal law—Progress report / Policy debate', Council doc 9804/16, 3 June 2016.

'Proposal for a Regulation of the European Parliament and of the Council on the European Union Agency for Criminal Justice Cooperation (Eurojust)' COM(2013) 535 final, 17 July 2013.

'Proposal for a Regulation on the European Union Agency for Criminal Justice Cooperation (Eurojust) [First reading]—General approach', Council doc 6643/15, 27 February 2015.

'Proposal for a Regulation on the establishment of the European Public Prosecutor's Office—Consolidated text: update of the provisional version', Council doc 11350/1/16, 28 July 2016.

Regulation (EC) No 1013/2006 of the European Parliament and of the Council of 14 June 2006 on shipments of waste [2006] OJ L190/1.

Regulation (EU) No 660/2014 of the European Parliament and of the Council of 15 May 2014 amending Regulation (EC) No 1013/2006 on shipments of waste [2014] OJ L189/135.

Regulation (EU) 2016/794 of the European Parliament and of the Council of 11 May 2016 on the European Union Agency for Law Enforcement Cooperation (Europol) and replacing and repealing Council Decisions 2009/371/JHA, 2009/934/JHA, 2009/935/JHA, 2009/936/JHA and 2009/968/JHA [2016] OJ L135/53.

'Report and Conclusions' of the Europol-OHIM Awareness Conference on Fake and Illicit Pesticides, held in Alicante, 26–28 November 2012 (2012) <https://euipo.europa.eu/tunnel-web/secure/webdav/guest/document_library/observatory/documents/Knowledge-building-events/1392909557_pesticides_report_en.pdf> accessed 18 September 2016.

'Report from the Commission to the European Parliament and the Council based on Article 10 of Council Framework Decision 2008/841/JHA of 24 October 2008 on the fight against organised crime' COM(2016) 448 final, 7 July 2016.

Report of the 'European action against the involvement of Organized Crime and Mafia-related crime in Waste Trafficking, in cooperation with Europol, owing to the emergence of the trans-national phenomenon', Council doc 16605/14, 8 December 2014.

'Report of the Expert Groups', UNICRI-UNEP International Conference on 'Environmental Crime—Current and Emerging Threats' held in Rome, 29–30 October 2012 (2012) <http://www.unicri.it/topics/environmental/conference/Report_of_the_Conference.pdf> accessed 18 September 2016.

'Report of the Strategic Meeting towards an enhanced coordination of environmental crime prosecutions across the EU: The role of Eurojust', Council doc 8101/14, 24 March 2014.

'Report to the European Parliament and national Parliaments on the proceedings of the Standing Committee on operational cooperation on internal security for the period July 2014-December 2015', Council doc 7033/16, 11 March 2016.

'Revised version of the European handbook on how to issue a European Arrest Warrant', Council doc 17195/1/10, 17 December 2010.

'Rules of Procedure of Eurojust' [2002] OJ C286/1.

'Summary of discussion of the meeting of 11 December 2014', Council doc 16163/14, 19 December 2014.

'The Bird-Egg case' (2013) 10 *Eurojust News* 15 <http://www.eurojust.europa.eu/doc library/corporate/Pages/newsletter.aspx> accessed 18 September 2016.

'The EU justice and home affairs agencies' (2014) <http://ec.europa.eu/justice/about/files/jha_agencies_en.pdf> accessed 18 September 2016.

'The Informal Network of contact points on the administrative approach to prevent and disrupt organised crime. A multi-annual Work Programme (2015–2017)', Council doc 16407/14, 9 December 2014 (document partially accessible to the public).

'The Manure Case' (2013) 10 *Eurojust News* 16 <http://www.eurojust.europa.eu/doc library/corporate/Pages/newsletter.aspx> accessed 18 September 2016.

'The Prestige case' (2013) 10 *Eurojust News* 14 <http://www.eurojust.europa.eu/doc library/corporate/Pages/newsletter.aspx> accessed 18 September 2016.

United Nations Convention on Transnational Organised Crime (2000).

UNODC, 'The Globalization of Crime. A Transnational Organized Crime Threat Assessment' (Vienna 2010) <https://www.unodc.org/unodc/en/data-and-analysis/tocta-2010.html> accessed 18 September 2016.

Case Law

Åklagaren v Hans Åkerberg Fransson (Case C-617/10) [2013] STC 1905, [2013] 2 CMLR 46, 15 ITL Rep 698.

Commission v Council (Environmental Crime) (Case C-176/03) [2005] ECR I–7879, [2005] 3 CMLR 20, [2006] All ER (EC) 1, [2006] Env LR 18.

Commission v Council (Ship-Source Pollution) (Case C-440/05) [2007] ECR I-09097, [2008] 1 CMLR 22, [2008] All ER (EC) 489, [2008] Env LR 12.

Commission v Council (Titanium Dioxide) (Case C-300/89) [1991] ECR I-02867, [1993] 3 CMLR 359.

Commission v Denmark (Danish Bottle) (Case 302/86) [1988] ECR 4607.

Commission v Italy (Case 92/79) [1980] ECR 1115.

Procureur de la République v Association de défense des brûleurs d'huiles usagées (Case 240/83) [1985] ECR 00531.

Interviews

Interview with Gowitzke W, Seconded National Expert at Europol, working in the fraud unit of Europol and dealing with environmental crime (Europol, The Hague, 21 April 2016; further clarifications have been provided in subsequent email exchanges).

Interview with Görts L, National Member for Sweden at Eurojust and Eurojust Contact Point for Environmental Crime (Eurojust, The Hague, 22 April 2016).

Interview with Jamin V, Head of the JITs Network Secretariat (1 June 2016, Skype interview).

Interview with Sacré V, EU-TWIX Project Manager (19 September 2016, email interview).

Websites

(All the webpages have been last accessed on 18 September 2016)

<https://cites.org/eng/news/pr/2013/20130218_operation-cobra.php>

<https://cites.org/eng/news/sundry/2014/20140210_operation_cobra_ii.php>

<https://ec.europa.eu/anti-fraud/media-corner/press-releases/substantial-quantities-smuggled-counterfeit-pesticides-seized-poland_mt>

<http://ec.europa.eu/environment/legal/crime/>

<http://ec.europa.eu/justice/criminal/criminal-law-policy/environmental-protection/index_en.htm>

<http://efface.eu/>

<http://inece.org>

<http://www.basel.int/Countries/StatusofRatifications/PartiesSignatories/tabid/4499/Default.aspx#enote1>

<https://www.cites.org/eng/disc/parties/chronolo.php>

<https://www.cites.org/eng/disc/what.php>

<http://www.eurojust.europa.eu/doclibrary/Eurojust-framework/Pages/agreements-concluded-by-eurojust.aspx>

<http://www.eurojust.europa.eu/Practitioners/JITs/Eurojust-JITsFunding/Pages/Eurojust-JITs-funding.aspx>

<http://www.eurojust.europa.eu/Practitioners/objectives-tools/Pages/6thRME.aspx>

<https://www.europol.europa.eu/content/eu-policy-cycle-empact>

<https://www.europol.europa.eu/content/megamenu/partners-1835>

<https://www.europol.europa.eu/content/page/europol-platform-experts-1851>

<https://www.europol.europa.eu/content/page/intelligence-analysis-1852>

<https://www.europol.europa.eu/content/page/strategic_analysis_reports>

<https://www.europol.europa.eu/content/operation-cobra-iii>

<https://www.europol.europa.eu/latest_news/environmental-crime-experts-meet-milan>

<https://www.europol.europa.eu/latest_publications/39>
<http://www.eu-twix.org/>
<http://www.impel-esix.eu/>
<http://www.interpol.int/Crime-areas/Environmental-crime/Environmental-crime>
<http://www.tecumproject.eu/>
<http://www.traffic.org/overview/>

www.ingramcontent.com/pod-product-compliance
Lightning Source LLC
Chambersburg PA
CBHW031326230926
51848CB00001B/114
9789004341548